THE
COMPLETE
BOOK
OF CHESS

I. A. HOROWITZ

P. L. ROTHENBERG

THE
COMPLETE
BOOK
OF CHESS

ORIGINALLY PUBLISHED AS

The Personality of Chess

COLLIER BOOKS, NEW YORK, NEW YORK

COLLIER-MACMILLAN LIMITED, LONDON

Library of Congress Catalog Card Number: 63-16107

FIRST COLLIER BOOKS EDITION 1969
FOURTH PRINTING 1971

The Complete Book of Chess was originally published in a hardcover edition
by The Macmillan Company as *The Personality of Chess*

The Macmillan Company
866 Third Avenue, New York, N.Y. 10022
Collier-Macmillan Canada Ltd., Toronto, Ontario

Printed in the United States of America

This Work
Is
Dedicated
to

M . L . PRESS , M.D .

Acknowledgments

In collating the material for *The Complete Book of Chess,* we have leaned heavily on the expertness of some and on the observations of others; moderately, on the views of still more; and widely, on tested reactions of many to this or that aspect of Chess. Our warmest thanks go to all.

Specifically, we acknowledge the gracious help of Dr. Albrecht Buschke, eminent authority on Chess literature; Mr. Walter F. Vella, Head of the John G. White Chess Collection at the Cleveland Public Library; Dr. Samuel Tabbat, whose cogent evaluation of the relationship of Chess to the human being has proved to be invaluable to us; Mr. Robert and (Mrs.) Lee Weinberg, graduate students in, respectively, the departments of Physics and English at Columbia University; and, assuredly, Edna Horowitz and Grace Rothenberg, who, in the course of preparation of these pages, avenged their "widowhood" by taking on the role of your authors' most severe (but, unbeknownst to them, most welcome) critics.

A special word of thanks is reserved for Mr. Peter Ritner, Editor in Chief of The Macmillan Company, who knows so much about so many things that even his offhand suggestions, in busy moments, have proved to be pointed.

I. A. H.
P. L. R.

Introduction

Your authors have lived in the *actual* world of Chess for the past fifty years. This, of course, spells out a *combined* interest embracing one hundred years. We are resolutely resisting the temptation of luring you, the reader, into the Chess world. It is our aim merely to offer you a more intimate acquaintanceship with Chess on a level of objectivity and detachment which, admittedly, is a great challenge to us.

Chess has offered us fun (much), frolic (some), and frustration (little, relatively)—all adding up to a happy balance. The energy we have expended has met with a significant recompense in the form of a potent truth, the absolutism and unequivocation found in Chess as against the varnished, shaded part-truths so prevalent in everyday life.

Chess has been variously considered a pastime, game, way of life, obsession, religion, waste of time, supreme intellectual challenge, curse, blessing, integrating force, and destroyer of family life. It is certain that it is not within the purview of this book fully to cover all aspects of Chess that have contributed to making it a significant social force in the course of the many centuries of its existence. On the other hand, the topics have been selected with care with a view toward presenting a comprehensive picture of a phenomenon that continues to arrest the avid attention of many millions throughout the world.

Introduction

In the Appendix you will find—in addition to the rules governing the game, and related material—an extensive bibliography of leading works on Chess. It follows that whether you know much or nothing about Chess, this book offers you the opportunity to explore more fully specific areas of interest.

The Complete Book of Chess is not planned as a continuous narrative, the context of each chapter necessarily depending on the preceding text. Proceed to read as you please, with the comforting assurance that not only do we not presume to exact from you a *pro* Chess verdict, but we do not even impose a prescribed reading sequence upon you.

I. A. HOROWITZ

P. L. ROTHENBERG

New York City
January, 1963

Contents

Table of Contents

Table of Contents

Table of Contents

I

The Everlasting Challenge

Man has faced and conquered many challenges, practical, intellectual, aesthetic, in the course of his transition from troglodyte to technologist. Each age has brought marvelous discoveries, the earliest of which, naturally enough, were concerned with basic survival.

When the cave dweller contrived a way of safeguarding a cut of venison, that was the deep-freeze of his day. When man conceived the amazing utility of the wheel, he foreordained the wagon, phaeton, horseless carriage, and the streamlined motorized marvels of our day. When he regimented the wind and the waterfall to grind his grain and otherwise to reduce the physical burdens of everyday existence, he predestined the push of a button which now performs thousands of tasks *beyond* human capability.

With trade and barter came the need for calculation and computation. The mathematics based originally on the use of fingers and toes (which, by the way, account for the term *digit* in our numbering system) gave rise to the abacus, the electronic computer of its day. The tradesman's crude till, employing one or more *secret* buttons, is the father of the present-day vault. The chiseling of characters on stone gave way to ink and parchment, and eventually to the miracle of the printing press. The feverish excitement stirred by the pony express a mere century ago is now unbelievable in a world of jet service, telegraphy, the telephone, and the fantastic exploits of the astronauts.

As man at last found himself able to take a minute from the overriding problems of survival, his intellect searched for hitherto untried activity. He became fascinated by the possibilities of another world—the aesthetic one. His hands began to shape this out of clay, that out of stone, and something else out of wood, and these nonutilitarian creations gave him delight. He found dyes in nature's vegetation which lent themselves to pictorial reproduction of things actually in existence or, what was more fascinating, things existing in his imagination. Thus man's early work in art presaged the scientific formulas for the applying of proper media and the using of suitable surfaces, all within the more exacting framework, of course, of the precepts governing creative art. Included in the general area of man's creativeness are astounding examples of early architecture which, produced in ages far removed from present-day technical aids in planning and construction, are destined forever to remain awesome sights.

But there was another activity: there was the search for fun, amusement, entertainment. This, to be sure, was initially reserved for the man of economic privilege. As a matter of fact, there are numerous examples of ancient art and architecture created by slaves for the delectation of the privileged one and gratification of the privileged one's ego—witness the Pyramids. Our blitz journey through the history of man brings us to Chess: a pastime, basically, which entails the matching of wits.

Compared with man's great achievements, what does Chess have to offer? Why be concerned about it? Strangely, Chess is one of the few man-conceived phenomena to which man has been enslaved, for he has not been able to solve the mystery of it. We are dealing with a *finite* concept—a board consisting of *exactly* 64 squares and two opposing forces each consisting of *exactly* 16 pieces, and each of the pieces locomoting within the bounds of the board in accordance with *specific* rules. Yet man, who has tackled the "infinity" of the cosmos with highly respectable results, has not been able to conquer Chess. Chess is fairly *countable* (*see* Chapter 2), yet man's mental capacity has proved to be insufficient to absorb the count and thereby gain *complete* mastery. True, the history of Chess includes the phenomenon of Paul Morphy (*see* Chapter 15) and long periods of invincibility in the lives of great Chessmasters, but no Chess expert or superexpert has had a career unmarred by lost games. At best, we can conclude that each Chess titan was at the peak of his career during his supreme reign, with none on the Chess scene to challenge his proficiency.

The world has been blessed with the superb brains of gifted men—in mathematics, science, law, medicine, *et al.* Many of these men, if not all of them, have showed the ability to relate themselves to their work, up to their last breath, on an intellectual level consistent with their earlier days. Rarely does such a development apply to Chessmasters. It may well be, of course, that the diminution of physical stamina, owing to advanced age, is accountable for the inability to withstand the rigors of competition inherent in Chess. But the sharp reduction in the skill of the Chessmaster as he ages is more logically to be explained by the fact that however superior his Chess talents may have been to those of any contemporary, at no time in his life did he have *complete* mastery of the game. On the other hand, we have the amazing alertness of the Einsteins and Holmeses up to the day of death.

Without entering into an idle assessment of the comparative intellectual powers of an Einstein and a world Chess champion —each, of course, with respect to his own field—we can with no strain conclude that the genius of each is established. In one of them we find that a sharp reduction of skill is concomitant with advanced age; in the other, we do not. How otherwise can this be explained than by the fact that mastery of his field —or, at the very least, a grasp as close as possible to mastery— is the *permanent* part of the one unaffected by age?

It follows that all the Homers in Chess are destined to nod: occasionally, even during the height of their achievements; decisively, at some point in later life. Chess remains the everlasting challenge.

We have no answer to this:

White to play.
Who wins?

2

Chess: Origin
and Durability

HISTORY

The invention of Chess has been credited to the Persians, the
Chinese, Arabians, Jews, Greeks, Romans, Babylonians, Scyth-
ians, Egyptians, Hindus, Irish, and the Welsh. Although the
precise origin has been lost in obscurity, it continues to excite
the speculation of men of learning at the one end and of
dilettantes at the other. The careful researchers have called it
an "ancient" game; the foolhardy are quite ready to underwrite
exact dates.

H. J. R. Murray's *History of Chess* (1913) is probably the
best known work on the subject. The best of the latest accomplishments is *A Short History of Chess* by Dr. Henry A. Davidson, whom we shall meet at greater length in Chapter 7. (Dr.
Davidson's *History* was serialized in *Chess Review* in 1956–57;
out of print, its re-appearance in book form is imminent.)

There appears to be reasonably compelling evidence that the forerunner to Chess was first known in India some fourteen hundred years ago, according to Dr. Davidson, and much, much earlier according to others. Its original name in Sanskrit was *Chaturanga,* literally, "four arms" or "four members." That was also the Indian word for army, more specifically the four components of the army: elephants, chariots, cavalry, and infantry (respectively, Bishops, Rooks, Knights, and Pawns). Significant, of course, is the fact that in the original concept, neither the King nor the then equivalent to the Queen was incorporated in the nomenclature assigned to the fighting forces. This royal pair remains to this day the superaristocracy of the Chessboard, the Queen having devastating power, as much directed toward guarding the safety of her spouse as it is toward demolishing the enemy.

Chaturanga traveled from India to Persia and thence Arabian conquerors brought it to Europe about a thousand years ago. By that time, as is usually the fate of "foreign" designations, *Chaturanga* had been changed in successive steps to *chaturang* and to *schah* (meaning *king*), in Persian, and to *shatranj* and *al-schah-mat* in Arabian. The *mat* is of Persian derivation, meaning *dead.* At last we have the etymological basis for the nomenclature in many modern languages, the designations, as is apparent, being *King* or *the King is dead,* as follows:

LANGUAGE	NAME
English	Chess
German	Schach
Dutch	Schaak
Danish	Schak
Icelandic	Skāk
French	Echecs
Italian	Scacchi
Russian	Shachmati

As played today, chess dates back to the sixteenth century. The rules now governing the game (except for minor changes) and the locomotive power assigned to the pieces had undergone significant changes during the preceding centuries. Outstanding was the transformation during the Middle Ages of the Persian *firz* (i.e., vizier) to Queen. This revolutionary step not only involved a change of sex but an astounding increase in the power of the piece. The vesting of such force in the Queen may well be *the* classic example of compensation for the centuries of delay in granting full civil rights and suffrage to women.

Curiously, the *al-schah-mat* of ancient days, meaning as it does that the King is dead, is a strange paradox in the history of the nomenclature of the game. As we shall see in Chapter 3, the Chess King *never* dies. His forces can be routed and he can be left by himself facing a relentless enemy, but, head up, he announces calmy and firmly: "You have won, but *I* am not to be captured. Understand?"

DURABILITY

Basic in the durability of a pastime is its inexhaustibility within a human life-span. That, to be sure, accounts for the consistent interest found in many card games. The bridge player, for example, who hopes to be dealt a 13-*spade* hand, with each of the other participants holding 13 in each of the other suits, should know that the odds *against* it are 9×10^{27} to 1, take or give several billion quadrillions. But this ratio, 9, followed by 27 zeros, to 1, the most impressive bridge statistic, is child's play compared with the fantastic permutation in Chess. The possibilities in Chess stagger the imagination. Lest one be accused of introducing a numbers game for the purpose of proving the superiority of Chess over bridge, we direct your attention to Chapter 13, where bridge, a superlative game, is given the recognition it richly merits. The bridge figure is given for purpose of comparison only.

Assume that there are twenty streets converging on the corner of your home; assume further that you walk daily to and from a given point forty blocks from your home, and that not only do you have an immediate choice of twenty routes, but that at the end of each of the first five blocks you have a similar choice of twenty routes, and thereafter, at the end of each block, a choice of thirty routes, right to your destination. The return tour, is of course, reversed, with a choice of thirty routes to the end of the first thirty-five blocks, and a choice of twenty routes at the end of each block thereafter, right to your home.

Is it possible for you to conceive how long it would take you to traverse every possible series of routes in your outward and return journeys? If you have concluded that all the people in the world cannot accomplish this in their combined lifetimes, you are correct.

Well, essentially your labyrinthian stroll is the mathematics of Chess. Maurice Kraitchik, stipulating most conservatively in his lovely *Mathematical Recreations* that a choice of *twenty* moves is available to White and Black for the first *five* moves and *thirty* moves thereafter, in an average game of *forty* moves, computes the following to be an *approximate* number of the different Chess games possible:

$$25 \times 10^{115}$$

We have two and a half times ten followed by 116 zeros. Says Kraitchik, "It is a very big number, in comparison with which astronomical numbers are miserably dwarfish."

In conducting an actual count of every possible move on every turn of a twenty-seven move game, your authors found a count of 115×10^{75} i.e., 115 followed by seventy-five zeros, for the possible permutations in that isolated game. In indicating that *every possible move* was taken into account, as is inherent in Kraitchik's computation, we are, of course, completely aware of the fact that some of the possible moves are murderously stupid, leading as they do to instant disaster. It may be forcefully argued that such moves should be disregarded in order to aim at a reasonably practical figure rather than an all-inclusive theoretical one. But such argument completely overlooks the purpose of the computation: a determination of possibilities *unrelated* to skill in playing the game. Moreover, if all possibilities are *not* cited, we arbitrarily disregard the thousands and thousands of players to whom a "murderously stupid move" is hardly a fatal step; they continue to play until their opponents manage to take a "fatal" step, and then until the inevitable ultrafatal disaster befalls the ultimate victim. If you do not agree, visit your neighborhood park on a mild Sunday and observe the suicidal performances of some of the Chess-players. And if you still insist that the theoretical computation is misleading, we allow you, without reservation, the privilege of chopping some zeros off the stated figures.

We shall now consider a number of other aspects of Chess, each offering a fascinating computation. Mercifully, the figures while astounding are nevertheless conceivable.

The first four (single) moves in Chess, that is, two by White and two by Black, can occur in 197,299 ways, leading to nearly 72,000 different positions, of which 16,556 result from Pawn moves only.

There are over 288 billion possibilities through the fourth move (by White *and* Black). (An amazing sidelight, by the way, is the fact that in some openings a misstep against a Chess expert at this infant stage of the game *can* prove to be fatal.)

Listed below are possibilities of legal positions on the Chess-board up to a maximum of three White pieces against a sole Black King. (A legal position is one that can be assumed to arise in a game of Chess in accordance with the rules governing the game.) According to T. R. Dawson, the late British genius who figures prominently in Chapter 9, enumeration of the possibilities of total number of pieces in excess of four appears to be beyond analysis because of the obstacles in eliminating illegalities. Dawson's observation, however, predated availability of electronic computers. The stated possibilities follow:

WHITE	BLACK	ON THE MOVE	NUMBER OF LEGAL POSITIONS
King	King	Either	3,612
King & Pawn	King	White	81,660
King & Bishop	King	White	193,262
King & Bishop	King	Black	223,220 *
King & Two Knights	King	White	5,748,640
King & Two Knights	King	Black	6,785,140 *

You will find in *Chessboard Recreations*, Chapter 14, more examples relating to the vast sea of permutations on which sails the Ship of Chess. In the meantime, it is possible that you may want to choose a rainy day to challenge the authenticity of the following two figures: 393 and 5704. The first, mathematicians tell us, is the number of ways in which the King, standing at K1 square, can reach K8 in 7 moves; the second, is the number of different ways in which His Majesty can accomplish this journey in *8* moves.

Or—do you concede?

* The sharp increase in each case when Black is on the move is, of course, explained by the fact that the Black King can stand in check; with White on the move, that is impossible.

TIME LIMIT IN CHESS

It seems incredible now that at one time Chessplayers were not subjected to time limit rules in critical matches and tournaments, to say nothing of encounters in less significant Chess events. Were no time limit in effect today, it is safe to guess that Chess would be reduced to a turtle-pace inanity, especially in important competition. Available to present-day masters is a vast literature of Chess analysis on which there has been more concentration during the past century than ever before in the history of the game. Picture, if you will, an adjourned game involving a complex position, under no time limit restrictions. The players might conceivably desire a year or more before resuming play.

But placed in effect, finally, were remedial measures, influenced by ridiculous experiences of the past and well-founded apprehensions about the future. Enforcement of the time limit in Chess started about a hundred years ago. The earliest devices were hourglasses, gradually advancing to various types of chronometers, until finally reaching the stage of the present Chess clock, a precise, convenient instrument for measuring the time consumed by each player.

The Chess clock consists of two dials, the time each player takes being governed by the dial nearer to him. At the start of the game, the time on each dial may be set on the hour (12 o'clock, say) and as each player moves, he presses a lever which stops his own clock and sets his opponent's in motion. If "time out" is required, for whatsoever reason—usually for settlement of a disputed point—both levers are set at "neutral," and no time is registered in either dial. Each player utilizes his time *cumulatively*, allowing as much for each move as he desires. If a player fails in the total time allowed to make the required number of moves (first forty moves in, say, two and a half hours, which is frequently stipulated) he loses the game, no matter how superior his position is. As a rule, however, the position of the player who loses a game "on time" is hardly the superior one. (Not infrequently a Chessplayer's ego finds solace in losing on time.) The number of required moves within a stipulated period is decided by the sponsoring bodies of matches and tournaments or, in lesser Chess events, by the players themselves. In all serious Chess competition the time limit is strictly enforced, usually by a referee to whom one or more Chess encounters are assigned for supervision.

In rapid-transit Chess tournaments, a designated person (or mechanical device) sounds off a gong at regular intervals (ten seconds, usually), and it is at that very moment that the player on turn must move—and not sooner. This assures equal advantage to both players for neither is ever allowed more than the allotted time for his next move. Moreover, confusion is obviated, for each knows exactly when he is on the move.

There is, finally, a move-on-move insanity, *Blitz,* which requires no clock, for *no time at all* is allowed the players. *Blitz* is a "relaxing" sport to topnotch players, each of whom *must* counter at the *very instant* a move is made by the opponent. Completion of a game in a minute or less is not unusual, provided the Chess pieces survive the punishment. *Blitz* is not recommended to persons afflicted with hypertension or cardiac disturbances. Nor is it recommended to persons who are not so afflicted.

3

Chess Is War

In this age of suspended animation, as it were—will or will not some megalomaniac press a button and destroy the world —it is reasonably comforting to examine an area of less lethal warfare, but warfare nevertheless: Chess.

The original array of the Chess pieces, the functions assigned to them, the terms used in describing these functions, the ultimate aim, the justified brutality in gaining the objective—all add up to war, no less.

OBJECTIVE

The object of a game of Chess is to force the enemy King into a position where he cannot, under any circumstances, avoid being captured. But a centuries-old fiction is maintained. The King, cornered and defeated, must never be captured. He has lost the war, but he must not be subjected to the indignity of removal from the board. *All* other pieces, as we shall see, *are* expendable.

ORIGINAL ARRAY

The King and his aristocratic entourage occupy the first rank. (Please see rules of Chess, notations, and basic terms in *Appendix*. A player's first rank is the horizontal row nearest to him.) Each of these eight nobles is shielded by a peasant directly in front. The Germans, with incredible magnanimity, have allowed this peasant to retain his bucolic identity; they call him *Bauer*. The Anglo-Saxons, more realistically, have reduced his status to that of *Pawn*. And that is precisely what this Mauldin's Willie is—a pawn!

In true feudalistic, monarchic tradition, the eight peers on the first rank are not exposed to the world. The Pawns are the buffers. At the outset, two of the lesser peers, the Knights, can hop over the Pawns in front of them, each to one of two squares, and each then closely guarded by at least one Pawn. ("My Lord, I am at your service.")

THE KING

The King is sacrosanct but he is not omnipotent. His function, passively enough, is to maintain the status of inviolable dignity, unapproachability, and regal aloofness. Stationed in the middle of the first rank in the original array, the King can betake himself to an inner sanctum as early as on the fourth turn of play. This is accomplished by means of a maneuver called castling, whereby the King slides two squares toward the edge of the board, and one of his titled subalterns, the Rook, obediently hops over him, thus allowing His Majesty complete privacy. Frequently, a Pawn directly in front of the castled King or diagonally adjacent to him is bidden to move, in order to provide access to the second rank (air raid shelter, if you will, in case of an enemy attack).

The King is really not expected to exert himself. If, of course, he is attacked, or if his army is depleted or routed, participation in battle becomes unavoidable. As a rule, the King is pressed into service (being actually awakened from his lethargy) when most of or all his nobles have fallen in battle. He is then, as a rule, pitted against the enemy monarch, each trying to outmaneuver the other with a minor peer and stray Pawns who have escaped annihilation. Since the opposing Kings must *not* attack one another, the maximum potential is being squeezed out of the remaining force (Pawns, usually) to the very end. If an impasse is reached, the war is over, and neither one is the victor. If the King is placed in a position of indefensibility, capture becoming inevitable, the war is over. The cornered King, *who must not be removed from the board,* is vanquished.

THE QUEEN

Her Majesty is the field commander of the armed forces of the realm; but unlike generals destined to die in bed, she furiously participates in battle, and if strategically wise, she sacrifices herself for her Sire's cause. This, to be sure, is quite in keeping with the traditions of absolute monarchy, for nobody, least of all a woman, is exempt from serving the interests of the King.

Endowed with devastating mobility, the Queen can swoop down from one edge of the battlefield to the other, horizontally, vertically, diagonally. In the center of the open field the Queen controls twenty-seven squares, more than two fifths of the total of sixty-four; in no case, when not obstructed, does she control less than twenty-one squares, one third of the total.

Usually, before the encounter is brought to a finish, the Queen falls in battle in exchange for her enemy counterpart. This is not considered a sacrifice. It is only when the Queen is deliberately lost outright or in exchange for a lesser warrior that a sacrifice occurs. The reason for sacrificing the Queen (or a less important piece) is, of course, the immediate prospect of gaining an advantage leading to victory. It is, by the way, the apotheosis of "beauty and brilliancy" in a game of Chess to effect a sound sacrifice of one's Queen. Says the famed Russian Chessmaster Eugene Znosko-Borovsky: "In a game of Chess . . . everything must be subordinated to the idea of victory."

THE ROOK

The Rook is, in effect, the *panzer* unit, pursuing his lethal purpose in straight-line tank marches. Vulnerable to diagonal attack, the Rook is not too concerned, for his orthogonal mobility allows him to travel from one edge of the battlefield to the other. On the other hand, the Rook must guard against being cornered, especially when hemmed in by his own pieces.

He alone, other than the Queen, has all-sufficient power to bring victory when, with the aid of his own King, he faces the lone enemy monarch after the other twenty-nine combatants have been dispatched to Valhalla.

THE BISHOP

The Bishop is a reconnaissance officer, who, as a rule, follows the other reconnaissance officer, the Knight, in finding a desirable vantage point from which eventually to penetrate enemy territory or to plague enemy forces. He can move diagonally only and is, therefore, doomed to live and die on a square of the same color as that of the square on which he was originally situated. This, of course, limits his powers materially as compared with the Rook, for example, whose mobility allows control of squares of both colors. On the other hand, the Bishop can also travel from one edge of the field to the other, and his control of the diagonal lines can be decisive in battle. As we can now readily understand, the Queen's mobility embraces that of *both* Rook and Bishop. As a rule, Rook cannot win against Bishop when each, aided by his respective King, is sole survivor on the battlefield. In certain positions, however, the Rook will prevail. A lone Bishop and King cannot deliver mate to the lone enemy King.

THE KNIGHT

The Knight moves *not* in a straight line to the *nearest* square of the color opposite the one on which he is situated. It is herewith unqualifiedly conceded that the definition of the move of the Knight is as grotesque as is indeed the move itself.

As a rule, the Knight is the first of the privileged gentry to leave the first rank. He is the only one in the first rank who need not depend on the move of a Pawn to create mobility for him, for he can hop to his destination square *over* his own or enemy forces.

The mobility of the Knight is limited. He attains a *maximum* possibility of reaching any one of eight squares when he is situated at a distance far enough from the edge of the board. On the other hand, his moves are deceptive and puzzling, especially since he is able to fork—i.e., attack simultaneously—two or more enemy units, as if he were situated on the hub of a wheel and aiming his fire at various points in the circumference. Picture also, if you will, a cannon, revolving on a pivot and shooting in all directions. Aptly enough, the full range of the Knight is called the Knight Wheel.

It follows that the Knight, denied long-range mobility, is amply compensated by reason of his unique locomotion. In certain battle positions, his maddening hop can prove to be far more devastating than the power of any other warrior.

The power of the Knight can perhaps be best appreciated when we realize that he is valued as much as the Bishop with his long-range mobility. On the other hand, not even two Knights, aided by their King, can mate a sole surviving enemy King.

THE PAWN

This miserable peon does everybody's bidding. He is the eternal footsoldier, expendable, yet all-important in winning a war—of prethermonuclear vintage, that is.

He can move forward *only,* one square at a time, except that at the very outset he is allowed the option of one *or* two squares. He can capture diagonally *only,* on a contiguous square, and he is given the extraordinary privilege of capturing an enemy infantryman *en passant,* that is, when the latter dares to move two squares from his original berth, thus landing alongside the advanced enemy Pawn. This "privilege," ironically enough, is less in recognition of the rights of the capturing Pawn than in contempt of the effrontery of the captured Pawn. How dare he pass over a square on which he can be liquidated according to standard rules of battle? But pass over it he does, and his fate is as if he did not.

The Pawn *can* be decorated on the field of battle, but he must reach the topmost rank before he gains the promotion. And then he has no assurance of maximum recognition (promotion to Queen), for the only consideration is his utility as a promoted man. How will he then fit into the scheme of battle? Is it perhaps strategically wise to sacrifice him after he is promoted?

Thus the Pawn starts on his *vorwaerts* journey, never to return to his homeland in his original image and seldom in any image. He blocks, shields, protects and, in turn, is frequently left to his miserable resources, which lack the one critical recourse in war, retreat. The King, in the safety of his cove, counts the casualties, with a solicitous concern for his first-rank aristocrats and with a wave of the hand at the stupid Pawn, one of eight, who got himself knocked off in battle.

TERMS

Given below is a *partial* listing of Chess terms of which many are commonly known to be used in warfare. When we recall (Chapter 2) that armed forces served as *the* basis for *chaturanga,* the precursor of modern Chess, the use of these terms becomes perfectly understandable.

Herewith, then, the lyrics to the *Marche Militaire* of Chess:

Offense, defense, attack, advance, retreat, block, salient, phalanx, enemy territory, enemy King, enemy piece, The Enemy, capture, isolated (Pawn), strategy, tactics, diverting move, maneuver, ambush, annihilation, wing (left or right), forces, guard, mobilize, immobilize, decoy, center, vacate, battery, firing the battery, interpose, fork, flank, reinforce, unguard, promote, sacrifice, gambit, weaken, concentrate, double guard, multiple guard, withdraw, line opening, obstruct, ambuscade, clearance, *coup de main, coup de repos,* waiting move, direct attack, indirect attack, flight, forced move, interception, interference, shutoff, field, territory, men, pin, paralyzing maneuver, protect, horizontal, diagonal, vertical, waiting (move or tactic), simultaneous attack, remove, face, back, front, rear, side, corner (as verb and noun), cluster, counterattack, abandon, closing, line of communication, mobility, trap, safe, saved, threat, cutoff, self-block, active (man), inactive (man), anticipation, plan (of attack), auxiliary maneuver, auxiliary forces, avoidance, critical (move), focal action, double attack, fringe forces, technique, line clearance, net, opposition, passive (move), tempo, self-interference, smother, retract, unblock, stroke, grab, infiltration.

Franklin K. Young, a Chess enthusiast who flourished during the early part of this century, wrote a number of books exclusively dedicated to the proposition that Chess and war are irrevocably one and the same thing. Mr. Young presents dozens and dozens of Chess positions tending to illustrate this or that maneuver. Our listing of war terms employed in Chess is completely eclipsed by Mr. Young's enthusiastic treatise. If we claim soberly that Young has overstepped himself in that his interpretation approaches fanatical proportions, we must nevertheless recognize that it is only the *degree* of his analysis to which exception is taken.

BATTLE GOALS

Although we frequently find a variety of descriptive synonyms for annihilation in sportswriters' accounts of victory on the playing fields, it seems that the lethal terms used by Chessplayers have more of the compelling ring of authenticity. "I killed him" or "I creamed him" or "I polished him off" or "he was murdered" conjures up a picture of the actual battle on the Chessboard, the snarling vehemence of the prospective victor's "check!" and his joy in observing his victim's doom. If this is not to suggest that the attitude of *all* Chessplayers is necessarily gory, it is definitely to note that the thrill of victory is, at best, but mildly restrained.

Known closely to your authors at one time were two men, Chessplayers both. The one, a gentle, soft-spoken scholar and aesthete—he was a music teacher—felt pained when his winning of a game of Chess entailed a depletion of the forces. The Chess pieces existed for him as animate beings, and he found no more joy in capturing an opponent's piece than in losing one of his own. Victory to him was a welcome prospect, for he truly had the challenge inherent in Chess, but he irresistibly subordinated victory to the means of attaining it.

Seasoned Chessplayers to whom this man has been mentioned regard him as a neurotic, a mystic, at best; as a nut, usually.

The other, an outgoing truculent extrovert—he was a lawyer —invariably held in one hand the pieces captured by him in the course of a game of Chess, while keeping the other hand free. The fuller his fist, the happier he was; and when his holding hand reached the limit of its capacity, he adroitly inserted the overage between his fingers. He loved Chess and he loved to win, admitting that the physical feel of his immediate conquests added to the thrill of ultimate victory or blunted the frustration of defeat.

Seasoned Chessplayers to whom this man has been mentioned do not regard him to be basically abnormal but merely more honestly unrestrained in pursuit of victory than most Chessplayers *pretend* to be.

We pose a question: Who of these two is temperamentally the more qualified to play Chess?

4

The Chessplayer's Mind

PATHOLOGY OF CHESS

Modern psychiatry has shown a live interest in the game of Chess, particularly in what is medically known as the "pathology" of the game of Chess. Pathology is, of course, the science of the study of diseases, their essential nature, causes, and development. Psychiatry has beeen keenly concerned with so much of Chess activity as tends to bring out manifestations of behavior that answer a Chessplayer's inner *unconscious* need for exercising hostility. In short, what role does Chess play in the behavior of the Chessplayer? What pathological tendencies exist in the Chessplayer?

PSYCHIATRIC INTERPRETATION
OF CHESS

It is to be regretted that some psychiatric tracts on this subject use a categorical, dogmatic approach, requiring a matter-of-fact, deductive application of allegedly established principles.

Psychiatric Interpretation of Chess

We are told that Chess, a game of war, is the release of hostility, primarily directed by the player against his own father (the enemy King) and coupled with a devotion for his mother (his own Queen). We are also told that the hostility is an oedipal tendency, that is, a neurotic (at best) disorder in adult life arising from the male child's unconscious attachment to the mother and hostility toward the father. Moreover, the antifather image can be traced to primordial warfare, entailing the prevalent custom of devouring the testicles of the chief of the conquered tribe. (In the interest of actual fact, neither of your authors has thus far encountered a Chessplayer so intoxicated with victory as to desire to partake of these anatomical morsels.)

On the other hand, the more moderate psychiatrist, though he fully subscribes to the hostility theory, does not go so far as to apply it on an absolute basis. He concedes that the Chessplayer may undergo various attitude stages, overcoming the inner hostility and eventually relating himself to the game as a casual or serious pastime, intellectual exercise, scientific challenge, or what have you.

It is also firmly claimed by psychiatrists that no matter what evidence there may be of *conscious* unawareness of the hostility and oedipal tendencies in the Chessplayer, this does not at all disprove the *unconscious* basis for the hostility.

It is best to certify at this very point that your authors, strongly resisting a popular laymen's pastime, the "practice of psychiatry," have no intention of offering a *professional* evaluation of the stated principles governing the "pathology" of the game of Chess. We do, however, offer our observations, based on exposure to Chessplayers all our lives and, indeed, on a rather suspicious look at ourselves.

First, we realize that once it is dogmatically decreed that the *unconscious* in us can be and frequently is *the* predominating force in our lives, there is nothing, but nothing, to say. We shall, therefore, judiciously limit ourselves to observations that relate to the *conscious* part of the Chessplayers we have known (some of whom, by the way, play Chess unconsciously).

In attempting to reach *lay* conclusions on the personalities of Chessplayers, we have conducted hundreds of tests, essentially of an elementary nature, which tend to furnish some key to the *offhand* relationship of the Chessplayer to the game. Perhaps you like to be tested? Whether or not you play Chess, you will be able to answer the questions given below. Ready? Get pencil and paper and put the answers down *instantly*.

1. Assume you are playing a game of Chess. Are you playing the White pieces or the Black pieces?

2. Assume you are winning the game. Whom are you beating?

3. Put down the *very first thing* that comes into your mind, but do not allow yourself a breath when reading *each* of the following:

    a. Knight

    b. Rook

    c. Queen

    d. Pawn

    e. Bishop

    f. King

The test is over.

Did you associate the Queen with anything feminine? We have found not a single instance of association of the

Queen with anything at all suggesting femininity. Most prevalent is the response of "power" to the Chess lady.

We have found that the more expert the Chessplayer, the more likely are his answers to Questions 1 and 2 to be "immaterial" and the more likely are his reactions to the Chess pieces, Question 3, to be fundamentally concrete aspects of the game, i.e., either the locomotive power of the piece, its location in the original array, or its relative value ("eh" for Pawn was most amusing!).

Contrarily, we have found that the more elementary the testee's knowledge of the game, the more likely is he to choose White for Question 1, and to name a *specific* opponent for Question 2; also, his flights of fancy with relation to the pieces are quite in evidence. The response of "moat" to Rook serves as a ready example.

We have discovered that consciously, at any rate, the Chessplayer does not confirm the psychiatric principle of hostility. Does this mean that the principle is discredited? Certainly not. We are presenting the results of our little fun-test for the little (or the nothing) it is worth.

It is, however, well to note that the absolutism claimed in behalf of any theory can fall short of stimulating absolute credibility. We have discovered that even respectable practitioners of *physical* medicine are not united in a burning resolve to bow at the altar of *all* psychiatric theories. They hesitate, of course, to make their reservations publicly known. First, they basically maintain a respect for psychiatry; second, and more important, a prudent physician is mindful of the dangers inherent in exposing to criticism *any* recognized branch of medicine.

We, of course, have been keenly sparked by the psychiatric conclusions about Chess. Our interest is hardly motivated by a desire to *protect* Chess against the onslaughts of the hostility theory. We have had discussion with psychiatrists of high professional standing. It is sad to report that, in the main, our uncertainties remain unresolved.

We have asked why hostility in males has not found more convincing (to us) outlets, such specifically as fencing, requiring as it does a weapon so obviously suggestive of the phallus, with which one can so lustily punish the hated father (substitute). We have been told that in fencing there is an absence of a critical oedipal factor, the mother-image; that such image *does* exist in Chess—the Queen, whom the Chessplayer guards and protects zealously. The role of the Chessplayer's *own* King, the principal unit in need of protection, is given little or no attention. The concededly conscious awareness of the male Chessplayer that his Queen is his most important fighting unit and his knowledge that uncompensated loss of his Queen means loss of the game do not, according to psychiatrists, lessen the force of the *unconscious* desire to protect her. (There is, by the way, a mild possibility that a Chessplayer may develop a resentment against *his own* King, as illustrated in a classical pleasantry. Said the defeated player: "I was doing fine, but my stupid King got himself mated.")

Is there human activity absolutely devoid of "pathology"? Are the attitude stages, previously noted, absolutely essential in the development of a Chessplayer from one governed by inner hostility to one who is not? In the spirit of fun, Murray Teigh Bloom, author of *Money of Their Own,* a fascinating documentation on the lives and deeds of master counterfeiters, has this to say, after noting that his research had failed to unearth a psychiatric study of counterfeiters: "All this may simply be a back-handed tribute to the fact that is perfectly obvious: counterfeiters counterfeit to make money, and not because they were taken off breast-feeding prematurely at six months or were forcibly toilet-trained at the age of two."

It is possible that the matter may resolve itself into a cart-before-the-horse consideration. Instead of automatically and peremptorily applying the theory to the person, why not the reverse? The excellent monograph on Paul Morphy (see Chapter 15), by the late Dr. Ernest Jones, eminent biographer of Sigmund Freud, illustrates the point. Dr. Jones shows no hostility to the hostility theory; as a matter of fact, he confirms it emphatically, but he applies it judiciously, among other incisive psychiatric findings, to a man whose case history he traces, step by step, with immaculate care and scholarly devotion.

It follows that a much-welcomed psychiatric study would be that of case histories of random Chessplayers, with a convincing analysis of how the hostility theory does (or does not, perhaps) apply.

If the theory is ascertained to be universally applicable on the basis of reasonably concrete evidence, then no room is left for doubt. But it may well be that the field of psychiatry is totally unconcerned about lay reaction to so profound a concept as is the human's unconscious self. We like to believe, however, that that is not so.

ANALYSIS OF PERSONALITY OF CHESSMASTER

Your authors have lived in the world of Chess and they have presumed to draw conclusions about the personalities and attributes of Chessplayers—i.e., the more advanced species.

First, we find a relentless will to win. As a rule, this consuming drive tends not to endear the Chessplayer to others, but there are highly skilled Chessmasters who are endowed with restraint and affability, and the serenity of their attitude serves as a restraint upon their opponents as well. We have in mind such personalities as Dr. Max Euwe, former World Champion, and Isaac Kashdan, an American Chessmaster.

Outstanding attributes of the Chess expert, purely with relation to Chess, are reliability of memory, power of visualization, alertness, calmness under fire, and the one intangible asset, the ability to assess an opponent's psychological reaction to a prospective move, position, or combination. As convincingly as we may argue that Chess is pure skill, with full development of the game in sight, it is nevertheless as frequently as not of basic importance to assess, *prospectively*, an opponent's reaction to a maneuver. "This will floor him" is much less silly than it sounds, even if the move is basically *unsound*, provided the elements of surprise, panic, and complications are carefully calculated to produce the desired effect, and all factors, including time pressure, are carefully taken into account.

Do the attributes of the advanced Chessplayer necessarily serve him well in other activities? The answer is an absolute no. As strange as it may seem, the Chessplayer's skill may have no relationship whatever to any other facet of his personality or activity. (In Chapter 7, you will find the low-rung extreme in the Chessplayer, the *idiot-savant*.) The common belief that expert Chessplayers are good mathematicians is a fiction. On the other hand, good mathematicians *may* turn out to be good Chessplayers. The common belief that expert Chessplayers show an alert reaction to any problems requiring quick analysis is also fiction. So is the belief that Chessplayers are necessarily intelligent. (Dr. Henry A. Davidson, however, in his *A Short History of Chess,* indicates that a study—limited admittedly—*does* disclose a correlation between skill in Chess and intelligence.)

One conclusion and one only is a safe one: Expert Chessplayers are able to play Chess expertly.

More often than not we find a unifaceted personality in expert Chessplayers, one that is consumed with Chess and nothing else. It follows that Chessmasters can be insufferable bores to all but their counterparts and adoring relatives. The reasons, not at all given in the spirit of defense, are basic. There are, in the United States at any rate, few Chessplayers who give their full time to the game. Chess, therefore, is usually an extraoccupational activity. We find the stockbroker, student, realtor, doctor, lawyer, clerk, teacher, each crowding the precious leisure hours into Chess, and showing a complete disinclination to give anything else any attention. "That train disaster in South America is dreadful, no?" "It sure is," comments the Chessmaster, "it reminds me of my game with Kalendosky, when I castled on the Queen side. . . ."

There is eternal speculation on the number of moves an expert Chessplayer can figure in advance. There is, moreover, a tendency to evaluate ability in terms of numbers: "He is a genius. He can figure fifteen moves ahead of time." Such an approach is rather naïve. One can see many moves ahead and fall a world short of being a genius. Successful planning in Chess must be on a configurative basis. The *likely* lines of play must be considered, along with the sequence of moves in each. Moreover, precautions must be taken against unexpected bolts, surprises that can bring crushing defeat at once. It follows that the mere figuring of x moves ahead of time is, relatively, no accomplishment. Various lines of play must be anticipated, in each of which the number of moves may vary. That is the kernel. Reshevsky has earned the reputation of a player deliberately inviting time pressure. That, of course, is false. The panic of time pressure is as unwelcome to him as it is to anybody else. What he does is give deep and long deliberation to the early stages of the game. He then has the various lines of play at his fingertips. It is certain that the spectators become more excited than Reshevsky when he has but a minute left to make a dozen moves or more. With calm and assurance Reshevsky proceeds to beat the clock.

It is also safe to conclude that the Chess ego of the Chessmaster is completely an integral part of him, and its emergence to the surface is only a matter of degree. The more proficiency in Chess compensates for other deficiencies in the life of the Chess expert, the more likely is his ego to dominate him. On the other hand, the more secure he is, the less is he enslaved by his conceit.

As against the expert, we have the thousands and thousands of casual Chessplayers who, to the master, exist as duffers, patzers, and Queen-odds nonentities. Essentially, the casual players embrace the full gamut of human society, from nitwit to sage. What is more, they enjoy the game with the sparkling delight of a child and they enthusiastically continue to repeat errors which could be quickly unlearned. They show actual contempt for study and analysis, the *sine qua non* to the expert, for essentially their interest lies in beating as weak a neighbor or an uncle. It is the casual player to whom Chess is a kind of primitive pleasure, not at all encumbered by a desire for skill. It is quite safe to conclude that better than 98 per cent of Chessplayers in the United States fall into this group. There is a sound basis for this conclusion. Millions of Chess sets are sold yearly in the United States, and thousands of books on the elements of Chess. The experts *and* strong players, so called, are a trickling minority.

ETHNIC FACTORS

Does Chess dominate the interest of *particular* ethnic groups in the United States? To some extent. We find that the closer is a person's origin to Europe or to those of its countries where Chess enjoys popularity, such as Germany, England, the Scandinavian lands, Russia (of course), the more likely (though certainly *not* necessarily) is he to have *some* interest in Chess. This is easily traceable to home influences which, in turn, stem from the social mores of the place of origin. The background of the original immigrants to these shores must necessarily be taken into consideration. Artisans, farmers, laborers brought with them comparatively less of a tradition of Chess than did persons in so-called white-collar occupations. On the other hand, as children of the non-white-collar European immigrants grew up in the United States, their parents encouraged Chess as a respectable symbol remindful of the way of life of the upper classes in their native lands. A chronological examination of listings of prominent Chess personalities in the United States from the time of Paul Morphy (the middle of the nineteenth century) to date is rather a review of the waves of immigration varying in origin from period to period in the history of this land. The farther back we go, the more the Anglo-Saxon names predominate, as in the rosters of many other fields of activity, such as those of our congressional bodies.

Whereas there is evidence that Chess has failed to arrest the interest of certain ethnic and racial groups in the United States, it cannot be as easily concluded that any *particular* ethnic group has dominated the Chess scene. We find relatively little interest in Chess in persons of Irish and Greek extraction, among others. This, understandably, reflects a relative lack of interest in the countries of origin. Interest in Chess is increasing among Negroes who, constantly maintaining a courageous fight for the attainment of civil rights, including desirable occupational activity, are finding more and more opportunities for utilization of leisure time along lines of general interest.

In examining the listings of hundreds and hundreds of persons who play "postal" Chess—that is, by correspondence, in successive pairings arranged by *Chess Review*—one finds the usual medley of names of many ethnic origins as one does in army rosters and the like, with no dominance of any particular nationality.

Leading United States Chess experts are urban dwellers. Logically enough, the cities, and the larger ones particularly, offer the best opportunities for practice, competition, and exposure to Chess talent. New York City, the Mecca of what have you, also leads in Chess talent.

It is frequently claimed that if any ethnic group dominates the Chess scene in the United States, it is the Jewish players. Cited as supporting evidence is the fact that every United States Chess champion since 1936 (after Frank James Marshall retired undefeated) has been at least partially of Jewish origin. This conclusion, finding its justification in a rather compelling consideration, merits analysis.

It is, of course, a fact that Chess has traditionally offered a keen interest to Jews. But again we necessarily speak of American Jews who are not too far removed from the home influence of Europe. Not too uncommon, though seemingly incongruous, is the bearded skull-capped Jewish patriarch engaged in a game of Chess. It is interesting to contemplate whether or not he—*and* his descendants—have originally been attracted by Chess because of a fascinating parallel between Chess and the study of certain complex commentaries on the Talmud, particularly the Gemara. In each there is the eternal challenge, "if." In the Gemara, the if's govern ever so many postulates, one outdoing the other in depth and intricacy, and each requiring a unique alertness and a quick ability to analyze and unravel. The "if" factor in Chess is, of course, self-evident. There is no contemplation of a prospective series of moves without the necessary "if" concomitants. Also, there is a distinct possibility that Chess has symbolized for Jews the struggle inherent in their history of persecution. In short, the bloodless fight, the battle of wits, the excitement of the intellectual argument (symbolized by action on the Chessboard), all traditionally dear to the Gemara Jew, may well have descended to his posterity. (Interestingly enough, not too significant is the contribution of Jews to Chess problem composition, a phase of Chess decidedly more passive than the game itself.)

Thus, we have established a traditional interest and the possible reasons therefor.

We now return to New York City, where we find the largest concentration of Jewish population in the world. The opportunities abound for the rise of great Chessplayers, and Jewish Chessplayers particularly. New York has produced all but one of the United States champions for the past twenty-six years. The exception, the late Herman Steiner, originally an immigrant from Hungary, was a Californian. And we now have a combination of interest in a concentrated ethnic colony, so to say, *and* the great opportunities to develop skills. We are, obviously, ready to conclude that there is indeed compelling evidence that *expert* Jewish Chessplayers have been prominent in the United States. *Does* that, however, mean domination of the Chess scene?

If top skill is the sole criterion, the answer is yes. If, however, other criteria are taken into account, including particularly a live interest in Chess in ever so many communities in the United States where Jewish participation is conspicuously absent, the answer is necessarily no. We then have a parallel in bridge. Bridge is a desirable pastime for millions who, as likely as not, are indifferent to the Gorens and Stones and Jacobys except for the possible purchase of bridge texts, usually written by top masters. Similarly many of the Smiths, Schmidts, Swensons, Kowalskys, and Whonots who play Chess throughout the United States may never have heard of Larry Evans, current Champion of the United States.*

The final word—and that is usually reserved *by* women—is about women in Chess. Bobby Fischer's estimate of the Chess talents of women (see Chapter 11) is perhaps *too* unkind. But the truth is that there is no counterpart in Chess of, say, a Helen Sobel of bridge fame. Top women players in the United States have failed to rise to the level of male masters. There

* Or Robert J. Fischer, Evans' successor. See Chapter 17.

have been expert women players in Russia and in England, but none approaching topmost rank in their own countries.

Psychiatrists have pointed out that women, as a rule, have no need for Chess, since they have no psychological drives like the oedipal tendency in man. Women, we are told, go through the Electra complex, which is love for the father and hate for the mother. Why they cannot direct their latent venom at the *opposing* Queen is not clearly explained. It is suggested further that when women do play, there is a *special* psychological reason, such as a strong emotional craving for revenge and self-assurance. But we have resolved not to tackle the Chesswoman's psychiatric entanglements beyond this point, for it is reasonable to rest on the fact that the world of Chess is essentially a man's world.

In 1961, a top United States Chesslady, Miss Lisa Lane of Philadelphia (who is mentioned also in Chapter 19) reaped a great deal of publicity because she decided to *quit* Chess. In the midst of a tournament in Hastings, England, Miss Lane, twenty-four and very attractive, announced to the world that first and foremost in her life was a man with whom she was deeply in love, and she had found it impossible to concentrate on Chess, and that it was definitely her decision to give up Chess altogether. About a year earlier she had announced that she was training for the *world* championship.

For some reason, it is difficult to visualize any *male* Chessmaster—take your pick—rising in the middle of a game and exclaiming: "My God! I'm in love and cannot continue to play." In any case, we are reasonably certain that if at that moment a colleague were to approach the lover and suggest calmly that Rook to Bishop Square definitely appeared to be a winning move in the latter's position, the object of the heart throb would be instantly forgotten.

5

The Favorite Chess Piece

"What is your favorite Chess piece?" a Chessmaster was asked. "The one that wins!" was the instant reply.

Chessplayers do not develop sentimental attachments to any one of the *dramatis personae* on the Chessboard. Logically enough, the safety of one's entire force is guarded zealously, and particularly that of the more powerful pieces. The peremptory claim of some psychiatrists (see Chapter 4) that a Chessplayer guards his Queen frenetically because she symbolizes his mother must indeed be measured against the prosaic fact that, as a rule, an uncompensated loss of the Queen spells out defeat, as does an arbitrary reluctance to part with the Queen when it is strategically wise to do so.

Isaac Kashdan, the American Chessmaster, is said to be partial to the Bishop as against the Knight. It would be inane to conclude that Kashdan, superb Chessplayer that he is, has become so enamored of the Bishop that he simply will not, under any circumstance, accept a Knight in return. What is certain is that Kashdan, as all top Chessmasters, is quick to recognize the *relative* utility of the Bishop (or any other piece) in a given position, and to plan his campaign accordingly.

RELATIVE POWER OF PIECES

The *relative power* of a Chess piece must, of course, always be assessed against its *absolute* value. The determining criterion is the role of the piece, presently or potentially, in a given position. It is fundamental, for example, that a securely protected Pawn on the 7th rank, about to be promoted, could be infinitely more powerful than any other piece on the board, for the very reason that the promotion of the Pawn to a strategically desirable piece may well bring victory. Similarly, a Knight about to execute a devastating fork cannot be denied his crucial contribution to victory. Other examples abound.

The *absolute* value of the Chess pieces has been mathematically determined, the lowest rating, a single unit, being assigned to the Pawn, and three or more units to the other pieces, as follows:

PIECE		UNITS
Pawn		1
Knight	} minor pieces	3
Bishop		3+
Rook	} major pieces	5
Queen		9

The King, once His Indolent Majesty gets into the fray, rates about three and a half units in playing power, for obviously enough his value is never assessed in terms of compensation for his demise. On the other hand, the absolute value of the other pieces does serve as a guide in securing recompense for the loss of any one of them. Thus we hear the term "even exchange," when a piece is exchanged for the identical enemy counterpart; or "exchange down," when a piece of a higher value is lost for a piece of a lesser rating (Rook for Knight, for example).

Is the rating chart an infallible guide? Certainly not! Much of Chess stubbornly refuses to lend itself to convenient formularizations. The absolute value of a piece may have little or no significance in a given Chess position. As a matter of fact, it is the *relative* power of the piece that is of prime import. To follow the chart woodenly is to invite disaster.

DEFLATION OF QUEEN

It has given us much pleasure to compose, especially for this Chapter, illustrative positions that emphatically deflate the major aristocrat of the Chessboard, the Queen. We must quickly add, however, that the exception *tests* the rule (*exceptio probat regulam*); it does *not* prove it. The Queen continues to reign supreme, except that it is well to know that the lesser pieces can have their hour of glory at the expense of Her Brazen Majesty.

The Favorite Chess Piece

Deflation of Queen

Drama in 5 Acts

(in each of which White performs first)

Act 1

*Rook Would Win but
Queen Can Only Draw.*

White plays 1 R-QB2, and Black must counter 1 . . . QxR (or else Black actually loses)—and what have we? A stalemate. But if Black's Queen were a Rook, White's position would be hopeless.

Act 2

*Bishop Would Win but
Queen Can Only Draw.*

White plays 1 B-B3, and again a stalemate of White after the forced 1 . . . QxB. A Bishop instead of a Queen would do Black very nicely, for he would win without much difficulty, as can be easily demonstrated.

Act 3
*Knight Would Win but
Queen Loses.*

Is there no end to degradation? Is this the way to treat a lady? White's Queen is completely helpless against the threatened mate by promotion to Rook or Queen (at Black's KR8). With a Knight instead of a Queen, White plays N-B5 ch, followed by N-N3 and Black can resign.

Act 4
*Pawn Would Win but
Queen Loses.*

But this is relentless! A Pawn?? A miserable Pawn, not even on the verge of promotion, is putting the Queen to shame??? How??

This way:

1 P-N4 ch QxP (forced) 2 PxQ ch K-R5 3 N-K5 P-N7 4 N-B3 ch K-any 5 N-Q2 and it is all over for Black. (If 3 . . . K-N6, White, of course, continues 4 N-Q3 and Black is kaput.)

If Black had a Pawn on KR5 instead of a Queen, Black's NP could not be stopped from queening, for then 1 P-N4 ch would be met with 1 . . . PxP *en passant,* and it would be White's turn to resign.

Act 5

> *If White Had No Queen,*
> *Black Would Lose. With*
> *Queen, White Must Lose.*

The brutal plot of this Chesspearean tragedy culminates in banishment of the lady. *Heraus,* Queen! "Why, why," weeps Her Squelched Majesty, "is this my fate?"

For this reason, Your Superfluous Highness:

Black threatens mate in 2 (Q-B8 or Q-N8, followed by QxN) which is irrefutable (except that White can play 1 P-R4 and delay execution by one move). If White had no Queen stationed on KB7, he would win easily: 1 N-K5 (threatening mate). Black must lose the Queen *and* the game. If White tries 1 QxN ch KxQ 2 P-N7 Q-N8 3 P-N8(Q) ch QxQ 4 NxQ P-Q6 wins easily.

6

The Deluge of Chess Literature

And out of the Chess shelves the books came tumbling—
Great books, small books, lean books, brawny books,
Brown books, black books, gray books, tawny books . . .

In appropriating Robert Browning's famed rodents, no in-
sidious analogy is intended; it is merely an attempt to describe
the fantastic variety of the shape, color, content, and purpose
of a myriad of books on Chess.

It may be said that the Chessplayer progresses from Tyro
to Messiah in direct ratio to the expertness he *believes* he has
developed. As a Messiah, of course, he has a burning message
to deliver—and that is a book on Chess. Violent is the com-
pulsion of the Chessplayer to see his name emblazoned as *the*
author of *the* last word on Chess. As often as not, the dream of

financial gain plays no part; the gratification of the ego is the dominating consideration.

The plethora of books on Chess has resulted in a frantic search for titles. The Chess scribes have appropriated *gems, brilliancies, cameos, garnets, treasuries, joys, enjoyments, thrills, miscellanies, potpourris* and, to be sure, an avalanche of *how-to-win*'s—in the *opening, middle game, ending,* as well as a sprinkling of flippant *how-not-to-win*'s, and coinages such as *Chesslets.* Curiously, the title *How to Win in the Post-Mortem* has not yet seen the light of day. But this is not an oversight exactly, for rare is the Chessplayer, howsoever suppressed his ego, who *fails* to win in the *post-mortem.*

CRITERIA FOR JUDGING MERIT

The outstanding contributions to Chess literature have, of course, serenely dominated the scene. The authors invariably are men whose accomplishments as players, discoverers of new lines of play, and profound students of the game are preeminent. For the most part, the lesser lights are egomaniacs at best; commercial hacks at worst.

Little has appeared in print to rival the *limited* output of such Chess giants as Emanuel Lasker; Capablanca (whose primers on Chess remain supreme); Nimzovich, (whose astounding knowledge of the game continues to amaze one and all); Alekhine (whose analyses are superb); and the outstanding American writer, Dr. Reuben Fine.

Dr. Fine is a psychologist, now in his late 40's, whose devotion to scholarship and painstaking research has been in evidence throughout his works on Chess and throughout his brilliant career as an outstanding Grandmaster. Fine concentrated on Chess writing during his early years; at present his dominant interest is his professional career. His books on chess openings and endings are classics, and none of his other works, including a splendid primer, fails to measure up to the highest possible standards.

Inclusio unius non est exclusio alterius. There are other authors of high eminence: Tarrasch, Euwe, Reti, Botvinnik, of course, and the perennially ebullient American Grandmaster, Dr. Edward Lasker, now a septuagenarian with an abiding interest in Chess for a period of some sixty years.

The all-time greatest authors of books on Chess problems are Alain White and T. R. Dawson. Their accomplishments are more fully covered in Chapter 9.

The secondary authors fall roughly into the two aforementioned groups: egomaniacs and commercial hacks. The former do produce a charming little opus once in a while. Their books, essentially harmless monuments to the ego, enjoy a limited market. The output of the commercial hacks, however, can and does undermine the standards of Chess literature, for the public can be easily misled by the high-power advertising puff of both work and author.

Chess book buyers in the United States consist principally of the following:

1. Those who have an authentic interest in the game of Chess or other phases of it, such as problems.

2. Those who are authentically interested in building a Chess library, regardless of their personal interest in the game.

3. Those whose book purchases and interest in the game are casual.

4. Those whose interest in Chess may be casual but who tend to purchase books as a symbol of status.

5. Public and school libraries, some of which make it a rule to acquire any Chess publications.

6. Miscellaneous persons or organizations, not falling into any precise category.

The book buyers who fall into categories 1 and 2 are obviously the book market. It is to them that we offer guides in the selection of Chess books, as follows:

1. Do *not be* impressed by publisher's blurbs stressing the *quantitative* output of the author. It is fundamental that the greater the output by the author, the more likely is his Chess product to be a crude *pastiche* or a rehash or an actual perversion of what already exists in much superior form.

2. Do *not* be impressed by an *extravagant* description of the author's qualifications. The qualifications of the eminent author—Lasker, Fine—need never be puffed; they are automatically known.

3. Do *not* fail to determine what actual contribution the author has made to Chess, as a person who has been authentically devoted to advancing the interests of the game rather than one who has, purely and simply, appropriated Chess as a commercial venture.

4. Do *not,* unless you can prudently rely on your own judgment, select books without seeking the guidance of recognized authorities of high professional standing. It is safer to acquire the work of a Fine, recommended by Fine himself, than anything recommended by a commercial hack.

5. Lastly, do *not,* as a lover of Chess literature, *fail* to acquire a book that reasonably appears to be an original approach to one or more phases of Chess in which you are interested, no matter who the author is.

At the risk of being duped occasionally, you will find that the joy of discovery will offer complete recompense.

THE JOHN G. WHITE COLLECTION

Curiously, there is a widespread misconception of the vast number of works on Chess in existence. Even so responsible an authority on games as Albert H. Morehead, Bridge Editor of *The New York Times,* who figures prominently in Chapter 13 of this book, estimates the number of books on Chess *and* Checkers to be "in the low thousands" (*The New York Times,* December 11, 1960). Actually, there are *at least* 15,000 Chess titles.

The largest and foremost Chess literature collection is to be found at the Cleveland Public Library, constituting but a part of over 100,000 volumes known as The John G. White Collection on Folklore, Orientalia, and Chess. To gain an acquaintanceship with this amazing Collection is to appreciate the little-known cultural oases throughout the United States: a charming art gallery here, a lovely museum there, and a splendid library elsewhere. All are, as often as not, gifts to the public from custodians of culture, as it were, whose exquisite taste for objects of great aesthetic value fortunately has been aided by financial means to acquire them. Appropriately enough, the John G. White Collection is in Cleveland, a city to which is often accorded the distinction of being called the cultural center of the American Midwest.

John Griswold White (1845–1928), an eminent Cleveland attorney, was a Chess *connoisseur* and an avid bibliophile. His love for books, as suggested by the title of the Collection, was not limited to Chess literature. Over a period of some fifty years he conducted a determined quest, throughout the world, for desirable additions to his library. As far back as 1914, H. J. R. Murray, famous Chess historian, referred to Mr. White's Chess library as the "largest" in the world. Mr. White, typically enough, shunned publicity. Casual references to him are found in the *Good Companion* magazine, an American periodical mostly devoted to Chess problems that flourished during the first quarter of the century. The vitality of the *Good Companion,* by the way, was traceable to Alain White

—no relative—of whom we have much more to say in Chapter 9. Mr. John G. White was vitally interested in the growth and progress of the Cleveland Public Library, serving at various times as its President and as member of the Board of Directors. Now, some thirty-four years after Mr. White's death, the Cleveland Public Library is the first to acknowledge that it owes its prominence in no small part to the pioneering zeal of such as Mr. White. The Cleveland Public Library has close to three million volumes, ranking second only to the New York Public Library; a staff of more than eight hundred, of whom over two hundred are professional librarians; a yearly loan volume of some seven million, constituting the largest per capita average, 7.45, for any urban area in the United States; three hundred fifteen thousand card holders (better than a third of the entire population of Cleveland) for the borrowing of books for home use; and close to four thousand daily visitors at the main branch only, to say nothing of thousands more who visit thirty-five neighborhood units.

This splendid *bibliothèque* was, of course, the logical heir to the collection of Mr. White, who also established a respectable fund for its growth. Since 1928, the Collection has been greatly increased. Some six thousand languages and dialects are represented in its more than one hundred thousand volumes. The inheritance was an automatic one, as a matter of fact, for the Collection, known by its present name since the death of Mr. White, had actually been made part of the Cleveland Public Library during Mr. White's lifetime. The Chess portion of the Collection has been increased from some five thousand titles to fourteen and a half thousand, the growth corresponding roughly to the rate of increase of the entire Collection. Duplicates account for about twenty-five thousand volumes. There are works in virtually every language in which Chess literature has appeared, including Latin, Arabic, Persian, Chinese, Japanese, Sanskrit, Bengali, Malay, and others. A rough breakdown of the Chess Collection into languages follows:

LANGUAGE	PERCENTAGE
English	35
German	20
French	15
Russian	10
Others	20

It is estimated that the collection is about five to six hundred titles short of *everything* ever written on Chess. The *total* Chess items in the Collection are considerably more than twice those in the world's largest printed Chess catalogue, that of the Royal Library in The Hague. Included in the titles are complete up-to-date volumes of Chess periodicals published throughout the world, pamphlets, and manuscripts. Clippings from newspapers and other sources, consisting of Chess columns and other Chess material, are kept in boxes, files, and in bound volumes. A so-called fugitive file is also maintained. This consists of advertisements, catalogues, pictures, and cartoons. In short, those in charge of The John G. White Collection have overlooked nothing of actual or potential importance in the world of Chess. It is their policy to buy every edition of any book published.

The earliest *printed* book on Chess in the Collection (*ca.* 1480) is Jean de Vignay's translation of *Solacium Ludi Scacchorum* by Jacobus de Cessolis, who wrote it at the end of the thirteenth century (*ca.* 1290). There are manuscripts of earlier date; the manuscripts include Cessolis' original Latin text.

Not available is a breakdown of the Collection into books, volumes of periodicals, manuscripts, and pamphlets. It is, however, reasonable to estimate that there are well over 10,000 *different* works on Chess in book or manuscript form out of an all-time total, as noted, of more than fifteen thousand titles. In making this estimate, we take into account the great number of abortive undertakings in the publication of Chess periodicals, as against the relative longevity of few: outstandingly, the *Deutsche Schachzeitung,* which has passed the century mark. If we allot a highly optimistic lifetime of five years per publication, and then assume that as many as five hundred Chess periodicals have appeared (and that each is included in the Collection), we arrive at a figure of twenty-five hundred. (The caution employed in this computation can be gauged by the fact that the United States, with a population of 185 million, has three Chess journals in circulation at present.) This leaves over twelve and a half thousand titles.

Gordon W. Thayer was Curator of The John G. White Collection from 1916 to 1956. It is to be noted that for many years, up to the time of Mr. White's death, Mr. Thayer shared his profound knowledge of books with Mr. White and continued for a period of close to thirty years to give his talents to the Collection. One conjures up a picture of the professional scholar and the scholarly *connoisseur* putting their heads together on such a noble project; one can almost visualize the excitement of these two men in acquiring a rare book, a "lost" manuscript, or an ancient tome resurrected from oblivion.

Mr. Walter F. Vella is now the Head of the Collection. Quite in keeping with the traditions of Messrs. White and Thayer, Mr. Vella's devotion to the Collection is completely in evidence. It is Mr. Vella, of course, who has furnished vital details, painstakingly gathered and patiently transmitted to your authors. So much of our story about the Cleveland Public Library in general and about The John G. White Collection in particular as is sprinkled with a warm adjective here and a word of praise there is *not* to be charged to Mr. Vella. This is the irresistible doing of your authors.

7

Chess in Literature

SELECTIONS FROM WORKS OF LEADING THINKERS

In literature, other than basic works on the game of Chess or other phases of it, Chess has played a respectable part, though not an overwhelming one. Its influence as a social phenomenon has been recognized by writers and thinkers throughout the ages; their observations have run the full cycle, from summary condemnation to warm endorsement. The game of Chess, nevertheless, has been incorporated in fiction and in mysteries. Of the latter, probably the best known is S. S. Van Dyne's *The Bishop Murder Case*.

Mysteries have also been built around retrograde analysis, that is, the reconstruction of the development of a game from a given Chess position, whereby the sleuth is aided in finding the criminal.

We find one of the earliest references in the *Analects* of

Confucius (*ca.* 200 B.C.). The Chinese philosopher, whose words follow, can hardly be considered a protagonist of the game:

I greatly admire a fellow who goes about the whole day with a well-fed stomach and a vacuous mind. How can one ever do it? I would rather that he play chess, which would seem to me to be better.

Chess is found in *The Arabian Nights,* in the *Rubáiyát* of Omar Khayyám and in Chaucer's *Book of the Duchesse.* Attributed to Pope Innocent II (1307–27) is the following didactic observation entitled *The Innocent Morality,* in which the treatment of the Pawns particularly is remindful of the discussion of the role of the Pawns in Chapter 3 of this book:

The world resembles a chessboard which is chequered white and black, the colours showing the two conditions of life and death, or praise and blame. The chessmen are men of this world who have a common birth, occupy different stations and hold different titles in this life, who contend together, and finally have a common fate which levels all ranks. The King often lies under the other pieces in the bag.

The King's move and powers of capture are in all directions, because the King's will is law.

The Queen's move is aslant only, because women are so greedy that they will take nothing except by rapine and injustice.

The Rook stands for the itinerant justices who travel over the whole realm, and their move is always straight, because the judge must deal justly.

The Knight's move is compounded of a straight move and an oblique one; the former betokens his legal power of collecting rents, &c., the latter his extortions and wrong-doings.

The Aufins are prelates wearing horns (but not like those that Moses had when he descended from Sinai). They move and take obliquely because nearly every bishop misuses his office through cupidity.

The Pawns are poor men. Their move is straight, except when they take anything: so also the poor man does well so long as he keeps from ambition. After the Pawn is promoted he becomes a Fers and moves obliquely, which shows how hard it is for a poor man to deal rightly when he is raised above his proper station.

In this game the Devil says 'Check!' when a man falls into sin; and unless he quickly covers the check by turning to repentance, the Devil says, 'Mate!' and carries him off to hell. whence is no escape. For the Devil has as many kinds of temptations to catch different types of men, as the hunter has dogs to catch different types of animals.

Johann Huss (1369–1415), famed Bohemian religious reformer, seeks repentance for loss of self-control at the Chess table:

You know how, before my priesthood (which grieveth me now), I have delighted to play oftimes at chess, and have neglected my time, and have unhappily provoked both myself and others to anger many times by that play. Wherefore, besides others of my innumerable faults, for this also I desire you to invoke the mercy of the Lord, and he will pardon me.

During the ensuing four centuries we encounter serious but scattered comment on Chess, outstandingly, Benjamin Franklin's *The Morals of Chess* (1779), but it was not until the nineteenth century that literary figures whose fame abides gave Chess considerably more attention. Understandably enough, the renewed literary preoccupation with Chess coincided with a renewed interest in the game itself. The nineteenth century saw the rise of analysts and students of Chess who have since done more in advancing the science of the game than had previously been accomplished in its entire history. Consider, for example, the fact that it was not until the middle of the nineteenth century that concentrated analysis, *continued to this very day*, was undertaken on a well-known opening, the Ruy López, discovered in the fourteenth century and initially given serious attention in 1561 by a Spanish cleric, Ruy López de Sigura. This spells out a lapse of four hundred years.

Lamb, William Hazlitt, Poe, Dostoyevsky, Tolstoi, George Eliot, Robert Louis Stevenson, John Ruskin, Dr. Oliver Wendell Holmes, Samuel Butler have their say, as does Lewis Carroll in his *Through the Looking-Glass.*

Poe, in his *Murder in the Rue Morgue,* indicates rather emphatically that Chess as against checkers (draughts) is overrated:

The faculty of re-solution is possibly much invigorated by mathematical study, and especially by that highest branch of it which, unjustly, and merely on account of its retrograde operations, has been called, as if par excellence, analysis. A chess-player, for example, does the one, without effort at the other. It follows that the game of chess, in its effect upon mental character, is greatly misunderstood. I am not now writing a treatise, but simply prefacing a somewhat peculiar narrative by observations very much at random; I will, therefore, take occasion to assert that the higher powers of the reflective intellect are more decidedly and more usefully tasked by the unostentatious game of draughts than by all the elaborate frivolity of chess. In this latter, where the pieces have different and bizarre motions, with various and variable values, what is only complex is mistaken (a not unusual error) for what is profound. The attention is here called powerfully into play. If it flag for an instant, an oversight is committed, resulting in an injury or defeat. The possible moves being not only manifold, but involute, the chances of such oversights are multiplied; and in nine cases out of ten, it is the more concentrative player who conquers.

Dostoyevsky (*Letters from the Underworld,* 1864) appears to be convinced about the brutality of the *goal* in Chess.

Ants are creatures of quite a different taste. They are constantly constructing marvellous edifices, but ones that shall be for ever indestructible. From the antheap all respectable ants take their origin, and in it (probably) they meet their end. This does credit alike to their continuity and to their perseverance.

On the other hand, man is a frivolous, a specious creature, and like a chess-player, cares more for the process of attaining his goal than for the goal itself.

George Eliot's passionate comments on Chess in *Felix Holt* and *Daniel Deronda,* respectively, are as follows:

Fancy what a game at chess would be if all the chessmen had passions and intellects, more or less small and cunning; if you were not only uncertain about your adversary's men, but a little uncertain also about your own; if your knight could shuffle himself on to a new square by the sly; if your bishop, in disgust at your castling, could wheedle your pawns out of their places; and if your pawns, hating you because they are pawns, could make away from their appointed posts that you might get a checkmate on a sudden. You might be the longest-headed of deductive reasoners, and yet you might be beaten by your own pawns. You would be especially likely to be beaten, if you depended arrogantly on your mathematical imagination, and regarded your passionate pieces with contempt.

Yet this imaginary chess is easy compared with the game a man has to play against his fellow-men with other fellow-men for his instruments. He thinks himself sagacious, perhaps, because he trusts no bond except that of self-interest; but the only self-interest he can safely rely on is what seems to be such to the mind he would use or govern. Can he ever be sure of knowing this?

Most of us remember Retzsch's drawing of destiny in the shape of Mephistopheles playing at chess with man for his soul, a game in which we may imagine the clever adversary making a feint of unintended moves so as to set the beguiled mortal on carrying his defensive pieces away from the true point of attack. The fiend makes preparation his favorite object of mockery, that he may fatally persuade us against our own best safeguard. He meddles so far as to suggest our taking out waterproofs when he is well aware the sky is going to clear, foreseeing that the imbecile will turn this delusion into a prejudice against water-proofs instead of giving a closer study to the weather signs. It is a peculiar test of a man's mettle when, after he has painfully adjusted himself to what seems a wise provision, he finds all his mental precaution a little beside the mark, and his excellent intentions no better than miscalculated dovetails, accurately cut from a wrong starting-point. His magnanimity has got itself ready to meet misbehaviour, and finds quite a different call upon it.

Oliver Wendell Holmes (*The Autocrat of The Breakfast Table,* 1892) is concerned with the behavior of the Chess-player, symbolic as this is to him of the behavior of man in general:

I say, averages of masses we have, but our tables of maxima we owe to the sporting men more than to the philosophers. The lesson their experience teaches is, that Nature makes no leaps,—does nothing *per saltum.* The greatest brain that ever lived, no doubt, was only a small fraction of an idea ahead of the second best. Just look at the chess-players. Leaving out the phenomenal exceptions, the nice shades that separate the skilful ones show how closely their brains approximate,—almost as closely as chronometers. Such a person is a *"knight-*player,"—he must have that piece given him. Another must have two pawns. Another, "pawn and two," or one pawn and two moves. Then we find one who claims "pawn and move," holding himself, with this fractional advantage, a match for one who would be pretty sure to beat him playing even.—So much are minds alike; and you and I think we are "peculiar,"—that Nature broke her jelly-mould after shaping our cerebral convolutions.

Samuel Butler (*The Notebooks,* 1893) voices, probably, the frustration of all writers, whose irrevocable words can plague them through life: "It [Chess] has this advantage that when it is done it is dead and buried; it is not like writing these stupid notes."

On the other hand, Stephen Leacock, the master humorist, in his delightful *Pawn to King's Four* (1943), recognizes that failure to make a proper move in a game of Chess can offer us much frustration. His verdict is crushingly terse: "Chess is one long regret."

Robert Louis Stevenson (*Talk and Talkers,* 1882) considers Chess a sublimation of a sort:

The spice of life is battle; the friendliest relations are still a kind of contest; and if we would not forego all that is valuable in our lot, we must continually face some other person, eye to eye, and wrestle a fall whether in love or enmity. It is still by force of body, or power of character or intellect, that we attain to worthy pleasures. Men and women contend for each other in the lists of love, like rival mesmerists; the active and adroit decide their challenges in the sports of the body; and the sedentary sit down to chess or conversation.

We have fiction fantasies centered about Chess by Lord Dunsany (*The Three Sailors' Gambit,* 1916), and E. M. Forster (*Chess at Cracow,* 1932). There is a devastating treatise on the game by the omniscient H. G. Wells (*Concerning Chess,* 1901), who equates Chess with perfidy, as follows:

The passion for playing chess is one of the most unaccountable in the world. It slaps the theory of natural selection in the face. It is the most absorbing of occupations, the least satisfying of desires, an aimless excrescence upon life. It annihilates a man. You have, let us say, a promising politician, a rising artist, that you wish to destroy. Dagger or bomb are archaic, clumsy, and unreliable—but teach him, inoculate him with chess! It is well perhaps, that the right way of teaching chess is so little known, that consequently in most cases the plot fails in the performance, the dagger turns aside. Else we should all be chess-players—there would be none left to do the business of the world. Our statesmen would sit with pocket boards while the country went to the devil, our army would bury itself in chequered contemplation, our bread-winners would forget their wives in seeking after impossible mates. The whole world would be disorganized. I can fancy this abominable hypnotism so wrought into the constitution of men that the cabmen would go trying to drive their horses in Knight's moves up and down Charing Cross Road. And now and again a suicide would come to hand with the pathetic inscription pinned to his chest: "I checked with my Queen too soon. I cannot bear the thought of it." There is no remorse like the remorse of chess.

Only, happily, as we say, chess is taught the wrong way round. People put out the board before the learner with all the men in battle array, sixteen a side, with six different kinds of moves, and the poor wretch is simply crushed and appalled. A lot of things happen, mostly disagreeable, and then the mate comes looming up through the haze of pieces. So he goes away awestricken but unharmed, secretly believing that all chess-players are humbugs, and that intelligent chess, which is neither chancy nor rote-learned, is beyond the wit of man. But clearly this is an unreasonable method of instruction. Before the beginner can understand the beginning of the game he must surely understand the end; how can he commence playing until he knows what he is playing for? It is like starting athletes on a race, and leaving them to find out where the winning-post is hidden.

Your true teacher of chess, your subtle chess-poisoner, your cunning Comus who changes men to chess-players, begins quite the other way round. He will, let us say, give you King, Queen, and Pawn placed out in careless possible positions. So you master the militant possibilities of Queen and Pawn without perplexing complications. Then King, Queen, and Bishop perhaps; King, Queen, and Knight; and so on. It ensures that you always play a winning game in these happy days of your chess childhood, and taste the one sweet of chess-playing, the delight of having the upper hand of a better player. Then to more complicated positions, and at last back to the formal beginning. You begin to see now to what end the array is made, and understand why one Gambit differeth from another in glory and virtue. And the chess mania of your teacher cleaveth to you thenceforth and for evermore.

It is a curse upon a man. There is no happiness in chess—Mr. St. George Mivart, who can find happiness in the strangest places, would be at a loss to demonstrate it upon the chess-board. The mild delight of a pretty mate is the least unhappy phase of it. But, generally, you find afterwards that you ought to have mated two moves before, or at the time that an unforeseen reply takes your Queen. No chess-player sleeps well. After the painful strategy of the day one fights one's battles over again. You see with more than daylight clearness that it was the Rook you should have moved, and not the Knight. No! it is impossible! no common sinner innocent of chess knows these deeps of remorse. Vast desert boards lie for the chess-player beyond the gates of horn. Stalwart Rooks ram headlong at one, Knights hop sidelong, one's Pawns are all tied, and a mate hangs threatening and never descends. And once chess has been begun in the proper way, it is flesh of your flesh, bone of your bone; you are sold, and the bargain is sealed and the evil spirit hath entered in.

The proper outlet for the craving is the playing of games, and there is a class of men—shadowy, unhappy, unreal-looking men—who gather in coffee houses, and play with a desire that dieth not, and a fire that is not quenched. These gather in clubs and play Tournaments, such Tournaments as he of the Table Round could never have imagined. But there are others who have the vice who live in country places, in remote situations—curates, schoolmasters, rate collectors—who go consumed from day to day and meet no fit companion, and who must needs find some artificial vent for their mental energy.

No one has ever calculated how many sound Problems are possible, and no doubt the Psychical Research people would be glad if Professor Pearson would give his mind to the matter. All the possible dispositions of the pieces come to such a vast number, however, that, according to the theory of probability, and allowing a few thousand arrangements each day, the same problem ought never to turn up more than twice in a century or so. As a matter of fact—it is probably due to some flaw in the theory of probability—the same problem has a way of turning up in different publications several times in a month or so. It may be, of course, that, after all, quite "sound" problems are limited in number, and that we keep on inventing and reinventing them; that, if a record were kept, the whole system, up to four or five moves, might be classified, and placed on record in the course of a few score years. Indeed, if we were to eliminate those with conspicuously bad moves, it may be we should find the number of reasonable games was limited enough, and that even our brilliant Lasker is but repeating the inspirations of some long-buried Persian, some mute inglorious Hindoo, dead and forgotten ages since. It may be over every game there watches the forgotten forerunners of the players, and that chess is indeed a dead game, a haunted game, played out centuries ago, even, as beyond all cavil, is the game of draughts.

The artistic temperament, the gay irresponsible cast of mind, does what it can to lighten the gravity of this too intellectual game. To a mortal, there is something indescribably horrible in these champions with their four moves an hour—the bare thought of the mental operations of the fifteen minutes gives one a touch of headache. Compulsory quick moving is the thing for gaiety, and that is why we revere Steinitz and Lasker, it is Bird we love. His victories glitter, his errors are magnificent.

The true sweetness of chess, if it ever can be sweet, is to see a victory snatched, by some happy impertinence, out of the shadow of apparently irrevocable disaster.

We also commend to the reader a featherweight zanyism by Robert Benchley, *How to Watch a Chess-Match* (1922).

PSYCHIATRIC ANALYSIS OF CHESS IDIOT-SAVANT IN STEFAN ZWEIG'S CLASSIC

No treatment of Chess in literature, howsoever limited or extensive, can possibly suffice without inclusion of a reasonably detailed account of the most fascinating and masterful fiction piece on Chess, the late Stefan Zweig's novelette, *The Royal Game,* his very last literary work.

The Royal Game appeared originally in the March, 1944, issue of the *Woman's Home Companion,* and it immediately fired the enthusiasm of those who value good literature. What is more, the principal characters have made a deep impression on all who have an interest in the phenomenon of Chess as it relates to human behavior and intellectual development.

The Royal Game is faithfully summarized by K. O. Mott-Smith, a prominent chess expert, in the March 1944 issue of *Chess Review.* Appearing in the same issue is a comment on *The Royal Game* by another Chess enthusiast, F. W. Thorne.

The questions raised by Messrs. Mott-Smith and Thorne aroused the professional interest of Dr. Henry A. Davidson, a psychiatrist, then in wartime service as a Captain in the United States Army. (Dr. Davidson, a dedicated scholar, had had a live interest in Chess for many years; he has since then written *A Short History of Chess,* a commendable piece of work to which reference is made in Chapter 2. Dr. Davidson's comments appeared in the November 1944, issue of *Chess Review.**)

---

* This and any other material in this book from *Chess Review* reprinted by permission.

Analysis of Chess Idiot-Savant in Stefan Zweig's Classic

We present the Mott-Smith–Thorne–Davidson observations *in toto:*

K. O. Mott-Smith: I would like to call your attention to the story by Stefan Zweig, the last ever written by the distinguished Austrian novelist, entitled "The Royal Game," and published in the March 1944 issue of the *Woman's Home Companion.* I do not ordinarily read the *Woman's Home Companion,* but I have a wife—bless her!—who does.

This is by far the best chess story I have ever read. Czentovic, an uncouth Yugoslav peasant of low mentality, has become chess champion of the world, thanks to his sole natural gift, and amazing aptitude for the game. On an ocean voyage he is prevailed upon, for the modest fee of $250 a game, to play against the ship's passengers in consultation. The passengers lose one game and are about to lose another when they are saved by a mysterious stranger who points out a masterly series of moves forcing a draw. The stranger proves to be Dr. B, distinguished Austrian lawyer, recently escaped from a prison hospital after having been imprisoned and tortured by the Nazis in an attempt to force disclosure of the whereabouts of certain trust funds. The torture, directed against the nerves and will rather than the body, consisted of prolonged isolation from human companionship and deprivation of all reading matter and other forms of intellectual diversion. About to succumb to the deadly monotony of his thoughts, Dr. B is saved by a book abstracted from one of his jailor's pockets, a collection of 150 master chess games. By following and studying the moves in his mind's eye (for of course he has no chess board or men), the prisoner is able to derive the mental vigor necessary to withstand the onslaughts upon his nervous system. But, after having learned all the games of the book by heart, he is driven, for a continuation of his chess calisthenics, to playing games against himself. The opposing stresses set up by this self-antagonism, the whipsawing of his mind between his White and Black selves, ultimately drive him insane.

After his escape and restoration to sanity, Dr. B avoided chess, lest renewed contact bring another breakdown. But the exhilarating sight of a game played with actual pieces and between living players had proved too great a temptation. He could not restrain himself from aiding the passengers in their contest with Czentovic.

Requested to play a game, Dr. B at first refused. On learning, however, that his opponent was no less than the world's champion, he agreed, despite his misgivings, to contest an even game against the champion. Beaten after a grueling struggle, Czentovic knocks the pieces off the board and coldly proposes another game. Now feverish with excitement, Dr. B consents. After announcing a nonexistent check to his adversary's King, he is forcibly prevented by the other passengers from continuing—just in time to forestall another mental collapse.

Could a blockhead like Czentovic become chess champion of the world? Could a sensitive soul like Dr. B be driven insane by too much analysis? These questions should furnish your readers with food for some interesting discussion. Personally, I am inclined to concur with Mr. Zweig, and if that be treason, etc. . . .

F. W. Thorne: *The Woman's Home Companion* has a story about a stupid dolt who became World's Chess Champion and remained stupid in everything but chess. I claim chess so stimulates the brain that he would have improved in manners and in many other ways—at least from traveling and association. Argument?

And Dr. Davidson's incisive article, entitled *Can A Dope Become A Denker?*

In the March *Chess Review*, Mr. Mott-Smith, recalling Stefan Zweig's last story, asks if a blockhead like Czentovic could become a chess champion and if a sensitive soul like "Dr. B" could be driven insane by too much analysis. And in the same column, Mr. Thorne asserts that a good chessplayer could never be as churlish as Czentovic was.

Being both a psychiatrist and a chessplayer, I have often thought about the problem of the intellectual assets required in playing a masterly game. Offhand, one would assume that the sole requisite is intelligence. But it is not so simple. It is well known that a man may be a brilliant braintruster, yet show an intellectual blindspot. For instance, an allround genius might be inept in the manipulation of mathematical concepts, stupidly trusting in business relationships, or gauche in the utilization of words. Ordinarily, all three of these activities require brains. But a man may be brilliant without covering every possible area of intellect. This is well known, but it does not answer Mr. Mott-Smith's query. He poses the reverse question. Granted that a smart man may have an intellectual blind-spot, the issue is: can a stupid man have an area of intellectual brilliance?

The answer, it appears, is yes. For instance, many reputable records attest to the existence of "idiots-savants"—persons of inferior, even defective intelligence, who show extraordinary clarity in certain compartments of thinking. There is one imbecile who can extract square roots in his head. This is not a matter of rote memory. He has not memorized a table of square roots. He performs the required arithmetical operation with dispatch and efficiency, even though his I.Q. is in the low fifties. Or consider the quality called "shrewdness." We bookish people show contempt for it because we don't have it and pretend that shrewdness has nothing to do with intelligence. We are kidding ourselves of course. Shrewdness is a form of intelligence, and if an unlettered yokel outwits you in a business deal, he has in fact "outsmarted" you; that is, he's smarter than you, even though you might win an encyclopedia from Clifton Fadiman when he can't. My point is that intelligence is not a measurable unit like height—something that you have so much of, and the next man has so much more or so much less. Intelligence is a mixture of skills including memory, curiosity, ability to generalize, ability to see comparisons, imagination, ability to put things together, and numerous other qualities—some of them still unnamed. When a man has a fair quantity of a number of these, he's a smart man. When he has large quantities of lots of these traits, he's a genius. But what is he, if he has an extra dose of one of these skills, while he has been short-changed on all the others? Then he is an *idiot-savant*, and that is what the surly master Czentovic was.

What is the pattern of intellectual skills that makes one man a good chessplayer while the other remains a duffer? Why is it that a superannuated quiz kid can persistently fall for the scholar's mate? I am not sure, but I think that these are some of the factors:

In the first place, topnotch chess requires visual imagery. Before you make a contemplated move, you have to visualize how the board will look after you make it, and then how it will be changed by your opponent's response, and how it will look after you meet this response and how it will look after you meet another possible answer. Now that takes visual imagery. Can you look at an empty apartment and imagine how your furniture would be placed there and what the rooms will look like after you have deployed the furniture? If you can, you are using visual imagery. Personally, I have a lot of trouble with that kind of intellectual exercise, which is one reason why I will never even be chess champion of New Guinea. But in self defense, I hasten to point out that an idiot may have good visual imagery. In fact, if his mind is uncluttered with the ideas that race through a busier head, he may have a nice clean tablet in his skull on which all sorts of pictures can find room. In general smart people have good visual imagery. In general. But some smart ones don't, and some alumni of our schools for the feebleminded do happen to possess this solitary intellectual asset. But even visual imagery isn't enough to convert a dope into a Denker.

You also need patience and restraint. The quick thinker is often a fool. To sit still without moving or talking and let the wheels go round takes patience, and to make yourself do it takes restraint. I know from personal experience that if I force myself to wait several minutes before making the "obvious" move, I use the time in thinking out other possibilities, and in the long run, win more games than I do when I move fast. But I usually make the "obvious" moves. Why? Because I have neither patience nor restraint.

Now these are the cornerstone qualities: visual imagery plus restraint and patience. But even that is no formula for a Fine. You need a good memory too. Memory has two components: ability to retain, ability to recall. The chessplayer needs both. You see how valuable that quality was in Dr. B's game against Czentovic. Chess plays constantly remind expert players of similar plays in other games. As a matter of fact, this humdrum quality of memory is probably the chief reason for the pedagogic value of "experience."

Finally, chess calls for a certain kind of "reasoning." Consider the mental processes involved in deciding whether to exchange that final pair of Rooks and take a chance on promoting one of the remaining Pawns. You need patience enough to sit on your hands while you think it out. You need memory —perhaps recollection of some formula for figuring out if the King can beat the Pawn, or perhaps recall some past experience in a similar situation. And you need visual imagery to picture how the board will look a few moves after those castles have been exchanged. You have to do all this before you elect to take that Rook. Now in figuring your chance to queen a Pawn before your opponent can reach home plate with his, you go through a reasoning process. You alternately put yourself in your colleague's place and figure what you would do if you were sitting on his side of the board, and then jump back into your own clothes. You use simple arithmetic. You use your imagination. You use your memory. You reason deductively, as when you say to yourself, "He'll probably clean up my passed Pawn first" or "he'll probably push his most advanced Pawn first" or "he'll hasten to move in with his King first" or whatever it is: that is, you take some general principle of endgame play and apply it. Now other things being equal, the more intelligent you are, the brisker your reasoning processes will be along these lines. But other things are not always equal. If you happen to have a mind which forms this kind of association easily, you will reason soundly even though you would never win a blue ribbon in an I.Q. derby.

This, then, is the putty which holds the blocks together. The blocks are memory, patience, and imagery. The putty is associative reasoning. In daily life you use some of these processes, but you also use other intellectual techniques. For instance, inductive reasoning (the ability to draw a general inference from an example) is not much used in chess, but it pays dividends in business and professional life. So your intelligent lawyer or merchant might be a bungler with the battling bishops. The answer to Mr. Mott-Smith's first question would appear to be "yes." The blockhead can become a chess champion. But he usually doesn't.

The number two question is: can a person be driven insane by too much self-analysis? Probably not. There is no provable case on record of anyone having gone insane because of overstudy, bereavement, or worry. We psychiatrists don't have the final answer as to what causes the psychoses. But there has been no evidence that introspection or self-analysis ever landed a man in a psychopathic ward.

Mr. Thorne wonders whether a chess genius would be as unmannerly as Mr. Zweig's mythical Czentovic. He certainly could. Manners, like morals, bear no relationship to intelligence. It is not a novel discovery that a genius can be a jerk. Many brilliant men have been surly and boorish; many have been arrogant, cruel, and bigoted; and some geniuses have been mad. Chess stimulates the brain, as Mr. Thorne points out. But kindliness arises not out of intellectual keenness, but out of poise, self-assurance, and emotional security. And on these qualities, the geniuses have no option.

8

Is Chess an Art Form?

Is playing Chess a creative activity? Is it an art form? Is it reasonable arbitrarily to include Chess in the family of universally recognized art forms: music, literature, painting, sculpture, the stage, choreography, architecture?

EXAMINATION OF CRITERIA FOR FORMULATION OF JUDGMENT

Let us first consider the basically essential ingredients of art. If we limit the definition of art to the unique (or original, at the very least) creation of something that has *form* and *beauty,* we are in trouble at once. Surely, the designer of a chic Ivy League vest will insist that his product is an artistic creation, falling squarely within the stated definition. We must, therefore, include in our definition a singular characteristic of art, which necessarily excludes fancy vests. And that is *permanence:* too sweeping a term perhaps for what is essentially *lasting value.*

Thus we have *form* as the basic substance; beauty and *lasting value* as the essential attributes. Lest we fall into a semantic morass, it is necessary to determine the standards employed in ascertaining what beauty and lasting value are. It takes no strain to conclude that they consist of a creative form which *continues* to *please* "us"—by line, color, proportion, texture, content, style, rhythmic motion, tone, depth, etc. And now, to dispose of the troublesome "us," and we have arrived at a workable definition of terms. The "us," necessarily, is that part of the human world which has made a reasonably painstaking effort to evaluate art forms not only on the basis of emotional response (which, admittedly, is an integral factor, more often than not) but on the basis of study, comparison, and, if you will, measured reliance on respectable authority. Are we now hopelessly bogged down? What is a "reasonably painstaking effort"? What is "measured reliance"? What is "respectable authority"? The standards are one's own. Is the judgment based on the reading of no books, one book, or a thousand? On the studying of one, fourteen, or five hundred paintings? On the blind reliance on someone whose qualifications are not known, or on the reliance on a proved authority?

So, finally, we can understand why we recognize art forms—whether or not they appeal to us individually—the creations of DaVinci, Shakespeare, Bach, Nazimova, Dostoyevsky, Christopher Wren, John Keats, O'Neill, and Jacob Epstein, and the reasons accounting for their lasting value.

But, if you will forgive our stubbornness, is Chess an art form? Concededly, unique skill is the *sine qua non* in art, and masterfully played Chess abounds with originality, superlative ability, incredible resourcefulness, and actual genius. It is, however, basic that the brilliance of the one participant in a game of Chess necessarily depends on lack of vigilance of the other. We deal with the matching of wits; we do not have essential elements for absolute creativeness. There are scores upon scores of brilliantly played games of Chess (see Chapter 17); they are the delight of the *connoisseur,* or even the player whose interest in Chess is casual; some of the games have earned eminence inherent in the titles bestowed upon them: "The Immortal Game," "The Game of the Century"; many more have earned a lesser yet permanent niche in the annals of Chess. Yet, none would have attained distinction had the victim anticipated the "brilliant" catastrophe about to befall him.

There are, however, many, non-Chessplayers among them, who claim vigorously that *expert* play of a game of Chess is quite analogous, say, to expert interpretation of a piece of music: each, therefore, a creative activity. This contention is implemented by the reminder that *any* art form, the tools for creating it and, to be sure, existing works of the same *genre* are necessarily interdependent; that strict originality is a rarity almost entirely limited to the works of the earliest pioneers; that the over-the-board brilliancy of the Chessmaster is no less an art form because of the interdependence that governs his performance. It is further contended that the more subtle the Chess brilliancy is, the more likely it is to merit recognition as an art form. In other words, when the opponent overlooks the possibility of an extremely obscure line of play that leads to the brilliancy (*against* him), the interdependence is reduced to a minimum. This, of course, is a necessary qualification, for rarely is a line of play credited as superlative if it arises as a result of an opponent's *obvious* error.

But it appears that those who believe the brilliancy in a game of Chess to be an art form do not take into account at least two vital considerations. First, the interdependence assigned peremptorily to all forms of art necessarily exists on a level much different from that governing a game of Chess. If we say that the painter and sculptor are slaves to their media, that the violinist is beholden to the musical score, that all of them, including the writer and artists in other fields, are restricted by what has already been done, we necessarily deny the possibility of original adaptation at the very least, to say nothing of actual creative genius. In such case, no Spinoza can follow a Socrates, no Joyce can follow a Dostoyevsky, no Cezanne can follow a Michelangelo. Clearly, in the most prominent art forms we have witnessed the creations, generation after generation, of gigantic works, each attesting to the uniqueness of the artist, and each *virtually* devoid of interdependence. Second, the *unplayed* brilliancy on the Chessboard is given no attention. We shall clarify. The annotations of many expert Chess games reveal that subtle brilliancies have been thwarted; the line of play was seen by the would-be victim, and he promptly took steps to prevent its coming to life. In no such case is the defensive player given recognition such as that freely accorded the one who performs the brilliancy. Why? It is placidly assumed that an aborted coup, whatsoever subtleties it may entail, does not earn the plaudits of an executed one. This is a strange paradox. We have, for example, the previously referred to *Immortal Game*. Certainly, if the victim had seen the possibilities against him and had taken defensive measures against them, this Chess encounter would now rest unsung in the prosaic archives of Caissa. It appears that the interdependence in the Chess game, distinguishing it so forcefully from that found in generally recognized art forms, must be recognized as a *dominant* feature.

It is quite possible that we are showing more concern for classification than substance. A game of Chess expertly played is an intellectual exercise of a high degree. Whether or not it is a creative activity—and your authors are reluctantly inclined to conclude that it is not!—is probably less material than a realization that outstanding over-the-board feats merit recognition as superlative mental achievements. One Chess titan outwits another in an astonishing manner. We must also consider, of course, that there are various levels of recognition of Chess brilliancies. The mortals find breathtaking features in, for example, many of Morphy's Chess exploits. On the other hand, Morphy fires limited enthusiasm in a Chessmaster of the standing of Dr. Reuben Fine, who knows at his finger-tips the outstanding games of leading grandmasters since Morphy's time, and as a superb Chess analyst is on sure ground in relegating Morphy's games to a much inferior level. It follows that the "best" in a game of Chess to a Fine may be a web of technical precision, such as is likely to escape the understanding (or the admiration) of the casual or even the more advanced Chessplayer. As a pointed illustration, we have included in Chapter 17 the game that Dr. Fine considers his best up to that time. In it you will find no sensational coups or brilliancies, no single stage in the course of play as striking as those in practically all other cited examples; but you *will* find a *complete* performance characterized essentially by the gradual, relentless, determined translation into victory of a thin, invisible (to most eyes other than Fine's) thread of ad-vantage.

There is, however, a phase of Chess that we definitely con-sider to be an art form. This consists of *composed* problems, endings, and various Chess settings, the relationship of which to the game of Chess may be fairly compared with that of poetry to prose. Implicit in this analogy is a recognition of the inevitable imagination, fantasy, subtlety, all expertly blended in superior Chess compositions and in good poetry, while sub-ject to basic precepts of discipline, as against an awareness of the pragmatic matter-of-factness and singularness of purpose in the game of Chess *and* in prose.

And so we come to the opportunity to muse on the creations inspired by the Erato of Chess.

9

The Poetry of Chess

**Masterpiece
by Eric M. Hassberg
New York Post, 1945**

**White to Play and Mate in 2 Moves
(Solution at end of chapter)**

COMPOSERS OF PROBLEMS
AND ENDINGS

The Chess problem and the composed Chess ending are *the* art forms of Chess, each embracing a wide area of creativeness. Chess problems have been called the *Poetry of Chess,* for the very good reason that their value is purely aesthetic and, like poetry, they serve mankind as a ". . . pastime and delight." [Actually, Longfellow speaks of poetry as mankind's *"universal* pastime and delight"* (italics ours), but in the light of relatively limited appeal, the *universal* can hardly be applied to Chess problems.]

A Chessboard composition is in essence an invented position calling for one side or the other (White, usually) to perform a stated assignment. Orthodox compositions consist of direct-mate problems, calling for a mate in a precisely stipulated number of moves; and of endings, calling for the demonstration of a win or draw. In both it must be conclusively shown that the solution is valid against best defense.

Whereas the earliest known compositions (dating back to the ninth century) consisted principally of mating nets (that is, a regimentation of forces, brutal frequently, for the purpose of delivering the lethal blow), Chess problem composition has developed in the course of the ages—and during the past century particularly—into a creative activity governed by rigorous standards. Stress is placed on originality, subtlety, and thematic content particularly. A composition without a theme— a plot, if you wish—is usually accorded little or no merit.

Chessplayers tend to frown upon the Chess problem, to be more receptive to the composed Chess ending. The former is considered a "puzzle" offering no particular aid in the improvement of one's playing skill, whereas the latter is looked upon as potentially if not actually related to positions that can conceivably be encountered in the game of Chess. On the other hand, there is a keen awareness of the inherent subtleties in good Chess problems. That accounts for the Chessplayer's tendency to refer to an unobvious effective move as problemlike.

VARIOUS TYPES OF COMPOSITION

If orthodox Chess problem compositions have invited the derision of Chessplayers, it is understandable that unorthodox settings, which *actually* have no relationship to the game, have all the more met with scorn. The unorthodox field of composition, known as Fairy Chess, is the surrealism of the Chessboard. (Fairy Chess is an unfortunate designation, by the way, for aside from the vulgar connotation of lack of masculinity it fails to convey the essence of its area of composition: fantasy, imagination, and flights of fancy incorporated into modes of play that blissfully take no heed of the rigid rules governing the game of Chess.) There is a menagerie of invented pieces: Grasshopper, Camel, Zebra, Nightrider, *et al.*, each endowed with a locomotion unlike that of standard Chess pieces. The stipulations include forcing the opponent to mate (*selfmate*), but some authorities place the selfmate in a class of its own, for basically the rules of Chess are strictly observed; helping the opponent to mate (*helpmate*) or to stalemate (*helpstalemate*). In *maximates* or *minimates,* one or both sides are limited, respectively, to the longest or shortest geometric move; in *reflex-mate* problems, each side *must* deliver mate on the move, if able to do so, and the ultimate object, in this variant of the selfmate, is to force the opponent to deliver mate in a stipulated number of moves; in *Grid Chess,* the Chessboard is subdivided into compartments, each piece being forced to move from one subdivision to another (and having no power to capture an enemy piece situated in the same subdivision), quite in the style of balkline billiards. Imagine the utter horror of the Chessplayer encountering opposing Kings in contiguous squares, but such juxtaposition is quite valid in Grid Chess.

It is altogether certain that, objections of jeering Chessplayers to the contrary notwithstanding, the amazingly rich literature on Chess compositions, problems, and endings is truly *the* repository of *the* art form of Chess. We find ingenious conceptions executed with unswerving determination. (Appended Problem No. 50 took some three years to compose.) We find beauty and precision reflecting the composer's stubborn battle against the geometric limitations of the Chessboard and the rigidly prescribed locomotive power of the pieces. We find the unfolding of subtle plots in settings of rich thematic content. We find, in short, man's perseverance in mastering a 64-square realm into which he has woven enigmatic patterns, while subject to a relentless discipline governing his creations.

The Russians are pre-eminent in the composition of orthodox problems and endings. They have given their talents principally to the ultraserious phase of problem composition, the dynamic subtleties of which are rather a mystery to the vast majority of solvers. This level of composition embraces two- and three-move direct-mate problems, with the former usually predominating, which, in effect, are artistic illustrations of original themes (the ultra in *all* problem composition), unique expressions of known themes with special stress on the mechanisms employed, or novel adaptations of related aspects. (It is, of course, to be noted that the terms *original, unique,* and *novel* are attributes of all problem compositions of merit.) In a word, the relationship of the ultraserious, dynamic Chess problem to the casual "cute" pleasantry is quite the same as that of the ultraprofound in poetry to light verse.

Among Russia's highest ranking problem composers are M. M. Barulin, A. P. Gulyaev (who has also composed splendid endings), and E. I. Umnov. (See *The Two-Move Chess Problem in the Soviet Union,* by Alain White, Richard Cheney, and Albrecht Buschke, Overbrook Press, limited edition, 1943.) Leading Russian composers of endings were the late A. A. Troitzky and K. A. L. Kubbel. (We have no immediate information as to whether the listed problem composers are still on the scene.)

Among the leading living American problemists are E. M. Hassberg, whose lovely 2-mover graces the beginning of this chapter; Newman Guttman, Kenneth S. Howard, Edgar Holladay, Julius Buchwald, Walter Jacobs, and P. L. Rothenberg. As these pages are being written, we learn with much grief of the untimely death (at age forty-six) of one of the greatest American composers of all time, Vincent Lanius Eaton. A graduate from Harvard at the age of eighteen, Eaton followed a scholar's career in the Library of Congress. For well over twenty-five years he excelled in every phase of problem composition. He was Problem Editor of *Chess Review* (1939–41). (Jacobs was one of his predecessors in that post; Rothenberg, his immediate successor.) Eaton's creations have been featured in Chess periodicals throughout the world.

Joseph Peckover is the best known American composer of endings, a field that has not attracted excessive talent in this country.

There are prominent composers in Europe (countries other than Russia), among whom Comins Mansfield and C. S. Kipping of Britain are two of the most distinguished.

The Chess problem scene in the United States is a limited one. The problem department conducted by Edgar Holladay in the *American Chess Bulletin* is the sum total of significant outlets. Relatively few show a burning interest in Fairy Chess, truly one of the most exciting forms of the Chess problem art. P. L. Rothenberg has been an outstanding devotee, a composer of superb settings (some of which are appended). Rothenberg is recognized as an authority on all phases of problem composition. All his life, he has had an uninterrupted, active interest in all phases of Chess in particular and in the world of enigma in general. He has invented a number of original games and puzzles; Rothenberg's Chess and related activities have been extracurricular, so to say. He is a social worker by profession. (We direct the reader's attention to Rothenberg's authoritative articles on problems and endings in the *Macmillan Handbook of Chess,* 1956.)

Among the few Americans who have showed a consistent interest in Fairy Chess is Mannis Charosh of Brooklyn, a mathematician, who has invented several Fairy Chess forms. *Relay Chess* is by far Charosh's most promising brainchild. It entails the transfer of locomotive power from one piece to another guarded by it. (For example, a Knight guarded by a Rook operates as both Knight *and* Rook.) There are astounding possibilities when Relay power is vested in either or both sides of the Chessboard. Unfortunately, the inspiration of a Dawson (of whom more later) is lacking to stimulate artistic exploration. As a matter of fact, since the death of Dawson (1951), the virtual father of Fairy Chess, expert composition has been on the decline. There are worthy composers in, for example, Yugoslavia, Hungary, and England, but there is no Dawson to take the lead. There is now an overabundance of the helpmate, which is the least gratifying of Fairy forms in the absence of compelling features justifying this type of composition. In the helpmate, White and Black cooperate in accomplishing the assigned task, usually mating the latter in a stipulated number of moves. The composer must guard against *too much* cooperation, resulting as this can (and frequently does) in unintended lines of play, which, of course, render the composition unsound. Once the cooperation is controlled, the composer can concoct for himself one piece of flimflam after another, with the illusion that he is a creative artist. It is safe to note that if 90 per cent of helpmates had never come to life, their permanent fetus stage would be a joy to one and all. On the other hand, much artistic value can be found in the (arbitrarily decreed) 10 per cent. Appended illustrations will prove the point.

GOLDEN ERA

The present moribund state of Chess problems in the United States hardly suggests a *golden era* of the not-too-far past. The halfway mark of the twentieth century brought an end to an enthusiasm for problem Chess which, though much on the wane then, had pervaded the American scene for seventy-five years or more, up to the early 1940's. In 1960 death claimed one of the most distinguished American problem composers, Geoffrey Mott-Smith. And now, aside from Howard, Jacobs, Hassberg, Rothenberg, and a few others, no ties are left with the titans, Shinkman and Wurzburg, and through them with the amazing Sam Loyd. There is no longer an Alain White, the Chess problem personality who is likely to remain *sui generis* for all time to come. Gone is the *Titanic Triumvirate,* Sam Loyd (1841–1911), the *Puzzle King* who casually antici-pated possibilities in composition fifty and more years ahead of time; William A. Shinkman (1847–1933), who enthusias-tically accepted the challenge of the Chessboard to reduce *it* to his will; and Otto Wurzburg (1875–1952), whose artistry kept energetic pace for more than fifty years with the standards set by Shinkman, Wurzburg's uncle. Gone are the *Good Companions,* an association of composers that flourished during the first quarter of this century and consisted of purposeful men who found delight in their devotion to problem Chess. But the creations remain, and the richness of the creations remains undiminished, and one sometimes wonders whether the men are really gone.

WHITE AND DAWSON

The world of Problem Chess can be spoken of in terms of the activity and accomplishments of two men, just two! It is not unlikely that the full gamut would be reasonably covered without so much as suggesting the contributions of anybody else. Seldom does any field of endeavor present such a phenomenon; rarely have talent, purpose, and determination found such concentration in men that the void created by their death suggests the possibility of an aching permanence. The two men were Alain Campbell White (1880–1951), an American, and Thomas Rayner Dawson (1889–1951), an Englishman, each endowed with a fantastic variety of superior faculties, and each, miraculously, able to perform prodigious tasks, within crowded hours, on a consistently high level.

To attempt to tell even a reasonably complete story of the accomplishments, talents, and traits of White and Dawson is to write an encyclopedia. We shall necessarily limit ourselves to a condensation of the highlights.

For a period of thirty-two years, 1905 through 1936, White * published at least one book yearly on Chess problems. These

---

* For the accomplishments of Alain White as all-time authority on Chess problems, and also as historian, literary scholar and naturalist, see *Chess Review* articles by Maxwell Bukofzer (May, 1935), P. L. Rothenberg (October, 1942 and June, 1951); *A Sketchbook of American Chess Problematists, Overbrook Series,* 1942; *To Alain White, Overbrook Series,* 1945.

were distributed as Christmas gifts to problem enthusiasts the world over, and to this day are known as the *Christmas Series* or *A.C.W. Series*. (See Bibliography.) He was the composer of hundreds of problems, none lacking in pointedness or basic originality, and he was the sponsor of numerous problem composing tournaments.

In 1941 White resumed compiling Chess problem books, under the sponsorship of Frank Altschul. During the ensuing four years, eight splendid books appeared, a fitting sequel to the *Christmas Series*. These, known as the *Overbrook Series*, consist of the most beautiful Chess problem books in existence, each a limited edition. (Again, see Bibliography.)

Whereas Chess problems received the lion's share of the talents of Alain White, a man of independent means and unshackled by occupational responsibilities, the amazing accomplishments of Dawson * were extracurricular. He was a leading engineer in the British rubber industry.

For a period of twenty years or more, up to the time of his death in 1951, Dawson was *simultaneously* the editor of *Fairy Chess Review* and of the problem pages of the *British Chess Magazine*. During the previous decade he had been the editor of *The Problemist,* the journal of the British Chess Problem Society. He published a number of books, principally on Fairy Chess, each a brilliant compilation. (See Bibliography.)

Dawson composed some 6,500 problems in all phases of the art; of these, over 5,000 were Fairy Chess settings. His *forte* was a relentless exploitation of all possible variants of a given theme or special aspect in composition. The resulting systematized classifications and anthologies, consisting of his own

* A splendid account of T. R. Dawson's all-around achievements can be found in the February, 1952 issue of *Fairy Chess Review,* by C. E. Kemp, successor to Dawson as editor of that publication.

compositions and those culled from all available sources, remain as models of scholarliness and precision. His work in the mathematical computation of various permutational possibilities on the Chessboard is outstanding. Examples of Dawson's wizardry appear in this chapter and in Chapter 14.

ETHNIC INFLUENCES

In no ethnic group except the Russians do we find a striking correlation between a live interest in Chess as a game and an enthusiasm for problem Chess. Noted in Chapter 4 is the fact that the *opposite* applies to persons of Jewish extraction, whose contribution to problem Chess as against that to the game itself has not been outstanding. In focusing our attention on the *total* picture of each of these phases of Chess, we can find a workable basis for the reasons governing ethnic influences, such as they may be.

Primarily, we are concerned with individual persons who fall into classifications. First, there is he who is genuinely interested in both phases of Chess. He may limit Chess activity to one or the other because of a realistic fear of diffusion or dilettantism; or he may participate superficially in both; or, if unusually gifted, he may concentrate on both and gain standing in each. (The Chess bird last mentioned, by the way, is the authentic *rara avis.*) Second, there is he who has no interest in any aspect of Chess but the area of activity he has chosen. It is he who accounts for the vast majority of Chessplayers and possibly to a lesser extent for problem composers. Third, there is he whose Chess interests undergo changes, but this one is necessarily related to his superficial cousin included in the first category.

It was the contention of the aforementioned Geoffrey Mott-Smith, who was a leading authority on games, that interest in *all* phases of a favorite game was the test of the authentic devotee. Implicit in this claim was no necessity for acquiring standing in all phases of the game but, Mott-Smith stressed, for the Chessplayer or bridge player to frown on problems was not only automatically to admit defeat but to betray a one-track preoccupation. The same in reverse, he argued, applied to problemists. As much as your authors, to whom all phases of Chess are ever of interest, would like to agree with Mott-Smith, they do not find it possible to do so.

Those who fear diffusion have a point. (Noted previously is that appended Problem No. 50 took some three years to compose.) There is ample evidence that Chessplayers who are devoted to the game must give time to study, especially in preparation for significant matches. Not to put in the time, in the absence of extraordinary endowments, is to invite disaster. Let us now combine the two: preoccupation with Chess problem composition (or even solving of problems) and keeping up with the demands of the game, and let us assume, reasonably, that each is a spare-time activity. Who, then, qualifies for multiple-interest activity in Chess? Clearly, he who is in the *rara avis* class.

We now have a controlling consideration in the attempt to determine whether certain ethnic groups are likely to be *more* attracted by one or the other Chess activity. There is evidence pointing to the affirmative. Let us return for a moment to our friends the psychiatrists. They indicate that the hostility factor in the game of Chess plays no part in Chess problems, for whatever resistance exists is under the *unilateral* control of the composer or solver. (Your authors have suggested to one psychiatrist that a composer, upon failing to acomplish an undertaken task, often showed inclination to kill everybody in sight, to say nothing of the loathed pater, but this has been dismissed as prosaic frustration.) If this verdict eliminates psychological considerations, it does not dispense with individual tendencies fairly traceable to ethnic influences.

The vast literature on Chess problems is most revealing. The dominance of the Russians in ultraserious composition is fairly recent, while their high-standard activity in endings dates farther back. It is difficult accurately to assess the state-controlled national pride as an effective spur for excellence in *all* phases of Chess. (Some conclusions, though scanty, may be drawn from the fact that Soviet Chess problem texts tend to stress the excellence of Russian compositions, while pointing to the *inferior* output of "bourgeois" countries.) On the other hand, the plodding, patient, determined way of the Slavs, critical attributes in problem work, must be taken into account.

We then find that the Germans have always been captivated by Chess problems, and so to a lesser extent have been the Dutch and the Scandinavians. Here, in the Germans particularly, we have the systematic mind, the predilection for precision, orderliness, and the finding of the solution. (A ghastly reminder is the "final solution," entailing as it did a methodical approach to a "problem.")

There are respectable contributions from the Hungarians, Czechoslovaks, French, Italians, some of the Balkan people, notably the Yugoslavs, and other Europeans, including Spaniards; also others from other parts of the world, such as South American countries, Argentina outstandingly.

We thus find a proclivity to Chess in the Slavs, the Germans and their ethnic cousins, and, to a lesser extent, in people of Latin and Gallic extraction.

Our survey brings us to the principal Anglo-Saxon countries, Britain and the United States. (We speak of America as Anglo-Saxon, taking the ethnic history and the majority of the population into consideration, as well as old-world influences in the political and economic development of the country.) A study of White and Dawson, both of Anglo-Saxon lineage, does suggest, whether with relation to problem Chess or any other purposeful activity, a dedication to the job, coupled necessarily with a scientific approach, such as may be reasonably considered an Anglo-Saxon trait. Is not the development as nations of England and the United States—the latter, of course, an offspring of the former—rife with evidence in support of that trait? Does not John G. White's bibliophilic activity (see Chapter 6), so orderly, so determined, and so destined to become the greatest of its kind, parallel the accomplishments of White and Dawson? More generally, is not the traditionally systematic, scientific approach of the Anglo-Saxon in practical matters—business, say—reflected in his aesthetic and intellectual pursuits? (In the latter case, we have the orderly acquisition of intellectual substance, but acquisition it is.) It requires no strain to understand the devotion of the Anglo-Saxon to a cultural pursuit, once he is attracted by it, and it is fascinating to observe the extent of accomplishment.

It may be argued, with reason, that both White and Dawson were *atypical* and that no conclusions can be drawn regarding ethnic influences. True, the uniqueness of their talents is undisputed. But is it really an accident that White and Dawson, and only White and Dawson, have been responsible for the greatest contributions to the Chess problem art? If that is so, and it may well be, then it does become difficult to understand lesser though singularly significant contributions by Englishmen and Americans, each pursuing his purpose quite in the tradition of White and Dawson, though not as intensely. We can mention great English problemists of the past: Godfrey Heathcote, George Hume, Philip Williams, along with the aforenoted masters, Mansfield and Kipping, and we have but scratched the surface. The same, to be sure, would apply to a random recital of American composers. (See *A Sketchbook of*

The Poetry of Chess

American Chess Problematists by Alain White, Edgar W. Allen, and Burney M. Marshall, 2 Vol., Overbrook Press, limited edition, 1942.)

The United States has been enriched, of course, by other than Anglo-Saxon strains. That applies to any field of activity. In problem Chess particularly, Sam Loyd, D. J. Densmore (Loyd's son-in-law), and William Meredith (1835–1903), the descendant of forebears in the diplomatic service of the United States, found rivalry of the highest type in Shinkman and Wurzburg, both of Bohemian stock.

Finally, we return to an earlier point. Is the significant contribution of Jews to the game of Chess necessarily indicative of a preference influenced by ethnic criteria?

Generally, Jews tend to adopt customs and manners, tastes and predilections of the majority, as do members of any other minority. (Chances are good that a sixteen-year-old boy in the United States, of whatsoever ethnic background, can identify a "stolen base" much more quickly than the Bristol theme in Chess problems.) What is more—and this has already been noted in Chapter 4—the longer the roots are established in the country of residence, the less likely is old-home influence to exert an effect. It follows, quite on the basis of fact, that the limited interest of the American Jew in problem Chess reflects the prevailing apathy. The same obtains in other lands. Of the persons of Jewish descent who are active in problem Chess, some are known to be newcomers to these shores, a score of years or so away from pre-immigration influences.

The disparity in the accomplishment of Jews in the one Chess activity (the game) as against the other (problems) may well be accountable by considerations also mentioned in Chapter 4. If the highly exciting competitive fight in the game of Chess symbolizes to the Jew his struggle in the Diaspora, the Chess problem, relatively void of battle, does not. Whether or not the Jew's inclination toward problem Chess is destined to increase in proportion to a rise in his personal sense of security one cannot categorically assume. The fact that there is some evidence of Chess problem activity in Israel means little. For all we know, the composer may be a border sentinel, setting his musket aside during relief hours and working on his Chessboard.

The honest fear of diffusion, responsible as this can be for the concentration on but one Chess activity and no other, plays a part in the attitudes of all people. This is an underlying factor that cannot be overlooked in our analysis. If the arrival at a decisive conclusion is not possible, at least it is reasonably certain that the prominent standing of Jews in the game of Chess, particularly in the past half century, *appears* to emphasize contrastively their role in problem Chess. Otherwise, the influences are *not* basically ethnic but are traceable in part to the impact of the mores of the country of residence, and are accountable to some degree to the force of traditional preferences.

In the interest of guarding against possible misinterpretation of our discussion of ethnic groups, with relation to problem Chess in this chapter and the game of Chess in Chapter 4, we stress that it is certain in our minds that Chess activity, limited or extensive, nonexistent or all-consuming, neither downgrades nor upgrades any individual, group, society, or nation. There are too many imponderables that play a part in assessing the worth of a person, Chessplayer or not, problemist or not. Anybody has a right, of course, to proclaim his Chess prowess from the rooftops; all others, we are convinced, have an essentially equal right to accord these proclamations the precise degree of attention they believe them to merit, covering the full gamut from wide-eyed admiration to abysmal indifference.

FIFTY-SIX SELECTED POSITIONS

To claim that our selections (or *any* compilation) can be considered *the* best compositions of all time is not only to be foolhardy but impudent. There are thousands and thousands of problem settings and endings in existence; thousands have been variously graded by authorities, in the light of *subsequent* developments in composition; hundreds have earned consistent applause; dozens remain highly significant in the art of composition. Which, then, are the absolutely outstanding? What are the standards to be employed, especially since there is not even reasonable agreement among experts on criteria governing absolute excellence? Except for basic considerations, such as thematic content, originality, economy of force, quality of key move, and fundamentals of like nature, what spells out top excellence to one authority may well be a matter of utter indifference to another. To enter into a detailed analysis is clearly beyond the scope of this book. It is certain that, in making a selection of superior problems, predilections play a part; but these must be controlled and disciplined. Mostly, the preferences of the selector must be based on a sound acquaintanceship with the entire field of composition.

The Chess problems and Chess endings that follow have been selected because (1) some *are* the best in their *genre;* (2) others (Loyd's especially) have had a lasting fame; (3) a few are superb examples of extraordinarily difficult tasks; (4) several are pleasantries of light *motif;* (5) one—Number 56—has been an unmet challenge to your authors for years, and the task is being offered you (for a prize!); *all* provide pleasure and entertainment on any desired level, from moderate to intense concentration required in finding the solution to a lighthearted examination of position *and* solution.

The solutions appear at the end of this chapter.

SAM LOYD'S MAGIC

No. 1
"Excelsior" by Sam Loyd
London Era, 1861

White Mates in 5 Moves

Perhaps you would like to select a White piece which is the *least* likely to deliver mate.

No. 2
"The Love Chase"
by Sam Loyd
Leipziger Illustrierte Zeitung, 1869

White Mates in 3 Moves

No. 3
"The American Indian"
by Sam Loyd *New York Sunday Herald*, 1889

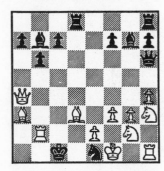

White Mates in 2 Moves

No. 5
Sam Loyd
N.Y. State Chess Association, 1892

White Mates in 3 Moves

No. 4
"The Steinitz Gambit"
by Sam Loyd
First Prize, *Checkmate*, 1903

White Mates in 3 Moves

No. 6
"She Stoops to Conquer"
by Sam Loyd
Schachzeitung, 1868

White Mates in 2 Moves

No. 7
G. F. Anderson
Il Secolo, 1921

White Mates in 2 Moves

No. 9
P. L. Rothenberg
Chess Review, 1942

White Mates in 2 Moves

No. 8
Geoffrey Mott-Smith

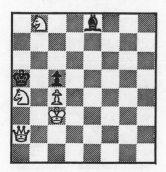

White Mates in 2 Moves

No. 10
"Into the Jaws of Death"
by P. L. Rothenberg
Popular Mechanics,
May, 1942

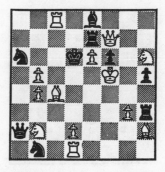

White Mates in 2 Moves

No. *11*
J. A. Schiffmann
Bristol Times and Mirror,
1927

White Mates in 2 Moves

No. *13*
G. Hoffman
First Prize, *Die Schalbe,*
1940

White Mates in 2 Moves

No. *12*
Alain White
First Prize, *Good Companions,* 1918

White Mates in 2 Moves

No. *14*
Newman Guttman
First Prize, *Chess Life,*
1958

White Mates in 2 Moves

No. 15
F. Gamage
First Prize, *Chess World,*
1946

White Mates in 2 Moves

No. 17
Newman Guttman
Christian Science Monitor, 1946

White Mates in 2 Moves

No. 16
F. Gamage and Eric M.
Hassberg
Chess World, 1946

White Mates in 2 Moves

No. 18
Eric M. Hassberg
First Prize, 1946

White Mates in 2 Moves

No. 19
Raymond Tump
First Prize, 1946

No. 19
Raymond Tump
First Prize, 1946

No. 20
E. L. Letzen

White Mates in 2 Moves

White Mates in 2 Moves

THREE-MOVERS

No. 21
Nathan Rubens
The Chess Problem, 1946

No. 22
Isaac Kashdan
Pittsburgh Post, 1925

White Mates in 3 Moves

White Mates in 3 Moves

No. 23
Vincent L. Eaton
Chess Review, 1941

White Mates in 3 Moves

No. 25
Otto Wurzburg
(after **N. Höeg***)*
Pittsburgh Gazette Times,
1914

White Mates in 3 Moves

No. 24
Otto Wurzburg

White Mates in 3 Moves

No. 26
W. A. Shinkman

White Mates in 3 Moves

No. 27
P. L. Rothenberg
Chess Review, 1938

White Mates in 3 Moves

No. 29
W. A. Shinkman

White Mates in 3 Moves

No. 28
F. Gamage
First Honor Prize, *Chess
***Correspondent*, 1946**

White Mates in 3 Moves

No. 30
Vincent L. Eaton
First Prize, *ex aequo*,
British Chess Federation,
1946

White Mates in 3 Moves

SHINKMAN'S PERIMETRIC MARVEL

No. 31
W. A. Shinkman

White Mates in 4 Moves

ENDINGS

No. 32
Richard Reti

White to Play and Draw

No. 33
Richard Reti
Koelnische Volkszeitung,
1928

White to Play and Draw

No. 34
Rev. Saavedra

Black to Play; White to Win

No. 36
H. Rinck

White to Play and Draw

No. 35
A. A. Troitzky

White to Play and Win

No. 37
H. K. Mattison

White to Play and Draw

No. 38
G. Sachodakin

White to Play and Draw

No. 40
K. A. L. Kubbel

White to Play and Win

No. 39
T. B. Gorgiev

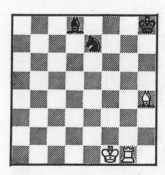

White to Play and Win

No. 41
H. Rinck

White to Play and Draw

No. 42

H. Rinck

White to Play and Draw

No. 43

S. Simkovich

White to Play and Win

No. 44
A. A. Troitzky

White to Play and Win

MOTT-SMITH'S SUI TASKER

No. 45
Geoffrey Mott-Smith
Chess Correspondent,
April 1941

**White Selfmates in
3 Moves**

DAWSON'S LUNAR FLIGHT

No. 46
T. R. Dawson
Caissa's Fairy Tales, 1947

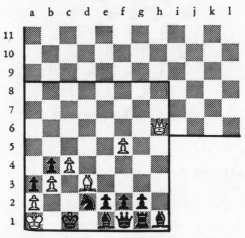

**White Mates in 7 Moves (on regular
8 x 8 Chessboard)**
**For explanation of extension of Chess-
board, see solution.**

FAIRY FANTASIES AND FLIGHTS OF FANCY

No. 47
Special Problem
"Four-in-hand"
In Memoriam Dedication to Sam Loyd by Alain White and P. L. Rothenberg
Chess Review, 1951

Black to Play and Help White Mate in 3 Moves in 4 Different Ways

In the Helpmate, Black moves first (as a rule) and *helps* White deliver mate in a specified number of moves.

In No. 47, there are four *intended* solutions (thematically related) in 3 moves. This and No. 48 were probably the very last composition work of Alain White.

No. 48
Alain White and
P. L. Rothenberg
Chess Review, July 1951

**Black to Play and Help
White Mate in 3 Moves
in 4 Different Ways**

Here, too, we have four intended solutions in 3 moves.

No. 49
P. L. Rothenberg

See Text

No. 49 was dedicated to Alain White in the 1945 Overbrook Press tribute previously mentioned.

The stipulation calls for adding *minimum* possible White and Black pieces, enabling White to:

   a. Mate in one move

   b. Selfmate in one move

   c. Stalemate in one move

   d. Selfstalemate in one move

No. 50
P. L. Rothenberg
Chess Correspondent,
1941

White Maxi-Selfmates in
4 Moves

In Maximate problems, one or both sides are restricted to the *longest possible* move on each turn. In No. 50, only Black is so restricted; White moves normally.

The longest move is the one which covers the greatest *distance,* not necessarily the greatest number of squares. (See Chessboard Recreation No. 3 for a detailed explanation of the greater distance covered by diagonal moves as against horizontal or vertical ones.) In essence, a one-square diagonal move may be counted as 1.41 units (assuming the area of each square on the board to be 1 unit squared), whereas a one-square horizontal or vertical move is exactly 1 unit. Thus, a traversal of 3 squares diagonally (4.23 units) is longer than a vertical or a horizontal move covering 4 squares (4 units). In the diagramed position, the longest move available to Black, obviously, is B-R6.

It took some three years to compose this problem, probably the most ambitious maxi-task in existence. One difficulty after another crept in until a sound position was reached. The solution is a very pleasing one.

No. 51
P. L. Rothenberg

**White Relay Mates in 2
Moves
(Both White and Black
Have Relay Power)**

In Relay Chess each piece assumes, *in addition* to its own locomotive power, the power of one or more pieces of its color which guard it. Thus, in diagramed position, Black Bishop at Q7 can move and capture both as a Bishop and as a Knight. No power is relayed to the King; nor can a Pawn use Relay power to move to its first rank (*never* accessible) or the 8th rank—which it must reach normally, as a Pawn, and convert itself to another piece of the same color by promotion.

No. 51 demonstrates a task which cannot be shown in an orthodox setting.

DOUBLE EXCELSIOR

Nos. 52 through 56 have been inspired by Loyd's famous *Excelsior* (see Problem No. 1). None has been previously published.

No. 52	No. 53
Geoffrey Mott-Smith	**P. L. Rothenberg**

Black to Play and Help White Mate in 7 Moves	**Black to Play and Help White Mate in 6 Moves**

The Poetry of Chess

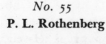

No. 54   No. 55

P. L. Rothenberg   P. L. Rothenberg

White to Play and Help
White Mate in 6 Moves

Black to Play and Help
White Mate in 5 Moves

No. 52 is a miracle of economy. No. 54 is one of the "luckiest" compositions, in that the White and Black forces are matched exactly. In No. 55, the White piece on KN8 and the Black piece on KN7 are Grasshoppers. A Grasshopper moves any number of squares—diagonally, vertically and horizontally—to the square *immediately* beyond the nearest piece of either color. It captures the same way. Obviously enough, the Grasshopper must depend on another piece for its locomotion. In the diagramed position, the White Grasshopper can move to KN1; the Black Grasshopper is immobile, for no piece is available over which he can hop.

PRIZE TASK

You have discovered, of course, that it is possible to demonstrate the *Double Excelsior* with Queen, Rook, Bishop, and Grasshopper. What happened to the Knight? Good question.

Your authors have struggled with this equine monster for many years, with no success. But if we have not been able to compose a sound position, that does not mean that everybody else is equally unequal to the task. (Nor have we been able to evolve a proof that it cannot be done.) We invite all brave hearts to join the good cause. Incentive?

We, the authors of this book, offer a prize of $100.00 for the first sound composition demonstrating the *Double Excelsior* with the Knight. Our offer is unqualified, once the composition meets basic requirements, as follows:

a. It must be a Helpmate in exactly 5 (five) moves. (It is child's play, relatively, to demonstrate the task in 6 moves or more.)

b. NO PROMOTED PIECES ARE ALLOWED. The composer must limit himself to the original forces on both sides. (Generally, if this requirement were relaxed, standards in Chess problem composition would suffer irreparably. Problem tasks have been given up as impossible because of inability to demonstrate them without promoted pieces. But we do offer commendation to two fine American composers, Nicholas Gabor of Cincinnati and Nathan Rubens of New York, who jointly succeeded in demonstrating the Knight task with a number of promoted pieces. Even that is a feat!) Also, no Fairy pieces are allowed. (Note that the Black Bishop in appended Problem No. 56 is a promoted piece. Even if No. 56 were sound, it would be disqualified.)

c. The position must be a legal one, that is, one that could conceivably have arisen from the starting point in a game of Chess. (This is another requirement in Chess problem composition which brooks no relaxation.) There must be no artificial conditions, such as stipulations that this or that specified piece may not move.

d. Finally, as in all sound Helpmates and as demonstrated

in our Nos. 52 through 55, there must be one solution (and one only) showing Black promotion to Knight on the fifth move, followed by White promotion to Knight delivering mate to the Black King. Neither side must have the possibility of any play whatever other than a precise sequence of 5 moves by Pawn starting from its home square and promoting to Knight.

No. 56

P. L. Rothenberg

(Experimental Position)

Position Deliberately

Unsound

Black to Play and Help

White Mate in 5 Moves

PRIZE TASK

We offer the position in Diagram 56 as an aid (hopefully) to those who will accept our challenge. As noted, the position is unsound. Black can help White mate in 3 moves, as a matter of fact: . . . P-N4 1 R-R6 K-N1 2 B-K5 B-B2 3 R-R8 mate. The intention, obviously, is . . . P-N4 1 P-R4 PxP 2 P-R5 P-R6 3 P-R6 P-R7 4 P-R7 P-R8(N) 5 P-R8(N) mate. Note that

Black must promote to Knight; otherwise, he either checks the White King or guards the square on which White must deliver mate.

The matrix in Diagram 56 is one of a number of possibilities. Unless the Black Pawn must move two squares initially in order to avoid checking the White King, finding a mechanism that forces the two-square move is a task in itself. The unintended lines of play that tend to creep in are *the* headache. We strongly suggest that composers check their settings thoroughly, and submit them to others for close scrutiny, before they are sent off to us as "sound."

Our offer of a prize of $100 will remain open indefinitely, or until such time as it is won. If we do receive a winning position, we shall have it published in one or more leading Chess publications and the "contest" will cease automatically.

SOLUTIONS

No. 1. This problem was published when Loyd was 20 years of age; he had composed it some 3 years previously, when he was 17. He won a wager from a friend who picked White's Queen Knight Pawn as the most improbable man to deliver mate. (Which one did you pick?) The principal variation: 1 P-QN4! (aiming for R-Q5 and R-Q1 mate), R-B4 ch 2 PxR, P-R7 3 P-B6, B-B2 (only way to stop mate by R-Q5 or R-KB5 etc.) 4 PxP, Black any 5 PxN (Q or B) mate. 'Nuff said.

No. 2. 1 Q-KB1! B-N7 or RP moves 2 Q-QN1 etc.; if 1 . . . B-B6 or B-Q5 2 Q-Q3 etc.; if 1 . . . B-K4 or B-B3 2 Q-B5 etc.; if 1 . . . P-N6 2 N-N6 ch PxN 3 Q-R3 mate. One of the loveliest examples of opposition play (Q vs. B), aptly titled.

No. 3. 1 B-B8!! (threatening 2 Q-R1 mate), BxR 2 BxQ

mate!! The earliest example of the most subtle ambush play in problem Chess. Loyd deliberately added a number of unnecessary pieces, in order to give the position a "natural" look and to confuse and divert the solver. Technically, adding superfluous force to a position is frowned upon, but who can presume to take the magnificent Loyd to task? (Hassberg's masterpiece, at beginning of this chapter, is the ultramodern expression of the American Indian theme, in a setting totaling 7 pieces: a miniature. The solution to Hassberg's problem appears at the very end of the solutions.)

No. 4. From a safe haven, the White King takes a walk, releasing a powerful yet helpless Black force. This daring key move has not been equaled in close to sixty years! The principal variations: 1 K-K2!! P-B8(Q) dble ch 2 K-K3 and White mates next no matter what Black does. If 1 . . . P-B8(N) dis ch 2 R-B2 disc ch and again mate follows.

No. 5. The fantastic Loyd with another setting featuring a fantastic key move. One is usually led to believe that you have to stick close to a King whom you intend to pulverize. Not so, says Loyd. The solution: 1 Q-KR5!!! K-N5 2 Q-B1 and mate follows. If 1 . . . K-R4 2 K-N3 and White mates next.

No. 6. And still another incredible key: 1 Q-R1!! rendering Black helpless.

No. 7. 1 K-Q6! This lovely crosscheck Meredith has been a favorite of problem lovers for over forty years. Note that Black obstructs the Bishop when he checks the White King, thus enabling White to mate by interposing *his* Bishop. (A Meredith setting consists of 8 to 12 pieces; a miniature, of 7 or less. The obstruction of B by R—or *vice versa*—is known as Grimshaw interference.)

No. 8. 1 Q-Q2! The late talented Mott-Smith specialized in slender settings. He has about 150 "gleams" (2-movers containing a total of 7 pieces or less) to his credit.

No. 9. This was a dedication to Geoffrey Mott-Smith and Alain White. The task is an *echo* mate on the 7th rank. (**An** echo is the repeated occurrence of a position, in a different part of the board, in identical or substantially identical form. If the mating position is repeated, as in this case, it is called an echo mate.) Note also that the Black King and Black Rook are in castling position. By convention, castling *is* allowed in problems, unless it can be demonstrated that castling is not allowed. The solution hinges on Black's castling privilege. If it were possible to prove that Black is not allowed to castle, then the meaningless 1 K-N7 would solve. The solution: 1 R(B5)-B7 threatening P-B7 mate, and leading to the echo mate as follows: 1 . . . R-Q1 2 R(N7)-K7 mate; 1 . . . O-O-O 2 R(B7)-B7 mate.

No. 10. 1 K-K4! The White monarch exposes himself to 8 different checks, each of which is countered by a mate of the Black King.

No. 11. 1 Q-B3!! This is one of the outstanding problems of all time.

No. 12. 1 R-QN4!! And so is this!

No. 13. 1 Q-K2!!! The Pickaninny theme is faultlessly presented in miniature form in this astounding first prize winner. The theme entails 4 different mates in response to each of 4 moves (maximum possible) of a Black Pawn on its home square. The differentiated mates are a joy.

No. 14. 1 B-Q4! This is a lovely example of modern composition by an able exponent of the art. The setting is completely integrated in a beautiful task entailing "false" tries. Note the reasons why neither of the Knights can unpin the Queen. Black has only one defense in each case.

No. 15. 1 P-Q7! A typical work of art by one of the most eminent of American composers.

No. 16. 1 Q-R8! Note the precision of the half-pin shut-off mates.

No. 17. 1 R-N6, leading to pretty effects in *third-degree* play. (The third degree, a complicated mechanism, entails differentiated mates arising out of Black's attempt to cope with successive White blows. In this case, the third degree is made cumulatively possible by Black's defenses of 1 . . . N-random move; 1 . . . N-Q5, not to allow the mate previously possible; and 1 . . . N-B5, not to allow both mates previously possible.)

No. 18. 1 K-B8! A first-class prize winner with a surprising key.

No. 19. 1 QxP! This is an elegant example of third-degree play.

No. 20. 1 R-QB4!! A very difficult key in a setting which features discovered mates by the White King limiting him to a different square each time.

No. 21. 1 RxP any, 2 R-N2 and mate follows. This is an old chestnut in miniature form, the work of an able American composer. The key allows the Black King the maximum number of flight squares: 8.

No. 22. 1 N-Q3, K-R3 2 R-N5 etc. 1 . . . P-R3 2 R-N4 and the mate which follows echoes the first one. White threatens 1 RxP ch and 2 P-B8(N) mate. If 1 . . . N-K4 2 N-B5 and mate follows. This is an accurate rendition by one of America's great Chessmasters. Known mainly as a superb player, "Kash" is one of the fastest problem solvers in the world and a fine composer.

No. 23. 1 B-R7, threatening mate with the Rook at B8 after the Knight clears the file, leads to 12 distinct variations following Black promotions and moves of Black Rook. It is a marvelous task achievement by a brilliant American composer of whose death we learn as this book goes to press.

No. 24. 1 N-R8, K-R2 2 R-Q7 ch etc.; 1 . . . K-R3 2 R-N4 etc.; 1 . . . K-N1 2 R-N5 ch etc.; 1 . . . K-B1 2 R-K7 etc.;

1 . . . K-B3 2 B-Q5 ch etc. and 1 . . . KxN 2 either R to
7th rank or QN-file. One would hardly expect such wealth of
play against a lone Black King—but this is by Wurzburg!

No. 25. 1 P-Q7, K-K2 (or K-B2 or K-B3) 2 P-Q8(Q) etc.;
1 . . . PxP 2 P-Q8(R) etc.; 1 . . . PxB 2 P-Q8(B) etc. and
finally 1 . . . K-Q3, 2 P-Q8(N) etc. This is the finest rendition of fourfold promotion in an orthodox setting.

No. 26. 1 Q-R3, K-N8 2 P-B8(B) and mate follows. This,
a Shinkman trifle, is accomplished with minimum force. The
key move is a restrictive one, cutting off two flight squares,
but is amply compensated by the futility of promotion to a
Queen and, generally, by the surprise element.

No. 27. 1 Q-R3! PxP 2 B-N1 etc.; 1 . . . P-N4 2 BxP
etc. This ambush setting has caused solvers much trouble.

No. 28. 1 K-R1!! P-R8(Q) 2 B-B5, KxP ch 3 B-N1 mate;
1 . . . P-R8(N) 2 N(R4)-B3, KxP ch 3 N-Q1 mate; 1 . . .
R-R8 2 BxR ch K-N8 3 N-Q2 mate; 1 . . . P-N4 (or P-R4)
2 R-KB6 (or R-N6) etc., and it is the last variation which
accounts for the wonderful key move in this lovely crosscheck
setting.

No. 29. White mates after 1 R-B4 threatening 2 R-KB3
mate. If 1 . . . B-Q5 2 R-QN4 and mate follows. Note that
in this perfectly symmetrical position, 1 R-QN4 will not do
on account of 1 . . . B-B6! That accounts for what is known
as an asymmetrical key move.

No. 30.

1 NxQP!	PxN(N5) ch	2 N-N5, P-K4	3 N-Q6 mate.
1	PxN(Q5) ch	2 N-Q5, P-K4	3 N-B6 mate.
1	B-N2	2 NxKP, PxN ch	3 N-B5 mate.
1	B-Q2	2 NxRP, PxN ch	3 N-B5 mate.
1	P-R6	2 N-N3, PxN ch	3 N-B5 mate.
1	P-K4	2 N-B3, any	3 N-Q2 mate.
1	R-N4	2 RxRP ch etc.	

Again Eaton at his best.

No. 31. This little perimetric marvel is generally credited to the great Shinkman (and why not?), but we have not been able to find verification. The principal variation: 1 R-R8, KxP 2 RxN, K-N1 3 R-R1, K-B1 4 R-R8 mate. Chessboard wonders never cease!

No. 32. This is one of the most famous endings in Chess literature. The composer, the great Chessmaster Richard Reti, has a number of superb endings to his credit. He was particularly captivated by the geometric possibilities on the Chessboard inherent in the fact that the King's diagonal *and* orthogonal locomotion offers him a great advantage, as is shown in the next setting also. 1 KxR, P-R4 and how in the blazes can White draw now??? This way: 2 K-N7, P-R5 (2 . . . K-N3 3 K-B6 leads to the line which follows.) 3 K-B6, K-N3 (If 3 . . . P-R6 4 K-Q7 draws.) 4 K-K5!! P-R6 (otherwise the Black Pawn is lost) 5 K-Q6 and draws!! It's true.

No. 33. 1 K-K7!! P-N4 2 K-Q6, P-N5 3 P-K7, B-N4 4 K-B5 B-Q2 5 K-Q4, K-N2 6 K-K4, K-B2 7 K-B4, K-Q3 8 P-K8(Q) just in time, BxQ 9 KxP draw.

No. 34. No compilation of endings can possibly be complete without the Saavedra gem. It continues to fascinate solvers and it has served as a basis for other fine compositions. The solution: 1 . . . R-Q3 ch 2 K-N5! (the only move) R-Q4 ch 3 K-N4, R-Q5 ch 4 K-N3, R-Q6 ch 5 K-B2, R-Q5!! (Now, if 6 P-B8(Q), R-QB5 ch 7 QxR stalemate.) But White plays 6 P-B8(R)!!! threatening mate in 2; therefore, 6 . . . R-QR5 (forced) 7 K-N3 threatening mate again *and* threatening to capture the Rook. Black has a Hobson option of saving the Rook and losing the King or losing the Rook and losing the King.

No. 35. White wins after 1 P-R7 and 1 . . . R-R7 2 R-B1 ch K-Q7 3 R-B2 ch and Pawn must promote to Queen.

If 1 . . . R-Q1 2 R-B6 ch K-Q7 3 R-Q6 ch and again Pawn must promote. Note the beautiful echo variations.

No. 36. 1 R-Q2, Q-R1 2 K-B2 disc ch QxR (one Rook gone) 3 R-Q1 ch (might as well get rid of the other one) QxR. What have we? Stalemate.

No. 37. 1 P-R4 ch K-N3 2 B-B2, P-B8(Q) 3 RxP, QxR 4 K-R1, QxB stalemate.

No. 38. 1 P-N8(N) ch RxN 2 R-B6 ch K-N2 3 R-B7 ch NxR ch 4 PxN, R(N1)-K1 5 P-B8(Q) ch KxQ 6 B-B5 draws. Remarkable as it may seem, two Rooks cannot prevail against one Bishop.

No. 39. 1 B-B6 ch K-R2 2 R-N7 ch K-R3 3 R-B7 K-N3 4 R-B8 and Black is in *Zugzwang,* losing a piece and the game. If 3 . . . N-B3 4 BxB, NxB 5 R-Q7, N-B3 or N-K3 6 R-Q6 and wins.

No. 40. 1 B-Q1 (must, else 1 . . . BxP is dead draw), P-B6! (deep, tricky plan) 2 NxP (best, obviously), B-N5 3 B-K2, B-Q2 (Black would welcome a repetition of moves leading to a draw) 4 N-K5 (unabashed), BxP 5 N-B4 ch K-N4 6 N-N2 disc ch K-R4 7 NxB??? Hold it! This is stalemate. What happened to the win? Believe it or not, the composer, the great Kubbel, originally presented this ending (colors reversed) as a draw! He overlooked 6 B-B1!! (instead of 6 N-N2 ch), after which Black is helpless, for he must lose the Bishop.

No. 41. 1 R-K1! (the only move to draw) Q-Q7! 2 K-B1, K-N6 3 R-K3 ch QxR 4 R-R3 ch KxR stalemate.

No. 42. 1 B-B6, BxB (forced) 2 R-Q2, QxR (forced), and now White has one Greek gift left: 3 PxP ch BxP stalemate.

No. 43. 1 K-B3, B-R7 2 R-QR4, B-N6 3 R-R8 ch!! and wins.

No. 44. 1 Q-B8 ch K-K4 2 N-B4 ch PxN 3 Q-B5 ch wins; 1 . . . K-K3 2 N-N7, Q-K8 3 N-B5 ch K-K4 4 N-Q3 ch PxN 5 Q-K8 ch wins; if, in second variation, 2 . . . Q-Q7

3 N-B5 ch K-K4 4 Q-R8 ch K-Q3 5 NxP ch PxN 6 Q-Q8
ch wins; or 2 . . . Q-B6 3 N-B5 ch K-K4 4 Q-R8 ch wins;
or 2 . . . Q-B2 3 N-B5 ch K-K4 4 Q-B4 ch wins; or 2 . . .
Q-R3 3 Q-R6 wins; and finally 2 . . . Q-N3 3 N-B5 ch
K-K4 4 N-Q7 ch wins. This is a typical illustration of
Troitzky's amazing skill in coordinating a campaign of Queen
and Knight. The Black Queen is captured on two files, two
diagonals and one rank, each time being unluckily stationed
behind the checked Black King. The Knight fork is an ancil-
lary feature. Mainly it is the precision of tactics in the chase of
the Black Queen, in an uncrowded setting, that emphasizes
the skill of this great composer. (Troitzky's treatise on King
and two Knights vs. King and Pawn remains a classical study
to this day.)

No. 45. When Dr. Roger Bannister broke the 4-minute
barrier in the mile run, other athletes followed suit, in reasonably quick succession. In Chess problems, the demonstration of a task long thought to be either impossible or brutally
difficult serves as an incentive to other composers. Geoffrey
Mott-Smith was the first to show four different mates, delivered
by each of four promoted pieces, in a 3-move Selfmate. Within
a month or so, P. L. Rothenberg found a different matrix, and
still another one soon after. The recognition goes to the
pioneer:

1 N-R3, P-N8(Q) 2 N-B2 ch QxN 3 Q-K2 ch QxQ mate.
1   P-N8(R) 2 N-N5 ch B-K4 3 Q-B1 ch RxQ mate.
1   P-N8(B) 2 Q-Q2 ch K-B6 3 Q-Q3 ch BxQ mate.
1   P-N8(N) 2 Q-B3 ch KxQ 3 N-Q2 ch NxN mate.

What is lovely appears so effortless!

No. 46. The brain of a Dawson can, naturally enough,
visualize and grasp quickly the potential infinity of a Chessboard. His *Caissa's Fairy Tales,* which appeared in 1947,

features a fantastic assortment of flights of fancy (sweetened by entertaining text) of which many are profound, some light —and none frivolous or insignificant. No. 46 could have been prophetically dedicated to the present Age of Space. The solution follows, in the words of TRD: "This is certainly a stimulating experiment. . . . I am not referring to the mate in 7 which (with Black moves consisting of shuffle of King between K8 and B8) is 1 B-N1   2 Q-Q6   3 Q-B4   4 Q-Q4   5 Q-K3   6 Q-Q3 and 7 Q-B2 mate, in a very clear recurrence manoeuvre of the White Queen; but I am referring to those extra squares you have added. I realise now that you are calling attention to the systematic lengthening of the play BACKWARDS. The White Queen could start at i-10 in a 9-mover, and so on to infinity. I wonder if you perceived that if we re-set the problem for mate in as few as 69 moves, since there are 2-inch squares on the board, the White Queen would start 240,000 miles away from White's QB1—ON THE MOON IN FACT—and we have a vision of a lunar Queen sweeping astronomically through space in a tremendous zig-zag path, converging remorselessly to strike the Black King to his doom —silver Fate swooping down."

No. 47.

. . . P-N8(N)	1 P-R7, N-Q7	2 P-R8(Q), N-B6	3 Q-R7 mate.
. . . P-N8(B)	1 N-R8, K-Q4	2 K-N5, B-K5	3 N-B7 mate.
. . . P-N8(R)	1 N-Q5, R-K8	2 N-N4, R-K6	3 N-Q2 mate.
. . . P-N8(Q)	1 P-R7, Q-Q6	2 P-R8(Q), Q-B6	3 Q-Q4 mate.

The essence of the fourfold promotion task is differentiating the mates for Q and B and for Q and R. The challenge arrested the attention of the composers when a rather incautious claim was made by several European composers that fourfold promotion by Black (with differentiated mates, necessarily) could not be accomplished in the Helpmate.

No. 48. The basic challenge was met with No. 47; this related task was thrown into the bargain. The solution:

```
. . . P-QR8(Q)    1 BxP, Q-R6    2 B-B8, Q-K2    3 B-N7 mate.
. . . P-N8(R)     1 PxP, R-N3    2 B-N3, R-K3    3 N-Q5 mate.
. . . P-K8(B)     1 BxP, BxP     2 B-N6, B-K4    3 B-Q8 mate.
. . . P-KR8(N)    1 BxP, N-N6    2 B-Q6, N-B4    3 P-K5 mate.
```

Note the successive promotions to Q, R, B, N, from left to right, and the promoted pieces serving, respectively, as blocks on Black's K2, K3, K4 and KB4.

No. 49.
  a. Q-R7 mate.
  b. Q-N7 ch QxQ mate.
  c. QxQ stalemate.
  d. Q-N8 ch Q(or K)xQ
     stalemate.
A lucky strike in composition.

No. 50. White's key move pins the Black Bishop—the piece which has longest mobility in the set position. Black is thereupon offered *four* alternative moves, each consisting of traversal of 5 squares horizontally or vertically—by the Q, each Rook *and* (lest we forget) by castling on the Q-side (which entails, of course, a two-square horizontal move by the K and a 3-square horizontal move by the R). The task which the composer set for himself was 1) to employ castling as a defense in one variation and 2) to force a mate by castling in another. The solution:

1 R-N8, O-O-O	2 P-K4, B-R6	3 R-B8, BxR	4 K-N8, B-R6 mate.
1 R-R6	2 P-B6, BxB	3 P-K4, R-R6	4 P-K5, B-N8 mate.
1 Q-Q7	2 RxB ch K-Q2	3 P-K4, Q-R3	4 R-Q8 ch RxR mate.
1 R-Q3	2 B-N6 ch RxB	3 RxR, B-R6	4 R-Q6!! O-O-O mate.

Note that the same mechanism is employed in the first and second variations—mate by discovery by each Bishop. Note also that in the first variation 2 P-K4 is White's only waiting move. No Chess problem task—aside from the unaccomplished No. 56, of course—has ever proved to be a greater challenge to the composer of No. 50.

No. 51. 1 R-N7 threatening 2 R-K7 mate, for the Rook will have the Relay power of the Pawn thus holding Black's Q1 and KB1. 1 . . . K-B1 (or K-Q1 or O-O-O) 2 R (respectively)—KB7, Q7, QB7 mate. The problem features a few amusing sidelights, arising necessarily out of Relay power. If 1 . . . R-N1 2 RxR mate is the only move, for the White Rook is pinned! If the White Rook moves out of the file, the Black Knight assumes Rook power and the White King is in check. If 1 . . . R-R3 2 R-K7 mate is the only move, for if 2 R-N8, there is no mate; the Black Rook (with Relay power from the Black Bishop) interposes at QB1. And again, the Black Rook can interpose at Q1 after 1 . . . RxP, thus limiting White to 2 R-K7 mate. The composer acknowledges indebtedness to Mannis Charosh, the inventor of Relay Chess, for testing the soundness of this problem.

No. 52. Queen Double Excelsior: . . . P-K4 1 P-R4, P-K5 2 P-R5, P-K6 3 P-R6, P-K7 4 P-R7 P-K8(Q) 5 P-R8(Q) ch Q-K1 6 Q-R1 Q-Q2 7 Q-QR8 mate.

No. 53. Rook Double Excelsior: . . . P-B4 1 P-R4, P-B5 2 P-R5, P-B6 3 P-R6, P-B7 4 P-R7, P-B8(R) 5 P-R8(R) R-KN8 6 R-R2 mate.

No. 54. Bishop Double Excelsior: . . . P-N4 1 P-R4, P-N5 2 P-R5, P-N6 3 P-R6, P-N7 4 P-R7, P-N8(B) 5 P-R8(B) B-R2 6 B-K5 mate.

No. 55. Grasshopper Double Excelsior: . . . P-K4 1 P-R4,
P-K5 2 P-R5, P-K6 3 P-R6, P-K7 4 P-R7, P-K8(G) 5
P-R8(G) mate. Black must promote to Grasshopper; otherwise,
a mate in 5 is not possible. Note that the Black Pawn must
move two squares initially, in order not to end up on the
Black K7 square on the 5th move, thus providing a move for
the Black Grasshopper and stopping a mate in 5. (By problemists' convention, by the way, promotion is limited to Fairy
pieces which are present in the setting *before* the promotion
takes place. This is in the interest of guarding against super-
fantastic developments. But an inevitable chicken-egg question has come up: How did the Fairy piece get there in the
first place? To which we offer Sam Loyd's reply—with relation to a questioned piece in one of *his* fantasies: "I put it
there.")

AUTHORS' PRIZE OFFER

No. 56. You are to furnish the solution. The $100 prize
offer still stands.

Solution to Hassberg 2-mover (at beginning of this chapter):
1 Q-B2! Loyd's American Indian theme (Problem No. 3) is
found in variation 1 . . . RxR(R2) 2 QxR mate. In all respects, this Pawnless wonder is one of the great achievements
in problem composition.

BUT OPTICS SHARP IT NEEDS, I WEEN,
TO SEE WHAT IS NOT TO BE SEEN.
— JOHN TRUMBULL

10

Blindfold Chess

REQUIRED SKILLS

Would you like to play blindfold Chess with your neighborhood druggist? This is the way to do it.

Tell him to stand in the center of his store, eyes closed. Then reel off the names of two or three dozen powders, pills, pellets, nostrums, and what not. You have several thousand items from which to choose. As you call out each product, your apothecary-oracle will *instantly* point in this or that direction, designating the precise portion of the precise shelf on which the unit is located.

That, essentially, is blindfold Chess.

Like those of the druggist, the attributes of the blindfold Chess performer are close familiarity, memory, visualization, and association. The task of the former is limited to instant location of each of thousands of individual things, with which he is closely familiar because of oft-repeated routine experience, and the arrangement of which on the shelves usually follows an organized scheme. The task of the latter is the more difficult, though not *basically* different, because more severe (or less automatic, if you wish) burdens are imposed on his memory and power of visualization, to say nothing of the pervading intricacies and complexities.

Blindfold Chess, a popular misnomer (for rarely, if ever, is the performer actually blindfolded) is the playing of one or more games of Chess without sight of the Chessboard and the pieces on it. The performer is, almost invariably, an expert player who has a close acquaintanceship with a myriad of Chess positions in various stages of the game. These he has learned to visualize and interrelate, thus being aided by a ready power of association. Moreover, at his mental fingertips, as it were, is the configuration (*Gestalt*) of the board—that is, the board in its *entirety*—for he is able to "see" it as if actually looking at all the pieces and all the occupied and unoccupied squares in every rank, file, and diagonal.

Examples of an elementary form of blindfold Chess are frequently noted in conversations about Chess, away from the Chessboard. Each of the participants suggests this or that move or series of moves in a particular game or opening, and each has a complete picture of the missing board and pieces. Some years ago, *Chess Review* published an amusing item faintly related to blindfold Chess. It described a telephone conversation between your authors, Horowitz and Rothenberg, with no Chessboard available to either of them. The preoccupation was with what *appeared* to be an enigmatic Chess setting that had been submitted to *Chess Review* by an enthusiast, with the firm claim that it was an absolutely legal position, having arisen from the starting point in a game of Chess. The poser stumped both Howowitz and Rothenberg, until the latter, with thundering finality, decreed that the position was "absolutely impossible!" and this was instantly followed by an ecstatic

". . . wait a minute!!" Rothenberg thereupon called off the moves leading to the puzzling position. (Failure to see the obvious in a Chess position, by the way, is known as Chess blindness, or, as suggested by the late great Chessmaster, Dr. Siegbert Tarrasch, *amaurosis schacchistica,* the title of Chapter 18.)

EXAMPLES OF ASTOUNDING FEATS

Blindfold Chess feats date back to the eighteenth century. The great Philidor first introduced the stunt in London to the frenzied adulation of his admirers. He played two games simultaneously without sight of the boards, whereon the *World* of London (May 28, 1783) commented as follows: "His performance should be hoarded among the best samples of human memory, till memory shall be no more." The first half of the nineteenth century witnessed the rise of Paul Morphy (see Chapter 15) and Louis Paulsen as blindfold artists, and there are records of blindfold duels between them, *each* playing *sans voir.* Paulsen was able to negotiate ten simultaneous blindfold games; Morphy made no attempt to outdo his eminent contemporary, being content with eight. Actually, Morphy found no particular merit in this form of Chess activity, saying that "it proved nothing." Typically enough, Morphy remained indifferent to the acclaim showered upon his brilliance in blindfold Chess. (After Morphy retired from Chess, Paulsen was able to better his earlier record of ten, with nobody on the Chess scene to challenge his prowess.)

It is fundamental that practically any Chessmaster is able to carry on at least one game of Chess without sight of the board. The most prominent performers necessarily are those able to play *simultaneous* blindfold Chess, and the goal, naturally, is to establish a record. The outstanding contemporary blindfold performers are George Koltanowski, originally a Belgian who has made his home in the United States, and Miguel Najdorf, a native of Poland and now a resident of Argentina. The former, a Chessmaster, specializes in exhibitions of blindfold Chess and related feats; the latter, a powerful international Grandmaster, has proved his astonishing prowess in blindfold Chess extracurricularly, so to say, for he has successfully participiated in leading Chess tournaments throughout the world.

In 1947, Najdorf played forty-five simultaneous blindfold games, in São Paulo, Brazil, winning thirty-nine, drawing four, and losing two. (It was the same Najdorf, by the way, who four years earlier, also in Brazil, had played two hundred two games simultaneously—not blindfold, of course—winning one hundred eighty-two, drawing twelve, and losing eight!) It is fundamental that players arrayed against simultaneous Chess game performers are hardly of the master class, but this need not reduce the magnitude of an outstanding feat.

Koltanowski's blindfold Chess exhibitions are frequently sweetened by stunts that leave his audiences breathless. For example, he conducts a blindfold Knight's tour (see Chapter 14), while the name of a city is assigned by members of the audience to each square, as the Knight hops from one square to another until the entire board is covered. A record is kept, of course, by someone in the audience, of the 64 "cities" successively covered by the Knight. Mr. K. then proceeds to recite the 64 cities in the precise order in which they had been visited by the Knight. This feat could lead one to believe that there is an accomplice in the audience, issuing invisible smoke signals, were it not for the fact that Chessmaster Koltanowski's integrity is unassailable, and that he is quite able to perform this trick while shut off in a cell, with a security guard solely entrusted to announce to him the selected names of the cities while maintaining constant vigil against foul play, such as writing implements.

Koltanowski's performance of the Knight-city-tour, astonishing as it may seem, can be accomplished by utilization of a basic mnemonic prop, association. It is, of course, possible to rely on straight memory, but few are endowed with the ability of committing to memory a long random series of unrelated things, such as Boston, Lublin, Pavia, in the *precise* order given. What is more, even given such ability, the memory expert would rather find an easier method of retaining the series in his mind than taxing himself with the brutal task of straight memorization. We do not know the exact method used by Koltanowski, but we assume, with reason, that it employs elements of association which, after repeated practice, have become an automatic part of his repertoire.

The steps entailed in performing the stunt *may* well be as follows. First, one must *faultlessly* commit to memory a Knight's tour, each hop, in the precise sequence, from first to sixty-third, being indelibly ingrained in the mind. (There are numerous symmetrical tours, by the way, which lessen considerably the task of mastering the first step.) Second, a *substitute* designation must be made, so that it assumes an identity that best suits the performer's sense of association. For example, he may choose to designate White's KR1 as "Tower," KB1 as "Church," etc., etc., thus creating a substitute designation for *every* square on the board. Thereafter the squares exist for the performer as "Tower," "Church," etc., and the Knight's tour now becomes a journey *not* from square to square, as each is known in Chess notation, but from one substituted designation to another, as devised by the performer. Third—and this is *the* crucial test of the performer's memory and power of association—as each city is called out by a member of the audience, an instant relationship must be formed between the city and the substituted designation. This calls for much ingenuity, for basic in formulating the relationship is a *recallable* association. (It is easy enough to remember "Tower of London," if, by propitious chance, London is called out for KR1, but what if Kalamazoo is the announced city for that square?) When the tour is completed, the performer, having mastered the necessary steps, proceeds to recite the cities, in precise order (Step 1), from one substituted designation to another (Step 2), depending confidently on recallable associations (Step 3).

As we can readily see, the subtituted designation may or may *not* be necessary. Koltanowski or any other expert may be able, without difficulty, to formulate associations between the ordinary Chess-notation designation of the squares and the announced cities. Moreover, the audience need not be limited to a recital of cities, for, obviously enough, it is possible to formulate an association between each square and anything at all. Now then, with full recognition of the exciting effect of Koltanowski's stunt and of the great skill required in performing it, we are nevertheless constrained to conclude that anyone with a good memory and a strong sense of discipline can learn to perform modest variations of this trick, on a limited scale initially, and more expertly in time. An illustration follows.

Create *your own* substituted designations for the numbers 1 to 10. Try to formulate a substitute for each number which, to you, offers a ready association with the number. (It is possible that for 1 you may choose the person who is most meaningful to you; for 2, something suggesting *two,* such as a married couple, etc.) Once you have mastered the substituted designations, have someone call out ten objects at random, one by one, for each of the ten numbers, not necessarily in chronological order. As each object is announced, you must quickly formulate a recallable association with your substituted designation for the number. (Do not allow yourself to be hurried; your "audience" will wait until you are ready for the next object.) Once you learn to recite the list flawlessly, in any desired order, or to announce object for number or number for object individually, if you are put to such test, your role as a welcome entertainer is assured . . . ; all the more so, if you keep on increasing your repertoire beyond 10. But since we do not desire to create a spate of competition for the redoubtable George Koltanowski, we suggest that you defer mastery of the blindfold Knight's tour stunt.

Najdorf's astonishing record of 45 simultaneous blindfold games remains *quantitatively* supreme. Curiously, it is *not* the outstanding feat in blindfold Chess. In 1945, the remarkable Reuben Fine played four simultaneous blindfold *rapid-transit* games (at ten seconds per move!!) and won every one of them! The magnitude of this accomplishment is still a wonderful memory to those who were privileged to observe it.

Dr. Fine's feat * remains unequaled. Attempts to minify its significance border on sheer stupidity. It has been suggested, for example, that the rapid-transit feature is not too overwhelming, for actually Fine (as one of the outstanding rapid-transit players of all time) was allowed more than ten seconds between moves on each board, since he played his four opponents in rotation, thus having the advantage of studying each position in the interim periods. Overlooked is the fact that relatively few players, even of master class, can negotiate *one* blindfold rapid-transit game. Secondly, each of Fine's opponents, while allowed no more than ten seconds per move, also had the opportunity to study his position in the interim periods, while unburdened by the necessity of carrying three other games in his mind. What is more, one of Fine's opponents was Robert Byrne, widely recognized as one of the leading

---

* See *Fine's Famous Feat* at end of this chapter.

experts in the United States. The magnificence of a magnificent mind remains unmarred, but it is nevertheless fitting to relegate carpers' carpings to the ashcan.

There is a fascinating point to be considered in connection with Dr. Fine's great feat. The exhibition took place at the termination of the United States–Soviet Radio Chess match, September, 1945. The United States had suffered a severe defeat, 15½ to 4½, with Fine himself earning ½ point out of a possible 2.

Why, we wonder, was this precise moment chosen by Fine for an exhibition of unparalleled prowess in blindfold Chess? Was there an acute compensating need for it—for Fine as an individual and as a key Chess representative of a country which had failed to acquit itself creditably, to say nothing of winning outright, in a significant international match? Did this young Chess genius succumb to a dominant tendency in man to look for the joy of victory in the wake of bitter defeat? But—and aside from all other considerations—was it not necessary for Fine to exercise iron-willed self-confidence, if the need for compensation depended so critically on a · *successful* outcome of his astounding performance? Or was there no connection between Fine's feat and the United States–Soviet match?

Perhaps Dr. Reuben Fine, able psychologist that he is, will one day favor us with an analysis, if the posed queries merit one.

But for considerations of *unusual* achievements, we have advisedly taken blindfold Chess out of the realm of amazement. To understand it intelligently is not to exaggerate necessary endowments of memory, visualization and association—all of them traceable to highly disciplined and concentrated periods of practice. In assessing skill in blindfold Chess, we again (as in basic skill in Chess, covered in Chapter 4) find no compelling evidence that it is necessarily correlated with an automatic facility for multifaceted intellectual achievements. Like it or not, a Czentovic (see Chapter 7) may come upon the scene tomorrow to surpass all records in blindfold Chess.

Lest it appear that we have reduced blindfold Chess to child's play—and that is definitely not the intention!—we caution that it is well to maintain an awareness of the sharp contrast between a close and a casual acquaintanceship with the Chessboard. Time yourself in answering the following question:

What is the color of Black's Queen's Bishop 5 square
(or c4, if you prefer algebraic notation)?

Finally, we guarantee that you, even if you have never seen a Chessboard in your life, can undertake to play two blindfold simultaneous games against Botvinnik and Reshevsky, with complete assurance that you will break even.

Have Reshevsky play the White side and give the Black pieces to Botvinnik. Then Reshevsky's first move will be *your* first move on Botvinnik's board, and the latter's rejoinder will be your counter to Reshevsky's first move, etc., etc. Mr. R and Mr. B will be playing each other, and *you* cannot possibly end up with a minus score. Cozy, no?

FINE'S FAMOUS FEAT

Following are the scores of the 4 rapid transit games—10 seconds a move—won by Reuben Fine on September 4, 1945, in a simultaneous blindfold exhibition.

KING'S INDIAN DEFENSE

	R. Fine *White*	R. Byrne *Black*		*White*	*Black*
1	P-Q4	P-Q4	21	Q-N7	P-R3
2	P-K3	N-KB3	22	QxR	PxN
3	N-KB3	P-KN3	23	N-K5	B-B4
4	B-Q3	B-N2	24	QR-B1	N-K2
5	O-O	QN-Q2	25	QxP	N/3-Q4
6	P-QN3	O-O	26	B-B4	N-B5
7	B-N2	P-B4	27	Q-B5	Q-Q1
8	QN-Q2	P-QR3	28	KR-K1	Q-R1
9	Q-K2	P-QN4	29	B-B1	N/2-Q4
10	P-B4	BPxP	30	P-B3	R-B1
11	KPxP	NPxP	31	Q-N5	R-B1
12	PxP	N-N3	32	P-QR4	K-R2
13	QR-N1	N-R5	33	P-R5	P-B3
14	B-R1	PxP	34	N-B6	P-N5
15	NxP	B-K3	35	PxP	BxP
16	N/4-K5	P-QR4	36	P-R6	N-B2
17	B-N5	N-N3	37	Q-N7	N/5-Q4
18	N-B6	Q-Q3	38	QxQ	RxQ
19	N-N5	B-N5		Black resigned	
20	QxP	N-B1		on move 48.	

TWO KNIGHTS' DEFENSE

	R. Fine *White*	M. Epstein *Black*		*White*	*Black*
1	P-K4	P-K4	4	N-N5	P-Q4
2	N-KB3	N-QB3	5	PxP	NxP
3	B-B4	N-B3	6	NxBP	KxN

Fine's Famous Feat

	White	Black		White	Black
7	Q-B3 ch	K-K3	20	Q-K4	R-R3
8	N-B3	N-K2	21	KR-Q1	R-B1
9	P-Q4	P-B3	22	R-Q7 ch	QxR
10	O-O	K-Q3	23	RxQ ch	KxR
11	PxP ch	K-B2	24	QxP ch	R-B2
12	B-KN5	B-K3	25	QxR	N-B1
13	QR-Q1	Q-K1	26	P-KN3	N-K3
14	N-K4	P-QR4	27	QxP	K-K1
15	N-B5	N-KN3	28	P-QB4	P-R3
16	NxB ch	QxN	29	P-QN4	B-Q1
17	BxN	PxB	30	P-B5	K-B1
18	RxP	B-K2	31	Q-R6	B-K2
19	B-K3	KR-KB1	32	QxN	Resigns

QUEEN'S GAMBIT

R. Fine   **A. Fomin**

	White	Black		White	Black
1	P-Q4	P-Q4	14	N-N5	Q-Q2
2	P-QB4	PxP	15	N-K5	Q-K1
3	N-KB3	P-K3	16	N-B7	Q-B1
4	P-K3	N-KB3	17	QxN	BxB
5	BxP	B-N5 ch	18	QxB	R-Q3
6	N-B3	O-O	19	NxR	BxN
7	O-O	P-QN3	20	Q-N3	R-Q1
8	Q-K2	B-N2	21	P-Q5	KPxP
9	R-Q1	P-B3	22	PxP	R-Q3
10	P-K4	Q-B2	23	PxP	NxP
11	B-KN5	B-K2	24	NxP	R-B3
12	QR-B1	R-Q1	25	N-K5 ch	K-R1
13	B-N3	N-R4	26	N-Q7	Q-B1
			27	NxR	Resigns

RUY LÓPEZ

R. Fine   K. Helander

	White	Black		White	Black
1	P-K4	P-K4	17	P-K5	PxP
2	N-KB3	N-QB3	18	BxN	NxB
3	B-N5	P-QR3	19	QxN	PxP
4	B-R4	P-QN4	20	B-B4	Q-K2
5	B-N3	P-Q3	21	N-Q2	B-K4
6	O-O	B-K2	22	R-K1	Q-Q3
7	P-QR4	B-N5	23	QxQ	BxQ
8	P-B3	N-B3	24	BxB	PxB
9	P-R3	B-R4	25	N-B3	P-B3
10	Q-K2	P-N5	26	NxP	QR-B1
11	R-Q1	O-O	27	QR-B1	P-QR4
12	P-Q4	BxN	28	N-B6	R-R1
13	QxB	KPxP	29	P-KN3	P-R4
14	PxQP	N-Q2	30	R-K7	R-B2
15	B-Q5	N/2-N1	31	QR-K1	R-QB1
16	B-K3	B-B3	32	NxRP	RxR

Black resigned on move 46.

I I

Leading American Chess Personalities

HELMS

> *On the eve of the publication of this book, the world of Chess sustained a grievous loss. Herman Helms died on January 6, 1963, one day after he reached his ninety-third birthday.*
>
> *Our deep regret is that Helms did not live to read the words which follow, constituting as they do a tribute to a lovely personality, written while he was alive and hardly intended as an obituary.*

The undisputed dean of American Chess is Herman Helms of New York City, a spare-boned, spry nonagenarian, whose name and (American) Chess have become fairly synonymous.

The life of Helms, who was born in 1870, has spanned *every* battle for the Chess championship of the world since establishment of the title in the nineteenth century. Helms was a toddler, age one, when the Franco-Prussian War was fought; he was fourteen years of age when the great Morphy died.

The official reporter of Chess events for several leading American newspapers, Helms has also been the editor and publisher of the *American Chess Bulletin,* now in its 59th year. Splendid as this publication is, Helms has been able to keep it alive—particularly during periods of sharp economic decline in this country—only by dint of iron determination and a fierce love for Chess. Helms also conducts a weekly Chess column in the *New York World-Telegram & Sun.*

Herman Helms is accepted in Chess circles with the affection and admiration he has so richly earned. As a matter of fact, it is rather monotonous to note that throughout the decades of his Chess activity, he has never invited a barb from any significant source. An expert Chessplayer, Helms was at one time champion of New York State. To this day, he dearly loves to engage in a bit of rapid transit Chess—10 seconds per move—and his "instinctive" knowledge of the game insures his status as a perpetually dangerous opponent.

Not talkative ordinarily, Herman Helms, upon being sparked, can regale his listeners with one delectable account after another of Chess tidbits of the far past, each spiced by appropriate histrionic furbelows.

HOROWITZ

As well known as Helms if not actually more extensively is I. A. Horowitz—"Al" to thousands of Chess *cognoscenti* throughout the land. (It may as well be noted at this point that the other of your authors is responsible for any *favorable* comment affecting either of them. . . .) A gangling, slow-moving, quick-thinking giant, Horowitz, in his middle fifties, is a prominent Chessmaster who, like Helms, has given his energies to but one activity, Chess.

So fired was Horowitz with a dedication to Chess that in 1933, not at all perturbed by a shocking depression, he founded *Chess Review,* now in its thirtieth year. At that time, Horowitz, a native of New York City, was a Chess veteran of some twenty years, having learned the game as a child. Initially, Horowitz was one of joint co-sponsors of the periodical; for the past fourteen years, he has been the sole editor and publisher. The *Chess Review* enterprise is linked with other commercial Chess activity, principal of which is the sale of books and equipment. It is quite likely that Horowitz, patiently and starvingly nursing his brainchild through multifarious diseases, some nigh lethal, is the first American Chess *entrepreneur* successful in forging a respectable livelihood entirely out of Chess.

His Chess business preoccupations are, however, quite incidental to Horowitz's ardent passion for all phases of Chess: the game, problems, endings, curios, and what have you. Characteristically enough, Horowitz can, with complete insouciance, allow himself to be captivated by a Chess morsel, while *seemingly* deeply concerned with one business responsibility or another. With it all, his prime undertakings have his unfailing attention. This is attested by frequent "rave" notes from readers of *Chess Review.* Serenely secure, Horowitz also makes a practice of publishing readers' complaints, none of which, unless palpably pointless, is ever summarily dismissed.

It is that attitude of Horowitz, essentially, which epitomizes his personality. Effortlessly affable, he is welcome in Chess circles everywhere. (His peregrinations, by the way, bring him to no other circles. . . .)

Holder (three times) of United States Open Championship

(first attained in 1936) and three times a member of the United States World Championship teams—Prague, 1931; Warsaw, 1935; Stockholm, 1937—Horowitz is assured of a respectable niche in master Chess.

A skilled teacher of Chess, Horowitz has had a number of prominent students, including the late Sinclair Lewis. He has written a number of books on Chess, being primarily concerned with introducing a unique, original touch in his writings. An outstanding example is *Point Count Chess,* the co-author of which is the late Geoffrey Mott-Smith, in which the popular point count in contract bridge is deftly applied to the game of Chess.

Like others who are forever sparked by an avid interest, Horowitz has faced the problem of necessary diminution of a wide scope of activity, and he has met it headlong, with "feverish, determined resistance."

FINE

Dr. Reuben Fine, the foremost American Chess author (see Chapter 6), retains his pre-eminence as an American Chess personality, although his activity in Chess is fairly of the past. Solemn, purposeful, scholarly and lightning-witted, Fine has had a brilliant Chess career, but one essentially characterized by paradoxes. It was Fine who, year in and year out, won the United States rapid transit championship, turning out flawless games at ten seconds per move. (Visualize, if you will, the type of stamina required for facing one opponent after another, hours on end, with a bell gonging every ten seconds: Move or perish!) It was Fine who played four simultaneous *blindfold* rapid transit games and won every one of them (see Chapter 10). It was Fine who, alone, contributed more to the science of Chess than any other author. It was Fine, the mathematician, philosopher, psychologist, to whom the Chessboard was indeed his breath of life. Yet, Fine was never able to win the United States Chess Championship. There is no implication that Fine was faced with inferior competition. Not at all. Time and again he earned second place to Reshevsky who walked off with the laurels. But why was it destined for this Chess Homer to nod at a most critical moment? In 1940, with the championship within easy reach in a crucial game, the great Fine slipped —and thereby handed the crown to Reshevsky.

Chess events are not likely to lack dramatic moments in the future, but long will the 1940 Fine-Reshevsky game symbolize the drama of paradox, in that a cool, calculating brain found a dreadful moment to veer, uncharacteristically but fatally, from the path of genius.

RESHEVSKY

Samuel ("Sammy") Reshevsky is, of course, the third vertex of the famed Chess-child-prodigy rectangle: Morphy-Capablanca-Reshevsky-Fischer. Now fifty years of age, this diminutive Chess giant is still remembered as the *Wunderkind* of the 1920's, his Chess fame having heralded his arrival in the United States.

Five times United States Chess Champion, Reshevsky has a formidable record in international competition, including victories over Alekhine, Capablanca, and Botvinnik. Mortally feared, especially by budding masters, Reshevsky is known as the "attrition" player, who seizes a thread of advantage and exploits it relentlessly. The respect for Reshevsky as an incredibly resourceful Chessmaster was exemplified in a rather amusing scene in a United States championship tournament in the late 1930's. A young master agreed to a draw with Reshevsky in a game which, at that point, appeared to offer the young master good winning possibilities. Some of the spectators began to taunt him for allowing Reshevsky to "get away" with a draw. Finally, the young man turned to one of his tormentors: "Would you, by any chance, like to continue the game with Reshevsky—and lose?"

In 1941, I. A. Horowitz was matched against Reshevsky in a series of sixteen games for the championship of the United States—resulting, by the way, in three wins for Reshevsky and thirteen draws. (Horowitz, severely injured in an automobile accident, had been unable to participate in the 1940 tournament, won by Reshevsky.) More than any game ever played by Reshevsky did the twelfth encounter of this match attest to his tenacity, much more attributable to his recognition of the exciting possibilities of a position than to a relatively prosaic will to win (or to avoid defeat). At that juncture, Reshevsky had won three games; eight games had been drawn; Reshevsky's eventual defeat of Horowitz in the match of sixteen games was clearly in sight. Horowitz, much to the delectation of a pro-underdog audience, acquired a winning position. It was the 50th move, and Horowitz, in pursuing a plan of action which was a "foregone conclusion," happily moved his King to N4—*instead of R4*. What difference did it make? Reshevsky's "I resign" was eagerly awaited by Chessmaster Horowitz and his coterie of admirers. It was midnight, and soon the battle would be over.

But—Mr. Samuel J. Reshevsky, having successfully passed the stages in a sparkling Chess career from *Schachwunderkind* to *Schachwundermensch*, began to study the position, rather intently. The kibitzers were visibly annoyed, but Reshevsky paid no heed; in good time, he moved. At about 4:00 A.M., 49 moves later, the game was declared drawn. The amazing Reshevsky, foreseeing a problemlike position some eight moves after Horowitz's casual K to N4 (instead of the fatal, to Reshevsky, K to R4), decided that he could squeeze out a draw. And he did. Really, it was simple as that. (The critical position is included in Chapter 18.)

Reshevsky continues to be active in Chess, but quite as in the case of Grandmasters who preceded him, he has not been able to withstand the onslaughts of time and of new generations of Chessmasters. In 1951 he experienced his first significant setback, losing the United States title to Larry Evans. Since then he has competed in four national tournaments but has not been able to regain the coveted crown. In 1960, when he last participated, he was in a triple tie for fourth place. In all, Reshevsky won the title in five of the ten national tournaments in which he played between 1936 and 1960.

In 1961, a match between Reshevsky and Robert Fischer, sponsored by the American Chess Foundation, ended in a victory (by forfeit) for Reshevsky, at a point where their scores were exactly even. This event, replete with heated charges and recriminations, has won a "distinction" as a melancholy chapter in American Chess annals. What is certain is that Reshevsky was *not* responsible for the impasse between Fischer and the ACF Arrangements Committee.

The story of the Chess genius of Sammy Reshevsky, encompassing a period of forty years or more, remains incomplete without a significant addendum. Necessarily, he has had to give his time and his energies to the support of a family. Chess, with its meager rewards, has become an extra-work luxury. One wonders how much *more* Grandmaster Reshevsky could have and would have been able to accomplish, had he had the independent wealth of a Morphy or the state sponsorship of a Botvinnik.

OTHER PERSONALITIES

Former United States champions who, in varying degrees, remain active in Chess, are Arnold Denker and Arthur Bisguier; the latter continues to participate in international tournaments, but his performance in the interzonal tournament in Stockholm, during the early part of 1962, was less impressive than usual.

The current United States champion is Larry Evans, who also won the title in 1951. Evans won the championship in the 1961 national tournament in which neither Reshevsky nor Fischer participated.

No mention of American Chess personalities can possibly be complete without including Harold M. Phillips, a New York attorney in his late eighties who, as an undergraduate, played Chess for the City College of New York in the 1890's. Phillips, a former President of the United States Chess Federation, is an honored elder in the Chess fraternity. He follows Chess with a youthful eagerness, and his presence in his favored Chess Club and at significant Chess events is automatically expected.

ROBERT J. (''BOBBY'') FISCHER

We come at last to *the* Chess phenomenon, Bobby Fischer, who, at the age of nineteen (as of March 1962), is a *veteran* international Grandmaster, a four-times holder of the United States championship (originally won in 1957, at the age of fourteen, and undefended by him in 1961 when the title went to Evans), and an aspirant, not with undue optimism, for the title of world champion. His most recent triumph—an incredible one!—is first place in the Stockholm interzonal tournament, with a record of thirteen wins, nine draws, and *no* losses. He outdistanced no lesser stars than Geller, Petrosian, and Korchnoi of the Soviet Union, and Dr. Miroslav Filip of Czechoslovakia. All five are now qualified to compete in the world challengers' tournament scheduled to take place in May, 1962 in Curaçao, Dutch West Indies. The winner of that tourney will then face World Champion Botvinnik.

Robert J. ("Bobby") Fischer

Overwhelming indeed is the Chess side of the Fischer ledger, and fairly unanimous is the acclaim of him as a Chess genius. As to his personality and development as a human being, there is a sharply divided camp, with ardent protagonists at the one end, bitter antagonists at the other, and few who have been exposed to Fischer inclined to take a neutral stand.

Bobby, a native of New York City, has concentrated on Chess since early childhood, to the exclusion of almost everything else. He left school as soon as he was legally allowed to do so, frowning upon the counsel of friends and relatives to continue, at the very least, until graduation from high school. He is the product of a broken home, and has maintained contact with his mother and sister, but not with the father.

In the January, 1962 issue of *Harper's*, Ralph Ginzburg, author of *An Unhurried View of Erotica*, wrote an article on Fischer entitled "Portrait of a Genius as a Chess Master." * This was based on interviews that had taken place some five months previously, and on background material consisting mostly of observations by prominent persons on the American Chess scene.

Chessmaster I. A. Horowitz is represented as deploring Bobby's tendency to "alienate and offend almost everybody . . . who might be in a position to help him in his career." On the other hand, John W. Collins, columnist for *Chess Life* and *Chess Review*, shows little or no concern for the development of Bobby's personality. Collins limits himself to an evaluation of Bobby's Chess prowess, indicating that he believes that the youth will "probably be the greatest chess player that ever lived." This estimate, though perhaps more conservatively, is shared by Frank Brady, business manager of the United States Chess Federation.

Ginzburg offers little editorial comment, beyond indicating

* © 1961 by Harper & Row, Publishers, Incorporated. Quoted portions in this chapter reprinted from *Harper's Magazine* by the author's permission.

that Bobby "does not show malice," although it is easy to see how Bobby can "offend people with his sweeping statements." Bobby's older sister is quoted: "Bobby is a boy who requires an extra amount of understanding."

The real meat of the article is, essentially, a series of direct quotations attributed to Fischer. We gather that, since appearance of the article, Bobby has disclaimed responsibility for some of the words charged to him, but we have seen no evidence of a firm protest backed by a bill of particulars. We proceed, therefore, to offer some of the *alleged* comments of Bobby Fischer—none, be assured, taken out of context. It is not unlikely that one or the other side of the aforementioned divided camp will beckon you, once you have gained an acquaintanceship with the observations of Robert J. Fischer, to wit:

ON WOMEN:

(In reply to Ginzburg's mention of Lisa Lane's estimate of Bobby as the "greatest chess player alive.")
That statement is accurate, but Lisa Lane really wouldn't be in a position to know. They're all weak, all women. They're stupid compared to men. They shouldn't play chess, you know. They're like beginners. They lose every single game against a man. There isn't a woman player in the world I can't give knight-odds to and still beat.

ON BOTVINNIK, TAL, KERES, SMYSLOV:
*They have nothing on me, those guys. They can't even touch me. Some people rate them better than me. That really bugs me. They think that no Americans play chess. When I meet those Russian potzers [sic] I'll put them in their place.**

---

* Robert J. Fischer finished *fourth* in the aforementioned Curaçao tournament, behind "Russian potzers" Tigran Petrosyan (first) and Yefim Geller & Paul Keres (tied for second & third).

Robert J. ("Bobby") Fischer

ON FISCHER AS EVEN GREATER THAN CAPABLANCA, STEINITZ, OR
MORPHY:

> *Well, I don't like to put things like that in print, it sounds*
> *so egotistical. But to answer your question, Yes.*

ON ATTRIBUTES OF A STRONG CHESS PLAYER:

> *A strong memory, concentration, imagination and a strong*
> *will. Very little* [mathematical ability].

ON MANNERS OF CHESS PLAYERS CAUSING PROSPECTIVE PATRONS OF
CHESS TO BE REPELLED:

> *It's the fault of the chess players themselves. I don't know*
> *what they used to be, but now they're not the most gentle-*
> *manly group. When it was a game played by the aristocrats*
> *it had more like you know dignity to it. When they used to*
> *have the clubs, like no women were allowed and everybody*
> *went in dressed in a suit, a tie, like gentlemen, you know.*
> *Now, kids come running in in their sneakers—even in the*
> *best chess club—and they got women in there. It's a social*
> *place and people are making noise, it's a madhouse.*

ON JEWS:

> *Yeh, there are too many Jews in chess. They seem to have*
> *taken away the class of the game. They don't seem to dress*
> *so nicely, you know. That's what I don't like.*

ON FISCHER'S OWN ETHNIC EXTRACTION:

> [I am] *part Jewish. My mother is Jewish.*

ON TACT:

> *Well, I'm not so sure I know what you mean by a prima*
> *donna, but if something doesn't interest me or if someone*
> *bores me, or if I think they're a phony, I just don't bother*
> *with them, that's all.*

ON EDUCATION:

> *You don't learn anything in school. It's just a waste of time.*
> *You lug around books and all and do homework. Nobody's*
> *interested in it. The teachers are stupid. They shouldn't have*

any women in there. They don't know how to teach. And they shouldn't make anyone go to school. You don't want to go, you don't go, that's all. It's ridiculous. I don't remember one thing I learned in school. I don't listen to weakies.* My two and a half years in Erasmus High I wasted. I didn't like the whole thing. You have to mix with all those stupid kids. The teachers are even stupider than the kids. They talk down to the kids. Half of them are crazy. If they'd have let me, I would have quit before I was sixteen.

ON MOTHER:

She and I don't see eye to eye together. She's a square. She keeps telling me that I'm too interested in chess, that I should get friends outside of chess, you can't make a living from chess, that I should finish high school and all that nonsense. She keeps in my hair and I don't like people in my hair, you know, so I had to get rid of her. Yeh, she moved in with her girl friend in the Bronx and I kept the apartment. But right now she's away on this trip with those people ** for about eight months. I don't have anything to do with her.

ON FISCHER'S PROGRAM OF ACTIVITIES:

Lots of time I'm traveling around. Europe, South America, Iceland. But when I'm home, I don't know, I don't do much. I get up eleven o'clock maybe. I'll get dressed and all, look at some chess books, go downstairs and eat. I never cook my own meals. I don't believe in that stuff. I don't eat in luncheonettes or Automats, either. I like a waiter to wait on me. Good restaurants. After I eat I usually call up some of my chess friends, go over and analyze a game or something.

---

* *Weakies* is Bobby's term for persons who play no Chess or a weak game, at best.
** The pacifists.

Robert J. ("Bobby") Fischer

Maybe I'll go to a chess club. Then maybe I'll see a movie or something. There's really nothing for me to do. Maybe I'll study some chess book.

ON TRAVEL BY SUBWAY:

Unfortunately, yes [upon being asked whether he uses the subway]. *It's dirty—kids there see I have nice shoes on so they try to step on them on purpose. People come in there in their work clothes and all, people come charging in like animals, it's terrible. People sitting and staring directly across the aisles at you, it's barbaric.*

ON FRIENDSHIP:

No. I don't keep any close friends. I don't keep any secrets. I don't need friends. I just tell everybody everything, that's all.

ON WARDROBE:

Yeh, I used to dress badly until I was about sixteen. But people just didn't seem to have enough respect for me, you know? And I didn't like that, so I decided I'd have to show them they weren't any better than me, you know? They were sort of priding themselves. They would say he beat us at chess, but he's still just an uncouth kid. So I decided to dress up.

Oh, I wouldn't touch them.* I have my shoes made to order, my shirts, everything. I like to dress classy. I have seventeen suits now, all hand-tailored.

No, just a strength (in noting that clothes were *not* a weakness with him). *I don't know. I've had suits made in Argentina, Trinidad, England, New York, California, East Germany, West Germany, and I guess that's all, so far. If you get seventeen suits, you can rotate them. They wear a long time. That's where the poor man gets it coming and going. His suits wear out fast and he never has a wardrobe*

---

* Ready-made clothes.

to choose from. Yeh, some Hungarian uptown makes them [the shoes]. *They cost a hundred bucks a pair. I've got five pairs, not counting ready-mades, which I don't wear anymore anyhow.*

This place called Sy's; they [the shirts] *cost twenty-five dollars each. It's the same place where Kennedy gets his made. I found out who Kennedy's tailor is in England. I might go up there, too.*

ON JOHN F. KENNEDY:

I don't think so [upon being asked whether he, Bobby, would have voted for Mr. Kennedy]. *I don't like to see millionaires in there. He has it too soft, you know. I don't think he's ever had any hardships. Besides, he doesn't have any class. He puts his hands in his coat pockets. God, that's horrible!*

ON DECLINE OF A NATION:

You know they say you can tell the decline of a nation when the people begin to lose interest in their clothes. Nowdays if you're dressed up people think you're a dandy. In the olden days the most virile men were men who dressed the best.

ON FISCHER'S INTEREST IN ANYTHING OTHER THAN CHESS AND CLOTHES:

Palmistry is a definite science; it's not just a bunch of nonsense like astrology. Like [as revealed by a study of his own palms] *I'm not as soft or as generous a person as I would be if the world hadn't changed me.*

ON RELIGION:

I read a book lately by Nietzsche and he says religion is just to dull the senses of the people. I agree.

ON CAUTION AGAINST FALLOUT:

(I am) *a cautious person. Every time you watch TV you get a little radiation.**

* Hence, no TV, or very little of it, for Bobby.

Robert J. ("Bobby") Fischer

Well, I . . . gee . . . I don't know.

Wait! There is: the aristocrats! Yeh, I admire the aristo-crats. You know, the millionaires, except that they're mil-lionaires the way millionaires should be, not the way millionaires are. They're the European millionaires. The French people, you know. Not like the American million-aires. Here you can't tell them apart from the other people. Some of them even drive Chevrolets. They dress casually and all, they're like afraid to be looked at. They should be setting the standards for other people. Instead, they dress like slobs, you know.

I haven't met any yet [European aristocrats]. But I've read about them . . . like in Charles Dickens' A Tale of Two Cities.

First of all I'll make a tour of the whole world, giving ex-hibitions. I'll charge unprecedented prices. I'll set new stand-ards. I'll make them pay thousands. Then I'll come home on a luxury liner. First-class. I'll have a tuxedo made for me in England to wear to dinner. When I come home I'll write a couple of chess books and start to reorganize the whole game. I'll have my own club. The Bobby Fischer . . . uh, the Robert J. Fischer Chess Club. It'll be class. Tournaments in full dress. No bums in there. You're gonna have to be over eighteen to get in, unless like you have special per-mission because you have like special talent. It'll be in a part of the city that's still decent, like the upper East Side. And I'll hold big international tournaments in my club with big cash prizes. And I'm going to kick all the millionaires out of chess unless they kick in more money. Then I'll buy a car so I don't have to take the subway any more. That subway makes me sick. It'll be a Mercedes-Benz. Better, a

Rolls-Royce, one of those fifty-thousand-dollar custom jobs, made to my own measure. Maybe I'll buy one of those jets they advertise for businessmen. And a yacht. Flynn had a yacht (referring to Errol Flynn). *Then I'll have some more suits made. I'd like to be one of the Ten Best-dressed Men. That would really be something. I read that Duke Snider made the list.*

Then I'll build me a house. I don't know where but it won't be in Greenwich Village. They're all dirty, filthy animals down there. Maybe I'll build it in Hong Kong. Everybody who's been there says it's great. Art Linkletter said so on the radio. And they've got suits there, beauties, for only twenty dollars. Or maybe I'll build it in Beverly Hills. The people there are sort of square, but like the climate is nice and it's close to Vegas, Mexico, Hawaii, and those places. I got strong ideas about my house. I'm going to hire the best architect and have him build it in the shape of a rook. Yeh, that's for me. Class. Spiral staircases, parapets, everything. I want to live the rest of my life in a house built exactly like a rook.

12

The Lighter Side of Chess

Johan Huizinga, the eminent Dutch historian, presents a fascinating study of the "play elements in culture," in his *Homo Ludens*. One of Huizinga's basic contentions is that play, a voluntary activity, is the direct opposite of seriousness; that the fundamental elements of play are mirth, fun, and tension. He then points out that participants in the game of Chess—among other forms of play, such as football outstandingly—are, more often than not, grave and solemn, applying themselves with a seriousness completely *un*characteristic of play.

How true!

Upon observing a Chessplayer absorbed in the web of the position facing him, one unaware of the nature of the activity can easily conclude that the player is, at the very least, in the process of demolishing Einstein's discoveries. As a rule, the very same solemnity governs a *post-mortem* analysis of a game. It is probably true that of Huizinga's three elements of play, fun and mirth, if at all applicable to Chess, are quite dormant, whereas tension is the dominant feature. Essentially, however, this conclusion governs "serious" Chess, played by experts. The duffers and casual players usually find a full share of mirth and fun in Chess, for their enjoyment is unstrained by considerations of skill. "Boy, did I give George a shellacking!"—in a game where George and the victor, for the nth time, each blissfully made the selfsame errors, except that George succeeded in making the fatal one.

HUMOR

In considering the "lighter side" of Chess, we necessarily limit ourselves to the skilled Chessplayers, for the absence of seriousness in the approach to the game appears automatically to eliminate all others. But we must keep in mind that much of humor arising out of Chess is of significance to the players only; more often than not, it can produce the impact of the fall of the doughnut on all others. In culling tidbits from here and there, the aim necessarily is to concentrate on what promises to have universal appeal.

THE IMPROVED SQUARE

Rare is the Chess Club not blessed with a generous complement of wags, zanies, screwballs, and pompous idiots who, naturally enough, spout omniscience on any and all subjects and on Chess particularly.

A wag in a leading New York City Chess Club chose a propitious moment to spring his trap on Mr. Omniscient, in the presence of a sizable audience.

"Tell me, Mr. O," Mr. W. asked, "what is an improved square? I have been trying to find out, and I don't find anything on it in any Chess text."

"Well, Sir, . . ." Mr. O began with some hesitancy, and, gaining momentum, went on and on and on, "explaining" how and under what circumstances a square on the board is *improved* in a game of Chess.

Mr. W. thanked Mr. O profusely and waited until the latter took his departure. He then turned to the *forewarned* listeners —all doubled with laughter. "Didn't I tell you? Nothing is hidden from the mind of this moron."

The wag had informed his coconspirators that on his way to the Club he had seen an advertisement in the subway, setting forth pridefully the matzoh (unleavened rectangular biscuit used in certain Jewish rituals) of latest vintage as an "improved square."

SELF-EFFACEMENT

Chess experts of genus shrinking violet are very scarce, practically nonexistent. The one willing to use himself as the butt of a witticism is *the* phenomenon.

"How did you make out with Smith?"

"Oh, him? I can beat him with my eyes closed."

"But how *did* you make out?"

"I was at a disadvantage. ·I had my eyes open."

(It is not unlikely that our friend had been influenced by Mr. Groucho Marx who, upon being asked what he thought of a Broadway production he had attended, remarked: "I was at a disadvantage. I sat facing the stage.")

MEMORY

Unless you are in the fold you have probably never been buttonholed (firm grip!) thus: "You remember my fifteenth move in the fourth game of the second elimination tournament, don't you? It was Tchigorin's suggested counter to . . .

etc., etc. Curiously, the buttonholed enthusiast *is* quite likely to remember it. Memory is the Chess expert's tool in trade. Following is a *modest* example.

Ephraim Sponge—ageless, rootless, mysterious—had two homes, the Chess Club and the law office where he worked; sandwiched in were his diggings, somewhere or other, where he slept. Sponge had been a law clerk for many, many years, never taking time from Chess to complete his law studies. On the other hand, full-fledged lawyer or not, Sponge was highly valued by his employer, Mr. Tort, because of Sponge's prodigious memory.

It was routine for Sponge to repeat, word for word, testimony heard by him in court, or to acquaint and reacquaint Mr. Tort with minute details of ancient documents and obscure citations. Sponge's memory was, of course, given full recognition at the Chess Club. It was routine for Sponge to cite this or that continuation in *all* Chess texts.

As luck would have it, Mr. Tort was visited by the Devil one day who announced that he, the Devil, had come to take Sponge. Mr. Tort was mortified. He pleaded, begged, cried, pointing out that it was absolutely impossible to run the office without Sponge and, as an afterthought, that Sponge was too young to go. The Devil was adamant.

Finally Tort thought of a daring stratagem, and turning to the Devil said:

"Are you a sport, Devil?"

The Devil looked at the lawyer quizzically and said:

"It depends."

Mr. Tort thereupon exacted a sportsman's agreement from the Devil that if the Devil ascertained Sponge's memory to be most phenomenal, as claimed by Mr. Tort, Sponge would not be taken.

Thereupon the Devil opened the door to Sponge's office and called out:

"Sponge, do you like eggs?"

"Yes, I do," said Sponge.

That was about six weeks before the attack on Pearl Harbor; late October, 1941, as a matter of fact.

Shortly after the war broke out, Sponge was drafted. Mr. Tort was frantic, but was unable to do anything about the inevitable loss of Sponge's services. Sponge, after receiving basic training, was sent to the Pacific theater of operations, and he acquitted himself heroically, particularly in Guam and Okinawa. He was wounded twice and decorated four times. Nothing was heard from him or about him, and Mr. Tort gave him up for lost. After three and a half years, Sponge was transferred to the European theater, and he again distinguished himself, particularly in the Battle of the Bulge. He earned two more medals.

In September, 1945, one month after the bombing of Hiroshima, Sponge was discharged from the service. He promptly reported to Mr. Tort.

The lawyer, not believing his eyes, was in ecstasy. He wined and dined Sponge, doubled his salary, and set aside a new spacious office for him. What a reunion!

But—three months later the Devil appeared.

Without much ado, he demanded to know where Sponge was. Tort, with trepidation, pointed to Sponge's new quarters.

The Devil opened the door and called out:

"How?"

"Scrambled," Sponge replied quietly.

JOSHING, GIBING AND JARGON IN THE CHESS CLUBS

Chess clubs throughout the country attract a consistent roster of membership. The nucleus, as a rule, consists of the best players in the community. Understandably enough, those who have an advanced knowledge of the game are interested in keen competition; contrarily, run-of-the-mill players may tend to keep away from clubs, in the interest of sheltering a vulnerable ego. The Manhattan and Marshall, both in Manhattan, are very likely the two outstanding Chess clubs in the United States, for the membership of each consists of some of the finest players in the country. Chess clubs are constantly in search of expert players, and it is traditional to offer honorary (gratis) membership to outstanding players, in obvious consideration of the prestige gained thereby.

Chess clubs are the second home to many Chess devotees whose interests one finds strictly and frenetically limited to Chess. Naturally enough, comradeship is developed, particularly between and among members of equal prowess in Chess, and that is characterized by a goodly bit of horseplay. In large urban areas such as New York City, the banter is stimulated by the polyglot influences of various ethnic groups. But any form of raillery is strictly taboo in serious games, such as intraclub and interclub championship matches or individual time-limit games of one significance or another.

When the gates are up, the joshing is the main order of business. Thus, a player will forcefully hammer a Chess piece down, looking the opponent straight in the eye and exclaiming ferociously:

"Pferd!" This gratuitous warning of an attack upon the opponent's Knight (pferd, horse in German; figuratively, idiot, jackass in Yiddish) is principally intended as an estimate of the opponent as a Chess player.

A more direct influence of German is found in still another form. Some of the German Chess texts are known for their ponderous annotations, terminating, wherever applicable, with ". . . *und der Bauer ist geschuetzt*" (and the Pawn is protected). This catchy phrase, switched into interrogative form, has become a kind of esoteric shibboleth among Chess experts, strictly in the spirit of fun. Thus, a nonserious game is in progress and in walks a habitué who, with simulated anxiety, addresses either or both participants—or, for that matter, nobody in particular: "Ist der Bauer geschuetzt?"

Extravagant mock courtesies are not uncommon. The player rises, bows deeply, and adresses his adversary: "Allow me to inform you, dear Sir, that you are a hopeless idiot! Check!!!" Mercifully, such panegyrics are reserved for the most intimate Chess friends.

An inevitable jargon has sprung up in the course of many years. A hopelessly poor player is a "patzer," used interchangeably with the more commonly known dub and duffer. A losing position is a "bust"; to "sac" is to sacrifice (a Chess piece); "pull" is a slight advantage in a game of Chess; "amateur" is somewhat of a euphemism for "patzer"; "strong amateur," on the other hand, connoting as it does a reasonably good player, though not one in the master class, is not necessarily derisive.

When the castled King is hemmed in by the Pawns in front of him, one of the Pawns is frequently moved for the purpose of creating an escape square in case of enemy attack. This move, in a casual game of Chess, is often accompanied by a cry of "Luft." (*Luft,* air in German and Yiddish; breathing space, figuratively.) This has given rise to what is likely the most outrageous pun in existence:

"Luft," exclaims the mover of the Pawn.

"De luftibus non est disputandum," his opponent notes.

Rare is the Chess Club which does not have a set of *mock* rules governing the game—as often as not prominently exhibited. There is, apparently, a universal penchant among Chess devotees to lampoon all basic principles related to the game and to the conduct of the player. Among the best is the following, of British vintage:

1. Never move any piece once until you have touched every other piece twice. Touch and move is a system adopted by some players to obtain a mean advantage when they fear they have a losing game.

2. If you have a piece "en prise," immediately put another so. It may confuse your opponent.

3. Bang your pieces down when you move. It intimidates your opponent.

4. As an onlooker, make your comments audibly, and never hesitate to move the pieces on the board. It will demonstrate the clarity of your thinking and the stupidity of the players, until you see the piece that you overlooked.

5. Never resign. There is always the chance that your opponent may drop dead before he mates you.

6. Always give a check if you can; it may be mate. Anyhow, it is better to have checked and lost than never to have checked at all.

7. Stick to one opening, even if it is bad and you don't know it. One day you will find somebody who knows it less.

8. Castle, take "en passant," promote Pawns to minor pieces whenever you can. It helps to create the impression that you have a deeper knowledge of the game than you really have.

9. Never think before you move. "Move and think afterwards" is more usual. You can always retract your move, but your opponent must never be allowed to retract his.

10. If you think you can "announce" a mate, do so; your opponent may resign on the spot.

11. Be prodigal with your Pawns. They only hamper your pieces and those of your opponent.

12. When you stumble on a win, at once declare noisily that

you had played for it. You may not convince your opponent, but it is comforting.

AT HOME

A Chess analyst, his attention riveted on a pocket Chess set, was a passenger on a train. Somehow he landed in a compartment carrying a number of men who were being transferred from one mental institution to another.

At each stop of the train, one of the guards carefully counted his charges, as a necessary precaution against escape. At the next stop, as the count was in progress—"53, 54, 55 . . ."—the guard stopped short, puzzled as he was by an unfamiliar face, that of the Chess analyst.

"What are *you* doing here?" the guard asked.

"I am doing the Schliemann variation in the Ruy López, and I have discovered that . . ."

"O.k., o.k., buddy," the guard said soothingly. "Where am I? Oh, yes, this guy's 56 . . . 57, 58, 59 . . ."

Culled from a gossip column in one of New York City's lusty tabloids:

"Miss ———, that tall sexy Off-Broadway actress, said: 'I love sex. I sometimes don't have time for it. But believe me there is no adequate substitute, not even chess.' "

The following tidbit by one of your authors (PLR) appeared in the December, 1941 issue of *Chess Review,* shortly after the tragic impact of Pearl Harbor. It was entitled "Blitz!" and it carried the Editor's legend—*Any similarity of names to persons living or dead is completely intentional.*

Once upon a time there were two great friends, Dolph and Hito. They loved to play Chess, for maneuvers with Pawns fascinated them.

They used to meet at an estate which once belonged to a neighbor whom they murdered and whose vassals, charged with the murder, were held responsible for the upkeep of the estate in a manner designed to suit the comfort and convenience of Dolph and Hito.

Their games were frequent and exciting. Dolph would sit himself down leisurely, using Boris as a footrest, and Hito would use Yi as a footstool. There were always servants at the beck and call of Dolph and Hito. Of these, Benny, Hermy the Elephant, and Henri were most loyally devoted.

One day Dolph and Hito, deciding to engage in a game, proceeded to determine who was to have the choice of White or Black. Yi was placed against the wall and each began to throw darts at him. The object was to strike Yi in the eye. On the third hurl, Hito—after expressing a supplication to his Ancestral Forbears for guidance—made a bull's-eye.

Hito chose White. Dolph looked at him contemptuously, exclaiming:

"Had I had my choice, I should have taken Black, the noble symbol of Death and Destruction, and not White, the putrid emblem of decency in a Decadent Civilization which has been doomed."

Hito felt humiliated but uttered not a word, for he realized that Dolph was right.

"I have the honor," said Hito, as the game began, "to move the Honorable Pawn from King Two to King Four."

"Pawns move by themselves when ordered," hissed Dolph and snapped his fingers, exclaiming "Ditto."

Hermy the Elephant, quick as a flash, executed the order.

"I have the further honor," said the patient Hito, "to move the Honorable Queen to the Rook Five."

"The place of women is in the kitchen," snapped Dolph,

"but I shall tolerate this female intrusion for the moment."

Dolph thought for a while, then motioned to Henri with a flick of his hand. With monarchial obeisance, the servant carried out his master's wishes, placed Dolph's King on the King Two square.

Hito could not believe his eyes. Seizing Dolph's King Pawn, he placed his Queen in its place. Addressing Dolph with diffident restraint, he said: "There is an honorable mate."

Dolph was seized with a paroxysm of laughter. He laughed and laughed, pounding his feet on Footstool Boris, who also laughed.

Suddenly the laughter ceased. Dolph sat upright in his chair, stuck out his chin, glowered at Hito with protruding eyes.

"My patience is exhausted," he screamed. "You have no alternative but to resign. My King will immediately remove your Queen from the board. You did not for one moment think that I would allow a female creature to have powers of locomotion superior to those of the Fuehrer, the King."

Hito quickly composed himself. With unmistakable admiration, he bowed deeply to Dolph and spoke these words:

"My Honorable Felicitations. This brilliant tactic is exceedingly superb. I shall at once acquaint the Gangsterial Council of Ministers in my Honorable Domain with its Honorable potentialities."

A favorite of the late Geoffrey Mott-Smith was this bit of insanity:

Once upon a time there was a college Chess champion who, at the drop of a hat, would undertake to play eight Chess games simultaneously and who, invariably, *lost every one of them.*

CLASSICAL TALES

TOUR DE FRUSTRATION

Common is the practice of recognized Chessmasters to stage simultaneous exhibitions throughout the country. The motives, as a rule, are much less altruistic than pragmatic. There are fees (howsoever modest), there is welcome publicity, there is adulation; there is, in short, an enhancement of the standing of the Chessmaster in the world of Chess. The promotion of the interests of Chess is a mere by-product.

Prominent Chessmasters arrange periodic tours, and they continue to return to familiar faces in this or that part of the country. A basic consideration, of course, is development and retention of the good will of Chess groups everywhere, for the elementary purpose of assuring re-invitations. Thus, the Chessmaster's personality comes into play, his ability to minimize the hurt feelings of his victims, and like attributes that make for good public relations.

The array of opponents against the Chessmaster usually consists of *relatively* weak players. Exhibition tours produce an overwhelming winning percentage for the Chessmaster, as against a few draws and a negligible number of losses. Those who succeed in avoiding defeat (to say nothing of attaining victory!) in simultaneous exhibitions are forever heroes in the eyes of their Chess confreres. (Prominently exhibited in the home of a late member of New York's Manhattan Chess Club was a Chess position on a gigantic board, captioned: MY DRAW WITH FINE.)

When the Chessmaster becomes reasonably well known to the local arrangers of the exhibition, they are not beyond testing his *human* qualities. The pitch—before the big event takes place—may take on the following form: "Mr. Master, as you know, Phineas Jones is the oldest member of our Chess Club. As a matter of fact, today is his 84th birthday. He was one of the charter members, 65 years ago, and he is a beloved citizen in this community. We are not asking you to do anything unethical, but if Mr. Jones succeeds in drawing against you, you can well appreciate what this can mean to him and to us. . . ." The Chessmaster who pays no heed to such blandishments is not likely ever to return to this community. . . .

A Chessmaster (who remains unnamed) faced a combination of circumstances precisely as described above, and he agreed to cooperate. (This, an actual occurrence, supports the contention that even invented anecdotes are closely related to fact.) The Chessmaster quickly discovered that the to-be-honored oldster was of the subtyro class, and he faced the task of employing a semblance of "strategy" short of making himself completely ridiculous. With a choice of evils, the Chessmaster fell upon the idea of *un*developing his pieces; he moved a Pawn here and a Knight there, and a third piece elsewhere, none beyond his fourth rank, with the burning hope that his octogenarian opponent would develop *his* forces, precipitating an unavoidable skirmish which, with a bit of finesse, could be steered into a draw. But Mr. Phineas Jones was not to be "trapped." He proceeded, resolutely, to emulate the great man's cautious maneuvers. The latter was in a sweat. In sheer desperation, he "ventured" into enemy territory; a piece of his reached the fifth rank. The ancient adversary pondered the "bold" challenge for a while and announced: "I resign."

Fortunately for the Chessmaster, his coconspirators knew enough of Chess to realize that he was not culpable. What is more, they were completely captivated by his comment:

"Gentlemen, sometimes no matter how hard you try, you cannot 'win.' "

The Lighter Side of Chess

AN AMAZING INCIDENT
FROM THE
TALES OF BARON MUNCHAUSEN
BY "E. J."

You ask me whether I play chess or not? said Baron Munchausen. Yes, of course I do. Who of us, my friend, has not at some time been fond of this fascinating game. If you have read your Kreutzik * you must know that I once saved my life by marvellous play and became the husband of a beautiful princess into the bargain. But the princess, unfortunately, turned out to have such an infernally bad temper that I gave up chess for ever.

Nevertheless, when the International Tournament opened in Moscow in 1935, I found I could no longer withstand the temptation and I set out for Russia. Though I travelled incognito, it was not very long before the participants in the tournament recognized me, and we spent a great deal of time together. I showed Lasker the special opening variations I had worked out, Capablanca showed me some of his most brilliant achievements, and Flohr consulted me earnestly on the postponed games, which by the way, accounts for his success.

The incident I was about to describe to you occurred soon after Botvinnik's victory over Chekhover, to whom he sacrificed, by way of preliminaries, at least half the pieces on the chessboard. The evening of that same day the chess players remained in the hall after the round, arguing about the correctness and the value of sacrifices in the game. Opinions differed widely. Spielmann asserted that 3 or 4 tempi were really not a bad compensation for a piece. Flohr said he would

---

* Kreutzik was the author of a series of chess "humoresques."

be glad even of a pawn as long as it was an extra one. Capablanca declared that he did not believe in the correctness of any sacrifices. In short, the atmosphere was tense and the weirdest moves were in the air.

I was sitting a little apart from the rest all the time and did not join in the discussion. At length, Capablanca turned to me and said:

"My dear Munchausen, do tell me what your opinion is on the subject."

Then very loudly and distinctly, I replied:

"To tell you the truth I am not much inclined to talking. It would be simpler, I think, if I agreed to play with anyone you care to name, *without any pieces,* receiving no more than a tempo for each piece."

Upon hearing these words, spoken with my usual sangfroid, the company was silent for a while. At last Capablanca said rather drily that audacity such as mine could not possibly be left unpunished and offered to play with me himself.

To tell the truth, I was a little taken aback myself by my own daring, but, reflecting that it was too late now to withdraw, I agreed. The board was arranged, the people crowded round in anticipation, the reporters got out their note books, the press-photographers prepared their cameras, and, in a tense silence, we seated ourselves at the board.

"Well now," said Capablanca with a smile, "I am going to take all your pieces, and we shall see how you play."

The game started in the interesting position shown in the first diagram.

Capablanca

Baron Munchausen

"Having given up seven pieces," I declared, "I shall now demonstrate that an equivalent number of tempi—or moves— is sufficient to win." Whereupon I played: 1 P-K4, 2 P-KN4, 3 P-K5, 4 P-N5, 5 P-K6, 6 P-N6, 7 PxBP mate.

"Perhaps I have been rather greedy," my adversary remarked. "I ought to have left you one piece, a Bishop at least."

"In that case," I replied, "I have only six moves."

Placing the Bishop on my King Bishop square, I immediately played: 1 P-K3, 2 B-B4, 3 P-KN4 4 P-N5, 5 P-N6, 6 BxP mate.*

"It is purely accidental," said Capablanca, "I had intended to leave you a Knight."

"It makes positively no difference to me," I replied, withdrawing the Bishop and placing the Knight on KN1. I then played: 1 N-B3, 2 N-N5, 3 P-K4, 4 P-K5, 5 P-K6, 6 PxBP mate.

"In that case," said my opponent, visibly embarrassed, "I insist that you play with both the Knight and Bishop."

---

* In the interest of keeping Baron Munchausen honest, it must be noted that here a mate in 5 is possible: 1 P-K4, 2 P-K5, 3 P-K6, 4 B-B4, 5 PxBP mate.

Black 16 Pieces

White 11 Pieces

"They will come in very useful," I agreed, mating in exactly five moves: 1 P-K4, 2 B-B4, 3 N-B3, 4 N-N5, 5 BxP mate.

This was too much for the ex-champion of the world. He fell down in a dead faint. Astonishment was general, and amid the general commotion, cameras clicked and pens scratched furiously. The sensation was all over the world next day. Alekhine invited me to play a match with him. Four clubs called after me were organized in America. A publishing house, specializing in books and periodicals on chess, offered to issue a complete edition of my games on the finest vellum paper, richly bound. The number of congratulatory telegrams and invitations to banquets obliged the management of the hotel where I was staying to double the staff. Delegations of enthusiastic chess fans arrived in shoals in Moscow, anxious for a glimpse of me. But with my usual quiet dignity I declined all honors and went into retirement once more.

Chess Review, June 1941

"AFFLUENCE"

It appears that the rich are not attracted to Chess, or rather, those who are do not reach the master class. (It seems that accumulation of wealth "interferes" with development of proficiency in Chess.) In any case, many *active* Chess enthusiasts are known to be in economic straits. Essentially, they are between Scylla and Charybdis. If they devote time to work, their Chess suffers; and *vice versa*.

When Chessmaster I. A. Horowitz embarked on his *Chess Review* venture, in 1933, he was quite prepared for the undertaking except for one minor consideration: funds. It was a bit of a problem, to be sure, how to conserve here and there and to manage to put out a Chess magazine. A *usual* item of overhead in such an undertaking is payment of rent for an office. But wait:

The late Fritz Brieger, Chess patron and Horowitz's friend, offered gratis accommodations in Woodside, Queens (N.Y.), and Horowitz was in business. After a while, it became imperative for Horowitz to move to Manhattan, in the interest of developing the enterprise in a more desirable location. Came the problem of "landlord references" and Mr. Brieger's deft (and completely honest) comment to the new lessor remains a classic to this day:

"Mr. Horowitz? He was one of my most desirable tenants. I never had to ask for the rent twice."

AN ANECDOTE IN MEMORY OF SCHOTTLANDER

The time was the beginning of the World War. I was a student in college and spent my spare time at the chess clubs in Breslau, as young Tarrasch had done a generation before me. There I made the acquaintance of the veteran master, Dr. Rosanes, who had played with the renowned Adolf Anderssen; also of Charles Bregmann, the creator of the Breslau variation in the Ruy López; and of Julius Steinitz, the problemist. All of them have since lost their last game, but in those days they enjoyed life, and from them I heard the story of the great Breslau master, Schottlander.

Once again he was playing with his favorite opponent who was known only by his nickname of "August, the Giant-Killer." Finally, they arrived at the following position:

August the Giant Killer

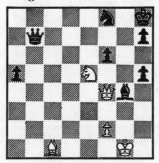

Master Schottlander

Schottlander played 1 QxP ch and August made the correct reply 1 . . . K-N1; seeing that if he played 1 . . . Q-N2 White wins by 2 N-B7 ch, K-N1; 3 N-R6 ch, K-R1; 4 B-N2!, N-K3; 5 Q-B7, etc. The master then continued 2 B-N2, and August replied 2 . . . B-R6 threatening mate. White now played 3 Q-R8 ch!! and the "Giant-Killer" grabbed it off without delay, 3 . . . KxQ.

Schottlander, when he saw the innocence of his opponent, decided to have a little fun, and exclaimed, "What have I done? Let me have my Queen back!" But August, feeling sure of a win, kept the Queen in his hand, refusing to give it back. Schottlander, loving a good joke, kept up the pretense for a few minutes. He rose from his chair and endeavored to take the Queen away. A chase around the room ensued to the enjoyment of the spectators. Finally, the "Giant-Killer" climbed a chair in self-protection, raised his right hand to show the Queen still clutched in triumph.

At last the master tired of the fun. "August," he exclaimed, "for the last time, are you going to return my Queen?" "I will not," said August. "Very well then," replied Schottlander, "I shall continue the game."

The two opponents returned to the board, and Schottlander, amid the laughter of the spectators, mated in two (as he naturally had intended): 4 N-B7 dble ch, K-N1; 5 N-R6 mate.

Hans Cohen in *El Ajedrez Americano*
English version, *Chess Review*, December 1938

•

CAISSA

Caissa, a dryad, heroine of a poem by Sir William Jones (1763), has been humorously appropriated as the tutelary deity of Chess. (The precise origin for the establishment of this role for Caissa (kå·ĭs′å) is obscure. In the Bibliography appended to this book, you will find Caissa incorporated in titles of works by T. R. Dawson.)

The finale to this Chapter is a hitherto unpublished limerick-acrostic, the authorship of which we are ready to confess *only* if it is well received:

> C aissa, the goddess of Chess,
> H as this task, no more and no less:
> E very game, match and damn bit,
> S icilian and gambit
> S he must ever be ready to bless.

[. . . and with great!]

13

Chess and Other Games

COMPARISON

In drawing a comparison between Chess and other games, we are, of course limiting ourselves to so-called indoor games that necessarily require equipment: board, dice, pieces, playing cards, and the like. Moreover, the "other" games are limited to the best known pastimes.

Generally, games may be subdivided into the following classifications: (1) pure skill; (2) combination of skill and chance; (3) pure chance.

The third category can be quickly dismissed. It consists of inanities requiring not a dram of marrow. Typical is the board game which has appeared under various names suggesting affluence: "Wealth," "Riches," "Cash." Each of a number of players (four maximum, as a rule) casts one or more dice, in turn, and moves a counter on a track a number of spaces corresponding to the total number of points in his throw of the dice. The advance of the counter determines the number and type of premiums gained or forfeited. These premiums—slips of paper, discs, or the like—are proportionately distributed to the players at the outset of the game; the object is to augment one's "fortune" after the counter has traveled the full circuit. This monstrosity, truly, is the nitwits' delight.

The second category includes practically all playing card games; Mah Jong; anagrams; *Scrabble,* a splendid proprietory game; and others. (A proprietory game, by the way, is one owned by a manufacturer who has sole rights to the name of the pastime and to the manufacture and sale of the equipment required for it.)

In the first category, Chess and checkers are the best known in Western countries, whereas Go has a strong following in the Orient.

In the history of games the most popular, unquestionably, have been the ones embracing a combination of skill and chance. Nothing is likely ever to surpass the popularity of playing cards. First, they offer the participant freedom from the brutal discipline inherent in games of pure skill. Second, they offer the excitement of the chance "draw" or "fall" of a coveted pasteboard. Third, they allow the opportunity to participate on *any* level of performance. (The duffer, to be sure, can find supreme enjoyment in, say, gin rummy, while making no attempt whatever to remember foregoing plays.) Fourth, they are made-to-order instruments for gambling. Fifth—and this is particularly significant—playing cards can and do attract the person of a keen mind whose power of analysis is called to the front as much by the necessity of utilizing to the maximum the advantages (favorable cards) as reducing to the minimum the disadvantages (unfavorable cards). It is this fifth consideration that sharply reduces the "chance" element in card games played by experts. A "bad run" of the cards is necessarily neutralized by the skills of the players.

Two of the enumerated elements, level of performance and playing for stakes, apply to Chess as well. But whereas good and bad Chess are everyday phenomena—with the latter dominating, incidentally—the playing for stakes is relatively negligible, limited as that necessarily is to players of *proved* equal ability or to rapid-transit sessions (ten seconds per move) in which the "pot" consists of a nominal ante by each of a number of participants. (In the latter case, the excitement and hilarity are, as a rule, no less an attraction than is the "pot" itself.)

G O

Go, invented in China some six hundred years ago and particularly popular among educated Japanese, is played on a board of 361 cells (19 x 19). Each of two players, in turn, places a counter on a vacant vertex; an opponent's piece is removed when it is surrounded. The object of the game is to occupy as many vertices as possible, the difference between the number of White and Black pieces on board at termination of the game being the margin of victory. Says Mauric Kraitchik (in *Mathematical Recreations*): "The Japanese claim that is a finer game than chess, but we don't have to believe them."

We gather that an energetic attempt is being made by manufacturers of the equipment to popularize Go in this country. Unquestionably, there is a great number of combinations and patterns in Go calling for much skill and concentration. A leading Go expert in the United States is Dr. Edward Lasker, the well-known Chessmaster. Why Go has not captivated Western man is open to debate. It may not be at all off key to assume that the Western mind, inherently restless, chooses to reject the extraordinary rigors of discipline and consummate patience required by development of skill in Go. It may also be possible that the sea of cells and the uniformity of the counters frightens the wits out of the Western uninitiate. In a word, Go may have proved to be too great a challenge, uncompensated—as in Chess —by the "fun" in handling dissimilar pieces, each endowed with a peculiar power of locomotion. It is well to note that even Nine Men's Morris, a relatively simple counter line-intersection game (but one requiring skill for expert play) has failed to gain an enthusiastic following in Western countries.

CHECKERS

Checkers is a splendid game, possibly *the* marvel of games of pure skill. It takes one minute to learn the rules and forever to master the game. Contrary to popular concept, checkers can boast of a respectable literature, beautiful problem settings, and complexities quite alien to the casual pusher. Attributed to Newell Banks, one of the all-time greats in checkers, is the following observation: "Everybody knows checkers and nobody knows how to play the game."

Curiously, there is at least one ending in checkers, First Position, which in spark and complexity is equaled by nothing (of *comparable opposing forces*) on the Chessboard. In First Position, we have two Kings versus King and Man, almost an equality, calling for the former to win against any defense. Remarkable as it may seem, the *stronger* side can actually lose by blundering fatally but not necessarily *too* stupidly. The nearest in Chess is King and Queen versus King and Rook, again calling for the former to win against best defense. The stronger side cannot possibly lose, except through ultraidiotic carelessness. Moreover, unlike the rigidly precise steps in First Position, inaccurate continuations in the Chess ending are *not* irrevocable.

On the other hand, checkers has its mathematically *countable* limits. (It is well to note that we are concerned with the game of checkers or draughts as it has been played for centuries in English-speaking countries. There are other modes of play, principally Russian or Spanish checkers, allowing for greater mobility of the King, with attendant strategy quite alien to the game as it is known to us.) The game has been so well analyzed that optional openings are *not* permitted in tournaments. The "restrictive move" limitation is applied by means of the chance draw of an instruction card, which stipulates a sequence of initial moves. In every case, of course, that sequence leads to *unanalyzed* developments. A checkers master carries thousands and thousands of games in his mind, ever prepared to take immediate advantage of an opponent's slip. More often than not, expertly played games end in a draw.

It is, of course, certain that—in the United States, at any rate—checkers is much more popular than Chess. The main attractions, aside from the principal one, the simplicity of the game, are the fun of capture and the backward move of the King. Checkers, however, has never attained the prominent standing of Chess, invariably accorded the distinction of the foremost game of pure skill. There is *relatively* but a fistful of permutations in checkers, as against the practically inexhaustible variations in Chess. (See Chapter 2.) Moreover, the monotonous uniformity of the pieces in checkers, whose locomotion is limited to Black-colored squares only, fails to captivate the searching mind as much as the Chess pieces, which operate in a much vaster arena.

In drawing a comparison between Chess and checkers, we have definitely not set out to "prove" the superiority of the former. Personal preferences play no part. The precision of expertly played checkers games, the intricacies of fundamental "positions"––the stock in trade of every skilled checkers player —the breath-taking beauty of a great number of superb endings and problems—all add up to an automatic recognition of checkers as an excellent game of pure skill. (Examples are given in *Chessboard Recreations,* Chapter 14.) On the other hand, the permutational riches of Chess and its wealth of variety of play remain supreme.

Chess is the foremost game of pure skill thus far conceived by the human mind. Its role of pre-eminence is principally accountable by the inability of man to exhaust its possibilities. Lines of play assumed to be sound for years and years are, after much back-breaking analysis, found to be otherwise. The reverse also holds true. In short, those who have proved themselves equal, consistently, to anybody opposing them in a game of Chess, have never succeeded in mastering the myriad of mysteries of Chess itself.

BRIDGE

We now come to *the* one chance-skill game which—in prominence, popularity, prestige—has easily outdistanced all others. That game, of course, is bridge; or more specifically, contract bridge. We hasten to add that the *chance* designation is not intended for duplicate contract bridge, especially team-of-four match play, for that has been generally recognized as a mode of play offering a reasonably authentic gauge of pure skill.

Contract bridge is the best known card game in the United States. There is hardly a newspaper of significance (none in New York City, for example) that does not have a daily column on bridge. National tournaments attract thousands of people from every corner of the land. Bridge enthusiasts look forward feverishly to sea trips, sponsored by bridge experts and dedicated to playing bridge. There is at least one prominent television show on bridge. There is a central authority that determines the ratings of players; designations of master and lifemaster are determined by the number of points earned in recognized tournaments. Periodically, international tournaments are held for the world championship (recently won by Italy). There is, in short, a widespread interest in bridge, kept alive by thousands and thousands who are frenetically attracted to the game.

Charles H. Goren, whose works enjoy a phenomenal market, is probably this country's best known authority on the game. Among the foremost experts and writers on bridge is Albert H. Morehead (also a recognized authority on games in general), bridge editor of *The New York Times.* As is typical of the *Times,* Morehead's daily and Sunday columns are second to none in style, accuracy, timeliness, and clarity of instruction. Like that of many of his colleagues, Morehead's interest in bridge is propelled principally by a genuine personal dedication to the promotion of the game. The refreshing tone of his writings offers a sharp contrast to a number of syndicated columns on bridge, which may be fairly characterized by their routine message: "Well, children, today's lesson is. . . ."

Another excellent bridge columnist is Miss Florence Osborn of the *New York Herald Tribune.* Her writings, too, are fresh, timely and lively.

As a rule, the bridge writers lay greatest stress—and understandably so—on major bridge events, which invariably consist of duplicate bridge competition. Since, as has been noted, duplicate bridge has eliminated to the limits possible the chance element in bridge, and since thousands and thousands of people of much lower than master standing play duplicate bridge, we are faced with a curious phenomenon: A game of skill, as close to "pure" as possible, has a fantastic popular following. Is this not an anomaly? Why not Chess, with its great tradition of supreme intellectual challenge? What is the difference?

The difference is tremendous, and the reasons are not too complicated.

Chess does not offer such elements of surprise, excitement,

uncertainty, need for self-confidence, *and* daring which, among other things, are peculiar to and serve as the basis for the magnetism of bridge—rubber or duplicate. First, there is the challenge of communication (bidding), subject to rigidly prescribed rules and conventions that allow for no deviations from fair play. Second is the challenge of *anti*-communication: How best to kill interchange of information between opponents, again in accordance with rules that call for meticulous observation of ethics—or else disqualification. Third, there is the perpetual excitement inherent in interchanging information, accurately and precisely, within the prescribed bounds. Fourth, there is the (completely legitimate!) double-cross and double-double-cross in the uncertainty deliberately created by the play of a card, or by the double, or by the redouble, or by the surprise bid. Fifth, there is the thrill of the daring bid or play, carrying with it as it does a keen psychological study of the opponents and the feverish (inward) but calm (outward) expectancy of the desired reaction. Finally, there is the disciplining oneself to maintain poise and balance when plans go awry, and to enter the next battle unshaken by frustrations.

Now then, do you wonder why many Chessmasters—to whom Chess, true enough, is *the* dominant interest—love to play bridge? The attraction to bridge has been explained by one Chess expert as "surcease from the rigors of the known," the open Chessboard sight of which is equally available to *both* opponents. Clearly, the excitement of the *unknown* in bridge cannot be found in Chess. This may well be the *basic* factor, differentiating bridge from Chess, on which the previously enumerated elements in the play of bridge are built.

Incidentally, do you know that many bridge experts love to play Chess? Why? We must leave that to someone who may one day write a book entitled *The Personality of Bridge.*

In 1904, a Briton (pseudonym Badsworth) wrote a eulogy on

bridge, then in its early stages as the successor to whist. (Contract bridge was invented by Harold S. Vanderbilt some twenty years later.) It is remarkable how Badsworth's words apply to present-day bridge *and* to Chess. We quote from Miss Florence Osborn's column, "The Bridge Deck," in the *New York Herald Tribune* (October 6, 1960): *

Bridge, with an alluring fascination which secures attention, teaches most of the lessons of life in the guise of amusement. The game calls for the prompt exercise of the soundest judgment in deciding whether the forces at your disposal justify an attack or compel a defensive attitude; it teaches you that there is a time to be prudent and a time to be bold, a time to accept responsibility and a time to transfer it to another.

It develops powers of concentration, the lack of which causes so many failures in life, by only demanding undivided attention to be given for the brief space of three minutes to a subject which interests and amuses you; the repetition of this a dozen times in an hour greatly increases the power of being able to devote all your thoughts to the one subject of the moment in the hurry and bustle of life.

It encourages careful observation and improves the memory, trains the mind to estimate probabilities accurately and to draw inferences from actual knowledge and marshaled facts, not to rest action on ignorance and guesses.

It gives a great insight into human character . . . teaches you . . . that a chance of success may be lost forever unless it is grasped at the moment.

Mah Jong is essentially a rummy game, enlivened by the attractiveness of the equipment: colorful tiles on which appear "occult" symbols. Invariably played for stakes, Mah Jong continues to be a favorite of women. A lady player carrying a Mah Jong case *can* be mistaken for a fife player on the way to or from a rehearsal.

No word game has as yet been invented to excel anagrams,

---

* Reprinted by permission of the *New York Herald Tribune*.

but *Scrabble* is the closest. In both, we have all the elements inherent in card games. What is more, choice of level of performance is here of extraordinary significance. The child and college professor can and do derive delight from play, each operating within the range of his vocabulary.

An outstanding feature of anagrams is the "stealing" of words from an adversary, coupled necessarily with protecting one's own words against theft by creating unchangeable combinations of letters. In *Scrabble* we have the excitement of the score, the defensive block of dangerous openings, and the feverish draw of critical letters. Anagrams can, of course, be incorporated into the game of *Scrabble*. The result is probably the most challenging word game extant. Essentially, each of the players is allowed to rearrange words, provided previously covered squares remain covered and the rearrangement is *necessary* for making the chosen play. Not unlike card games, moreover, both anagrams and *Scrabble* can be played for stakes and prizes.

CHESS VARIANTS: KRIEGSPIEL

In the course of years, ambitious attempts have been made to stimulate interest in a number of Chess variants. The forces have been increased, decreased, given different locomotive power; the Chessboard, correspondingly, has been extended, contracted, reshaped, all to no avail. Chess is taken in its traditional form or not at all. There is, however, one variant, *Kriegspiel*, which has enjoyed more than fleeting popularity.

It is quite possible that *Kriegspiel*, while retaining substantially the basic aspects of the game of Chess, offers enough of the excitement of the *unknown* to attract persons who are primarily interested in Chess but welcome the added features as a release from the (aforementioned) "rigors of the known." Indeed, *Kriegspiel* has had a respectable following. Chessmaster Kashdan ranks as an expert player.

Bridge

Kriegspiel requires three Chess sets and the services of a referee. Each player makes moves on his own board out of sight of his opponent. The referee keeps track (on *his* board) of the *actual* moves made by White and Black, and acts as go-between, informing each player that the other has moved. When the move is neither a check nor a capture, the referee announces that the side (White or Black, as the case may be) has moved. When a capture is made, the piece is removed from the board of the player who has lost the piece, while the other is informed that he has made a capture. If the move is a check, both players are so informed and the referee specifies whether the check is along the file, rank, diagonal or by a Knight.

Each player must maintain his own forces in accordance with his actual moves and in compliance with the directions of the referee. He can arrange the enemy pieces as he imagines them to be. Implicit in the acquiring of skill is the ability to draw quick inferences as to the actual distribution of enemy forces.

If an attempted move is an impossible one, the referee says "No." A player, on turn, may always try to determine whether any of his Pawns can make a capture by asking "Any?" If the referee says "Try," the player must make at least one attempt. When an *en passant* capture is made, it is announced by the referee. In no other case is the identity of the captured piece made known.

The players are usually in the same room, back to back or otherwise out of each other's sight, with the referee between them. It is perfectly ethical to listen alertly to exchanges between the referee and the opponent. Inferences *can* be drawn. *Kriegspiel* is, essentially, a battle of deductive reasoning, and even a thin clue can offer advantage.

Mostly, the biggest attracton of this Chess variant is that the ostensible mystery of it begins to dissolve quickly, once the first plunge is taken.

14

Chessboard Recreations

The Chessboard, with or without the aid of Chess pieces or checkers, has been found to be readily adaptable for stunts, puzzles, arrays, arrangements, patterns, games (other than Chess and checkers, of course), gamelets, and jigsaw designs of dissected components of the very board itself. The extensiveness of this area of recreations attests compellingly to the magnetism of the realm of enigma for the human brain; to challenges overcome by painstaking perseverance; to formidable tasks undertaken with but a single gratification (though a superbly significant one!) as the reward: the answer, the solution!

Chessboard recreations are mostly in the public domain; few, if any, have been conceived throughout the ages as means of promoting personal material gain. They well symbolize, therefore, the human satisfaction in giving and sharing the fruits of the intellect: whether a charming puzzle of joy to relatively few or a discovery in medicine and science of benefit to millions.

As often as not, that satisfaction may be essentially *un*altruistic, being primarily based on the aggrandizement of the ego of the creator, but the gain to all others is not at all affected thereby.

We are including some of the classical recreations, along with others less known but offering an appeal all of their own. You will find some of the outstanding accomplishments of the amazing Sam Loyd, the American "Puzzle King," and charming creations—including the greatest puzzle ever conceived by man —of the brilliant English puzzle artist, Henry Ernest Dudeney. Included also are posers especially composed for this chapter by one of your authors (PLR). The solutions will be found at the end of the chapter. There is a good measure of amusement in store for all, in proportion, of course, to the interest generated by this compilation of enigmas, whether the solutions are worked out—with the reward of *Eureka!*—or simply looked up, with an irresistible "How lovely!"

1. EIGHT QUEENS

This classical challenge is undoubtedly the most popular of all stunts having some relationship to Chess. The stipulation calls for arranging eight Queens on the Chessboard, so that none can capture any other. (The provision "can capture" rather than "is guarded by" is abritrary. The Queen moves horizontally, vertically, and diagonally, any distance along a straight *open* line; she *can capture* the nearest piece of *opposite* color situated on the line, whereas a piece of the *same* color so situated *is guarded by* the Queen.)

The Eight Queens puzzle is known to millions, but not many have an awareness that there is a precise solution embracing *all* possibilities. It has had the attention of superb mathematicians and determined analysts; essentially mastery of the puzzle requires a systematic, orderly process of attack in what is virtually a jungle of permutations. Any one desiring to find all possible solutions by trial and error is quite welcome to take some 240 lifetimes for the job. The total number of all possible arrangements of eight Queens on a Chessboard is 4,426,165,368. Assuming that one can exhaust 1,000 positions per day, at the constant rate of 125 per hour, working eight hours *every* day for an uninterrupted period of fifty years, it will take more than 240 lifetimes to complete the job. We suggest, therefore, that you may as well accept the findings that follow.

There is a total of ninety-two arrangements of which twelve are *basic*. A basic arrangement is one from which other views of the *identical* pattern are obtained by rotating the Chessboard and reflecting each time the position then in view. A rotation of the board allows, in essence, a view of the pattern with each side of the board at the bottom (say); a reflection is the mirror image of the view thus obtained. More specifically, assume, as in bridge, that the bottom of the board is South, the top North, the right edge East, and the left edge West. When the board is given a quarter turn to the right, North is now to the right, East at the bottom, etc. Another quarter turn to the right places North at the bottom, and still another quarter turn gives us North at the left edge of the board. We thus have all possible positions for *each* side of the board. In each case, of course, the mirror image of the position is its reflection.

Obviously enough, a nonsymmetrical arrangement yields eight different views of itself by rotation and reflection. Four views only are possible in a symmetrical pattern (consisting, essentially, of homogeneous pieces or wholly balanced arrays), for a view from the top is the same as a view from the bottom and two rotations and their reflections are necessarily eliminated.

In the Eight Queens puzzle, one of the twelve basic arrangements is symmetrical; we therefore have a total of ninety-two (instead of ninety-six) views. Formulas have been evolved for boards of $n \times n$ squares, where n is necessarily greater than 2. Thus, there are 40 solutions on a 7×7 board (6 basic, of which 2 are symmetrical), 724 solutions on a 10×10 board (92 basic, of which 3 are symmetrical), 14,200 solutions on a 12×12 board, etc., *ad infinitum*. (It is, of course, obvious that n is the number of Queens used on an $n \times n$ board.)

The solver who finds one or more basic patterns in the Eight Queens puzzle is good; he who discovers all twelve is superb!

2 . Knight's Tour

Another of the great classical stunts relating to Chess is the Knight's tour, on which there is an extensive literature dating back to the beginning of the eighteenth century, possibly earlier. The stipulation: Move the Knight from an optional starting point in such manner that it shall have successfully entered, once and once only, *every* square on the Chessboard. Obviously enough, 63 moves are required.

Basically, the problem is twofold, embracing (1) the open path, in which the last square on which the Knight lands is *not* a Knight's move away from the square on which the Knight is originally situated; and (2) the re-entrant or closed path, in which the last square *is* a Knight's move away from the point of beginning, thus allowing for an endless circuit. The latter is considered the more elegant solution, for the very good reason that the tour can begin or end on *any* desired square.

The move of the Knight is best defined as one *not* in a straight line to the *nearest* square of a color other than the one on which the Knight is originally situated. (As noted elsewhere in these pages, the definition quite matches the grotesqueness of the move itself.) The Knight has a maximum of 8 moves, a minimum of 2, depending on the square of the board on which he rests. In Diagram 2*a,* below, all ranges of the Knight's mobility are given for the 6 *basic* squares on which he can be stationed.

In Diagram 2*b* is indicated the number of moves available to the Knight when stationed on any square in each of the enclosed areas. As is obvious, the corners of the board offer minimum mobility; the 16 squares in the center, maximum.

Diagram 2*a*

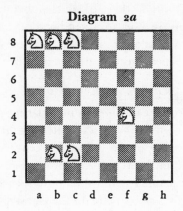

Diagram 2*a*. Knight at *a*8: 2 moves, *b*6,*c*7.

    "   "   *b*8: 3   "   *a*6,*c*6,*d*7.

    "   "   *c*8: 4   "   *a*7,*b*6,*d*6,*e*7.

    "   "   *b*2: 4   "   *a*4,*c*4,*d*3,*d*1.

    "   "   *c*2: 6   "   *a*1,*a*3,*b*4,*d*4,*e*3,*e*1.

    "   "   *f*4: 8   "   *e*2,*d*3,*d*5,*e*6,*g*6,*h*5,*h*3,*g*2.

Diagram 2*b*

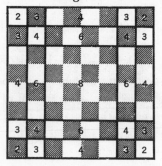

Diagram 2*b*. Note subdivision of areas covering all squares variously corresponding to those specifically selected in Diagram 2*a*.

The total number of Knight's tour possibilities has *not* been determined. It has been authoritatively estimated, however, that the number lies between 122,802,512 (a definite figure of re-entrant paths of a particular type) and—hold your breath—168 units taken 63 at a time, i.e.

$$\frac{168!}{105!63!}$$

a figure which, in the absence of aid of electronic devices, we promise that we shall determine *exactly* (use of logarithm tables being barred, of course) as soon as we consider ourselves ready for the booby hatch.*

Now that you know that there are zillions of solutions, get ONE, and you will have accomplished a feat! (We suggest, by the way, the use of likely indicators, such as counters, to cover the squares visited by the Knight in the course of the journey; otherwise, utter confusion.) You will find in the appended solutions an example of the open path and an illustration of the re-entrant one, along with an explanation of a rather simple *modus operandi* for one of them. Compare also discussion of Knight's tour in Chapter 10, in connection with blindfold feats.

---

* The exclamation mark (!) is the mathematical symbol for "factorial." It denotes the product of the number so designated multiplied by the one lower, and the next lower, and so on down to 1. Thus, $4! = 4 \times 3 \times 2 \times 1 = 24$. 168!, obviously, is the product of $168 \times 167 \times 166 \ldots \ldots \times 3 \times 2 \times 1$. It follows that the given expression is factorial 168 divided by factorial 105 times factorial 63, i.e.,

$$\frac{168 \times 167 \ldots \ldots \times 2 \times 1}{(105 \times 104 \ldots \ldots \times 1) \times (63 \times 62 \ldots \times 1).}$$

3. QUEEN'S TOUR

Diagram 3

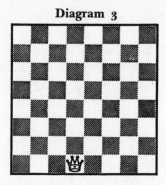

What is the *greatest distance* the Queen can cover in 5 (only!) continuous moves, from starting point indicated in above diagram, without crossing her path (that is, entering any square more than once)? This delectable morsel, generally credited to Dudeney, features a diabolical point. Note that we have italicized *greatest distance*. And now—think!

4. TYRANNY OF WORDS

Diagram 4

Move the Rook "Home" from the square on which he is situated, so that in the course of his journey, moving one square at a time, he enters every square once, and once only.

When you have decided that it is impossible, read the stipulation once more.

5. ANOTHER QUEEN'S TOUR

Diagram 5

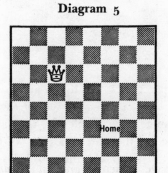

The Queen can reach "Home" in 15 continuous moves, covering the entire board and not ever crossing her path. How is that done? The solution, a unique one, is a lovely pattern. (This charming poser appeared in *The Tribune,* London, in 1906: another brainchild of Dudeney's.)

6. HODGEPODGE

Diagram 6

This twofold poser is essentially for arithmophiles.

Not a single piece, in either portion of the board, has been placed in its "home" square, i.e., in the square where it is originally situated at the start of a game of Chess. Moreover, in the lower part of the board, the two Bishops are on squares of the same color.

a. In how many different ways can the 8 pieces be set up so that each is on the *wrong* square, the Bishops, as in the lower position, being allowed to occupy squares of the same color?

b. The stipulation is the same as above, except that the Bishops, as in the upper position, must occupy squares of different color.

No distinction is to be made between Queen's Rook and King's Rook, Queen's Bishop and King's Bishop, and Queen's Knight and King's Knight. In the diagramed positions, for example, an interchange of the Rooks, or of the Bishops, or of the Knights, does *not* produce a *different* setting. This necessarily adds a bit of zest to the task of finding a precise computation. Good luck!

7. ALL ROADS LEAD TO . . .

The mischievous, fun-loving Sam Loyd became somewhat annoyed with the alibis of a group of would-be Chess problem solvers. He·stumped them time and again, but invariably they would insist: "Oh, we thought *that* was the White side of the board, not *this*. No wonder we couldn't get it." Loyd's next composition, sure enough, had a distinct solution for White to play from *either* side of the board, and he had his revenge.

Loyd was the pioneer in many phases of problem composition, but threadbare now are problems with even four intended distinct solutions: that is, for White to play from *any* side of the Board. We do, however, have a bit of a novelty.

What, do you guess, is the minimum number of pieces required for a 2-move mate from *every* side of the board, the mating position in each of the four solutions being different from any of the others? Less than 10? Exactly 7? More than 10?

8. DETECTIVE WORK

Would you care to be a Chess sleuth? It's fun, and we shall initiate you painlessly.

As noted in Chapter 7, retrograde analysis of Chess positions has been used as a crucial prop in murder mysteries. In essence, retrograde analysis is a determination of how a given position could possibly have developed from the starting point in a game of Chess, in accordance with the rules governing the game. There is a respectable literature on retrograde analysis, consisting of ingeniously conceived and highly complex settings. We shall limit ourselves, however, to three reasonably elementary morsels.

Diagram 8a

Diagram 8b

Diagram 8c

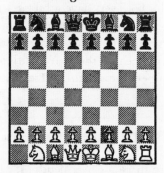

In each of the diagramed positions (arranged by PLR), can it be determined whether White or Black is on the move? If not, why not? Specifically, if you can ascertain whether each side has made an *odd* or an *even* number of moves, then the following possibilities *must* govern your conclusions:

White	Black	To Move
Even	Even	White
Even	Odd	Black
Odd	Odd	White
Odd	Even	Black

In other words, if both sides have made an odd or an even number of moves, then it is White's move; if not, it is Black's. We offer a hint in the form of a query: If a Knight is situated on a square of the same color as his home square (i.e., the one on which he is originally stationed at the outset of a game of Chess), has he made an odd or an even number of moves?

9a. YOU ARE DRAUGHTED

Diagram 9a
BLACK

WHITE
White to Play and Win

In Chapter 13, we accord checkers (less commonly known as draughts) the recognition it merits as an excellent game of pure skill. Few, relatively, are acquainted with its complexities and with a rich selection of splendid problems and endings.

The above is an incredibly beautiful conception, the brainchild of Hugh Byers and known as *Byers' Gem*. To find the critical maneuvers in so slender a setting is to derive much joy.

9b. KING DEFLATED

Some years ago, one of your authors (PLR) was challenged to construct a position in checkers answering the following stipulations:

1. It must consist of a *minimum* total number of pieces.

2. Each piece in the original setting *must be* mobile. No blocks allowed.

3. The forces of the two sides must be numerically equal, that is, no side may have more pieces than the other, but either may have more men (or Kings) than the other.

4. Now, it must be possible to demonstrate conclusively that if a specified piece of a given side (White, say) is a King, White loses; but if that piece is a man, White wins.

This is probably the only task in checkers (aside from related challenges, such as drawing with a man instead of a King) where we find considerations inherent in the examples appearing in Chapter 5, which deals with the *relative* value of the Chess pieces.

But for stipulations 1, 2, and 3, the task is not a difficult one. If a disparity of forces and block clusters are allowed, appropriate settings suggest themselves quickly. And there is the rub!

The task was accomplished with a total of 8 pieces: a hint to the brave and the bold who may desire to undertake this sleep-robber. If anybody *dares* meet the challenge with less than 8 pieces, we vow solemnly to include the new discovery in a future opus to be entitled "Chessboard Exasperations."

10. Still Another Queen's Tour

Diagram 10

This is one of the great Loyd classics. Begin the Queen's tour from the square on which the Queen is stationed in the above diagram. In 14 continuous moves cover every square on the board and return to point of beginning. The Queen *is* allowed to cross her own paths, i.e., re-enter squares which she has previously visited.

Few Chessboard conceptions have gained as many accolades as this one. Dudeney, for example—Loyd's contemporary and friendly rival—published a tribute and a scholarly analysis, in recognition of the unique features of the solution to Loyd's challenge.

11. FLATTERY

Diagram 11

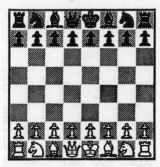

Imitation, we are told, is a sincere form of flattery—and we must hasten to add that in Chess it can lead to a great deal of trouble. When the great Loyd was twenty-five years of age, the original array of the Chess pieces suggested to him the possibility of beautiful effects based on Black's making *exactly* the same moves as White. He demonstrated, for example, the possibility of a self-mate in 8 moves, and of a mate in 4. The latter, however, was inaccurate in that it was possible to accomplish it in more than one way.

Inspired by Loyd's offhand experiments ninety-six years ago

(doesn't one feel puny, though?), we pose two tasks, in both of which Black must make exactly the same moves as White, starting from original array (Diagram 11):

a. Demonstrate a mate by White in 6 moves, entailing one specific sequence of moves (and one only) and involving *no* captures.

b. Demonstrate a discovered mate by the White King in 18 moves, where King and Pawns (*only*) may move. (No pieces other than King and Pawns may move; a promoted piece may *not* move, for it is no longer a Pawn.) Here a precise sequence of moves is not required, for it cannot be forced.

The second of the two *flattery* tasks (both composed by PLR) is particularly difficult. It was conceived more as a most surprising effect than a challenge to solvers.

12. PAWN ARRAY

Diagram 12

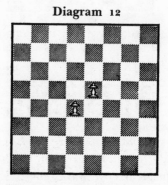

This poser, a Dudeney conception, is tactically related to the Eight Queens classic.

Place the remaining 14 Pawns on the board so that no three of the total of 16 (i.e., including the 2 already placed, as indicated in Diagram 12) will be situated in a straight line: horizontal, vertical, or diagonal.

13. DECONTROL

Diagram 13

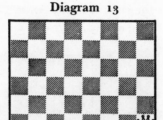

It is obvious, of course, that the 8 Queens, as situated in Diagram 13, control the entire board. Transfer 3 of the Queens (and 3 only) to other squares, thereby leaving 11 squares unguarded.

It is believed, by the way, that it is impossible to place 8 Queens on an open board so that *more* than 11 squares are unguarded. No rigorous proof is available, however.

14. KING'S MAGIC TOUR

Diagram 14

In an $n \times n$ magic square (where n, necessarily, is a number higher than 2), the consecutive numbers 1 through n^2 are so placed in the cells that the sum in each row, column, and long diagonal is exactly the same as in any other. Thus, for example, we have the sum of 15 in a 3 × 3 magic square:

8	1	6
3	5	7
4	9	2

In an 8 × 8 magic square (corresponding to the Chessboard), the numbers placed are, obviously, 1 through 64, and the sum in each rank, file and long diagonal is 260.

Believe it or not, it is possible for the King to conduct a *magic* tour. He can start from Square 1 (Diagram 14, above) and, in successive King moves, to be designated 2, 3, 4, 5, etc., he can reach the indicated Square 64, and his numbered steps will form a perfect magic square, the sum in each rank, file, and long diagonal adding up to 260.

The starting point (Square 1) and last step (Square 64) are offered as a hint. There are other ways of accomplishing this exciting task. Note also that the tour forms a re-entrant path. (See Knight's Tour, Number 2 in this chapter.) The King can continue from Square 64 to Square 1, 2, etc., retracing his steps in an endless circuit.

May we be so presumptuous as to suggest that you do not attempt to solve this lulu *sans voir?*

15. QUO VADIS, KING?

Diagram 15

This is another *early* Loyd composition. His genius, throughout his fruitful career, simply refused to recognize the "inexperience" of youth, the mental decline of advanced years, or any other limits. You will find in Number 17 of this chapter two astounding conceptions of Loyd's, composed forty years apart!!

In the above pleasantry, the Puzzle King challenges you to find the following:

a. Square on which the Black King stands stalemated.

b. Square on which the Black King stands checkmated.

c. Square on which the Black King can be mated in one move. (Curiously, this is more difficult to ascertain than either of the preceding.)

d. Square on which the Black King can *never* be mated— i.e., by the given White forces. [Not at all surprising is that this was a unique discovery by Loyd, to whom the Chessboard was a perpetual fascination. The stipulation, in effect, is an incredible one: Demonstrate that White King, Queen, *and* Bishop cannot possibly mate the (unaided) Black King when the latter is situated on a specified square. This is the classical example in Chess of adamant regal resistance.]

16. LONESOME TWOSOME

Diagram 16

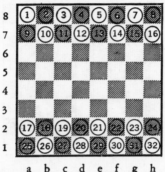

This is an elegant Chessboard solitaire pastime, an adaptation by Dudeney. Numbered counters, such as appear in the accompanying diagram, are not required; they are used as an aid in the explanation of the stunt. Hence, the 32 Chess pieces can be used.

The object is to remove all men except two, the *Lonesome Twosome,* but these two must originally have been stationed on the *same side* of the board. (Obviously enough, if you start with the original array of the Chess pieces, two Whites or two Blacks can be left, but *not* one of each.) The rules governing removal of the men follow.

Each man may remove the one adjoining it horizontally or vertically—but *not* diagonally—by jumping over it—if, of course, the square immediately beyond the jumped-over man is vacant. No moves other than jump-moves are allowed. In other words, the task must be accomplished in 30 moves.

Illustrations: 1 moves to *a*6 removing 9; 2 to *b*6 removing 10; then 1 can go to *c*6 removing 2. If in the original setting, 3 goes to *c*6 removing 11, then, of course, 1 can go to *c*8 removing 2. But note that 1 to *c*6 removing 10 is not possible, for diagonal jumps are not allowed. When the upper men and the lower men merge, one can jump the other at will, in accordance with the stated rules.

For economy, the moves listed in the appended solution consist of two characters only, the jumper and the captured man, respectively. Thus, 1–9, 2–10, 1–2, for example, means that 9, 10, and 2 have been respectively removed by 1, 2, and 1.

Have fun.

17. LOYDOWN ON STALEMATES

Stalemates do occur, of course, in games of Chess: as a rule, in the late stages, after 50 moves or more, when the stalemated King is the sole survivor or accompanied by several blocked Pawns. The ever-curious Sam Loyd set out to determine the *theoretical* possibilities in effecting stalemate in fewest possible moves, from the starting point in a game of Chess. Implicit in this challenge is the cooperation of the side to be stalemated. Thus, Loyd created a humdinger of a task for himself: What is the fewest possible moves in which a stalemate can be accomplished *cooperatively?* (This, in effect, is a *help* problem of which examples are given in Chapter 9.)

In 1866, when Loyd was twenty-five years of age, he established the minimum-move record for the stalemate of Black. He allowed himself the "luxury" of captures in accomplishing the task. The record has not been broken and there is good reason to believe that it never will be.

In 1906, when Loyd was sixty-five years of age, the challenge caught his fancy once again. (It is unlikely, by the way, that it ever left him.) "It is inelegant to resort to captures," said he to himself, "and I must find a way of accomplishing this with *no captures at all.*"

He did!

The astonishing result was a stalemate (of White, this time) with the *entire* White and Black forces intact! Not a single

Pawn or piece captured! In how many moves was Loyd able to accomplish this feat? Two more—two!—than required in his first effort.

The reason, incidentally, why Black is stalemated in the one case and White in the other is accountable by a consideration of economy: the saving of a move. In the latter case, for example, if Black is to be stalemated, an additional White move is required.

This indeed is the classical tale of tenacity. But tenacity to a mortal was usually child's play to Sam Loyd. What elevates Loyd far and above his eminent contemporary puzzle-maker, H. E. Dudeney, is the former's miraculous knack for instant recognition of potential fun and excitement, through the medium of enigma, in everything about him, *including* Chess problems. Loyd's artistry as a Chess problem composer remains unique. Dudeney, on the other hand, saw in the Chessboard little more than permutational possibilities for tours and the like (an area, by the way, which did *not* escape Loyd's talents) and a *milieu* for occasional Chess settings of a puzzling type. Yet, it was the same Dudeney who presumed to excoriate Chess problems as unworthy of serious attention or recognition. We wonder what subjective human elements motivated Dudeney to issue the tirade. Was there possibly a pique born out of a realization that he had no talent for Chess problems? If so, it is highly regrettable, for greatness as a puzzle artist can never be denied Dudeney, one of whose marvelous creations, generally regarded as the greatest puzzle ever conceived by man, appears as the last item in this chapter.

We return to Loyd's Stalemates. What is your guess?

    a. Was the first, captures allowed, accomplished in 10, 14, or 17 moves?

    b. Was the second, no captures, accomplished in 12, 16, or 19 moves?

18. PERMUTATIONAL PICNIC

Chapter 2 offers a glimpse of the fantastic permutations in Chess. Here we supplement with specific examples in the form of a multiple-choice game. You are completely at liberty, of course, to work out your own calculations, but you may prefer the fun of guessing.

a. In how many different ways can the King go from K4 to Q4 in 8 moves? Closest to 100,000? 200,000? 400,000?

b. In how many ways can the White King and Black King, each starting from his home square and playing alternately, exchange places in 7 legal moves? Closest to 25,000? 30,000? 35,000? (In stipulating that the moves must be *legal*, it is fundamental that neither of the Kings is allowed ever to be in a square adjoining that on which the other stands.)

c. In how many different ways can two White Rooks and two Black Rooks stand on the board so that each has two captures? Closest to 500? 1,000? 1,500?

d. Same for two White Bishops and two Black Bishops. Closest to 300? 400? 500?

e. Same for two White Knights and two Black Knights. Closest to 300? 400? 500?

f. In how many different ways can a Bishop moving from K1 square, one square at a time, reach K7 in 8 moves? Closest to 300? 400? 500?

g. In how many different ways can a Bishop moving from K4, one square at a time, return to K4 in 6 moves? Closest to 300? 400? 500?

h. In how many different ways can a Knight, allowed to visit squares *more than once* in the course of his journey, move from K4 and back in 4 moves? Closest to 50? 100? 150?

i. In how many different ways can a Knight, *not* allowed to visit any square more than once in the course of his journey, move from K4 and back in 4 moves? Closest to 50? 100? 150?

All of above are from a compilation by the late T. R. Dawson, *Chess Pie*, August, 1936.

19. COVER THE WORLD

Diagram 19

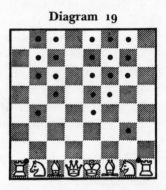

This lovely tidbit dates back to the middle of the nineteenth century. We have not, however, been able to trace precise authorship.

You will note that in the diagramed position, consisting of the original array of the pieces on the first rank, the marked squares, including the two on which stand the Rooks, are *not* guarded. 41 squares, including 6 on which all pieces but the Rooks stand on the first rank, *are* guarded. Now comes a tri-fold task.

   a. Rearrange the 8 pieces so that a *maximum* number of squares, including those on which the pieces are situated, is guarded.
   b. Same as above, except that you are allowed to place the two Bishops on squares of the *same* color.

c. Arrange the 8 pieces so that a *minimum* number of squares is guarded. (The count must necessarily include absence or presence of guard of the squares on which the pieces themselves are situated.)

You will find this an extraordinarily pleasant Chessboard recreation. We suggest your employing counters, or other likely indicators, for guarded squares.

20. CORNUCOPIA

There are amazing possibilities for changes of fortune in a game of Chess. Basically crucial in many positions is the extent of mobility of the pieces available to one side or the other. Two theoretical examples have been composed by one of your authors (PLR) to illustrate the *extreme* possibilities of increasing the mobility of the enemy, an admittedly insane maneuver in a practical game of Chess. But an awareness of the existence of a theoretical possibility, howsoever ruinous, need not influence your game of Chess.

a. Black is in a stalemate position. White is on the move. What, do you guess, is the maximum number of moves which White, in releasing the stalemate, can create for Black? Would you say less than 15? More than 20? Closer to 30?

b. Black is *not* in a stalemate position, and again White is on the move. By how many moves, would you guess, can White increase Black's mobility? More than 20? About 40? Close to 50?

We believe that you will find the answers rather surprising.

21. MAXIMA & MINIMA

In Chapter 2 we cited Kraitchik's computation for the possible number of different games of Chess, a fantastic figure running into well over 100 digits. Yet, this incredible total is based on conservative considerations. Kraitchik allows a *maximum* of 30 moves for each side in any stage of the game. Following are splendid examples of maximum and minimum mobility positions, and a diagramed answer to each one is included in the solutions appended to this chapter. In the meantime, we can have a bit of guess fun.

a. What is the maximum number of moves available to White *and* Black, in a legal position containing no promoted pieces? Under 100? Over 150? Over 200?

b. Same, but promoted pieces allowed. Over 100? Over 200? Over 300?

c. What is the maximum number of moves available to White *and* Black in a legal position consisting of *all* 32 pieces? Over 75? Over 125? Over 150?

d. Ditto, for a total of 16 pieces only (no Pawns). Would you say that the mobility is or is not greater than in the preceding?

e. Ditto, for the 16 White men alone. Over 100 or under 100?

f. Ditto, for the 16 White men *plus* a desired number of Black pieces. Would you say that preceding can be increased by more or less than 25?

g. Ditto, for the 8 White pieces alone (no Pawns). What do you believe is the difference between the mobility of this and *e*?

h. What is the *minimum* number of moves available to White *and* Black in a legal position containing all 32 pieces? Would you say less than 5? More than 5? Exactly 9?

i. Is it possible to allow mobility to one piece and one piece only in a legal position consisting of all 32 pieces?

j. What is the maximum total number of pieces in a legal position with no move available to either side? 20? 26? 30?

k. What is minimum number of moves available to Black *and* White in a position consisting of the 16 pieces alone (no Pawns)? 10 exactly? 12? 18?

22. KING IN THE CORNER

Diagram 22

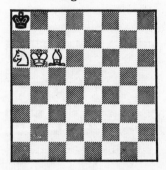

In the above diagram we have a simple mating position: King, Bishop, and Knight cooperating nicely in delivering the lethal blow to the enemy King in the corner. Interestingly enough, this gave rise to a bit of mischief by the late T. R. Dawson. His challenge is, superficially at any rate, quite elementary: In how many different ways can King, Bishop, and Knight deliver mate to the enemy King stationed in each of the four corners of the board? (It is, of course, implied that in testing all possibilities, you are allowed to place the Bishop on a Black Square *or* White square. In the above position, for example, place Bishop on R7 and Knight on B7 and you have another legal mate.)

In any case, this bit of something appears to be much ado about nothing. All that is necessary, apparently, is to determine the number of different mates in one corner, multiply by 4 and we have the answer. Or have we?

Whether or not you proceed to solve this, the twist in the solution should prove to be titilating. (By specifying, incidentally, that each mate must be *legal,* it is merely stipulated that it could have arisen only in accordance with the rules of the game of Chess.)

23. FINALE: DUDENEY MASTERPIECE

Diagram 23

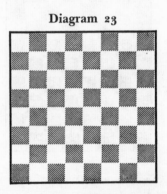

What, a blank Chessboard? That is right. What is more, it is the only prop you need for what is the greatest puzzle ever conceived by man. You need no knowledge of Chess, checkers, or any other game or stunt on the Chessboard to appreciate the wholesomeness and beauty of this poser. But you do have to muster that little bit of common sense and elementary reasoning which is often *the* key to ostensible mysteries. In short, finding the answer is most gratifying; failing to find it exacts a gasp at the fiendish simplicity of this gem. Observe.

Two men sit at a perfectly constructed Chessboard each square of which is, to the nth fraction of an inch, exactly like any other. Each man has an unlimited number of Pawns at his disposal, each of which is also perfectly constructed, so that the diameter of the base of any one Pawn does not vary, by so much as the *n*th fraction of an inch, from any other. Each of the two men, in turn, places a Pawn—always in upright position—*anywhere* on the surface of the Chessboard, in the center of a chosen square, or at the edge, or at the line of intersection between one square and the one contiguous to it, or, actually, at the very edge of the board with but part of the base of the Pawn resting on the board.

Now then, it is stipulated that he who succeeds in placing the last Pawn on the board, with no space whatever left for his opponent to place an additional Pawn, is declared the winner. Who wins? The man who is first to place a Pawn on the board, or his opponent?

In the interest of guarding against captious stratagems, we add that the base of the Pawn is *not* larger than the surface of the entire Chessboard. This would be a bit too inanely simple. It may be reasonably assumed that the base of the Pawn is much smaller than the area of each square.

In bringing *Chessboard Recreations* to a close, we do hope that we have succeeded in conveying to you the enthusiasm that has gripped us anew in going over old favorites and in creating several original ones. The solutions follow.

SOLUTIONS

[NOTE: Each of the diagrams below is designated by "S" (for solution), followed by the appropriate number.]

1. EIGHT QUEENS

Following are the 12 *basic* solutions in notation. The last one listed is the symmetrical pattern that also appears in Diagram S-1:

$a4$, $b1$, $c5$, $d8$, $e2$, $f7$, $g3$, $h6$
$a4$, $b1$, $c5$, $d8$, $e6$, $f3$, $g7$, $h2$
$a4$, $b2$, $c5$, $d8$, $e6$, $f1$, $g3$, $h7$
$a4$, $b2$, $c7$, $d3$, $e6$, $f8$, $g1$, $h5$
$a4$, $b2$, $c7$, $d3$, $e6$, $f8$, $g5$, $h1$
$a4$, $b2$, $c7$, $d5$, $e1$, $f8$, $g6$, $h3$
$a4$, $b2$, $c8$, $d5$, $e7$, $f1$, $g3$, $h6$
$a4$, $b2$, $c8$, $d6$, $e1$, $f3$, $g5$, $h7$
$a4$, $b6$, $c1$, $d5$, $e2$, $f8$, $g3$, $h7$
$a4$, $b7$, $c5$, $d2$, $e6$, $f1$, $g3$, $h8$
$a4$, $b8$, $c1$, $d5$, $e7$, $f2$, $g6$, $h3$
$a4$, $b6$, $c8$, $d2$, $e7$, $f1$, $g3$, $h5$

Diagram S-1

You have, of course, discovered that the $a4$ square (or wherever it may be situated correspondingly by rotation and reflection) *must* be covered. Sam Loyd was among the first to notice that feature, and he promptly incorporated it into a puzzle. Note also that the inclusion of the $a4$ square in every one of the basics listed above is *not* mandatory, for any position arising by rotation or reflection from any one of the above may be used as a basic.

2. KNIGHT'S TOUR
Diagram S-2a

34	49	22	11	36	39	24	1
21	10	35	50	23	12	37	40
48	33	62	57	38	25	2	15
9	20	51	54	63	60	41	26
32	47	58	61	56	53	14	3
19	8	55	52	59	64	27	42
46	31	6	17	44	29	4	15
7	18	45	30	5	16	43	28

OPEN PATH

The *modus operandi* for the open path is not too difficult. Place the Knight on the edge of the board and move, always in the *same* direction and always to a square from which there are *fewest* exits to unoccupied squares. Obviously enough, the initial journey will be concentrated in the ranks and files nearest the edges of the board. When the outer ring of the board is filled, it will be found that completion of the tour in the 16 squares in the center is, by pursuing the same method, reasonably automatic.

CLOSED OR RE-ENTRANT PATH
Diagram S-2b

22	25	50	39	52	35	60	57
21	40	23	36	49	58	53	34
24	21	26	51	38	61	56	59
41	28	37	48	3	54	33	62
20	47	42	13	32	63	4	55
29	16	19	46	43	2	7	10
18	45	14	31	12	9	64	5
15	30	17	44	1	6	11	8

The closed path, as already noted, is considered the more elegant solution. The method—and there are numerous ways of accomplishing the task—is somewhat more involved than that employed in the open path, but it can be mastered by a determined examination of Diagram S-2*b.*

Those interested in the Knight's Tour beyond the fundamentals covered in this chapter may consult the references listed in the bibliography appended to this book.

3 . QUEEN'S TOUR

Diagram S-3*a*   **Diagram S-3*b***

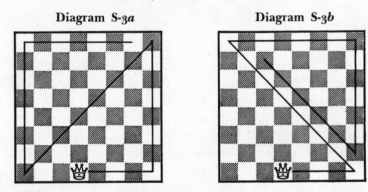

Most solvers, despite pointed warning, interpret *greatest distance* in the stipulation as *greatest number of squares,* and are pridefully satisfied with the tour in Diagram S-3*a,* as the solution. Strange as it may seem, the journey in S-3*b,* where the Queen covers 29 squares, as against 31 in S-3*a, is* the solution, for basic is the fact that a diagonal move is longer than a vertical or horizontal one (each, of course, covering the same number of squares).

Assume that the side of each square on the Chessboard is exactly 1 inch. (The arbitrary assignment of a dimension does *not* affect the problem. We have chosen a convenient unity to facilitate the explanation.) It follows that the distance of the diagonal of each square is 1.4142 inches. The Queen—as any other piece—moves from the center of the starting square to the center of the destination square. More specifically, if the Queen moves to an *adjoining* square, it covers exactly 1 inch, horizontally or vertically, and it traverses 1.4142 inches, if the move is a diagonal one. (The 1.4142 dimension is based, of course, on the elementary Pythagorean theorem governing determination of length of the hypotenuse of a right-angled triangle.)

In S-3a we have 24 squares covered orthogonally, i.e., horizontally and vertically, and 7 covered diagonally, accounting for a total of 31; in S-3b, 17 are reached orthogonally and 12 diagonally, accounting for a total of 29 squares. But the distance covered in the latter is the longer one—fiendishly enough, by .071 of an inch, but longer nevertheless. The computation:

S-3a	Orthogonal	24 × 1	24	
	Diagonal	7 × 1.4142	9.8994	
		Total	33.8994	inches

S-3b	Orthogonal	17 × 1	17	
	Diagonal	12 × 1.4142	16.9704	
		Total	33.9704	inches
		—	33.8994	"
		Difference	.071	" Q.E.D.

4. TYRANNY OF WORDS

Diagram S-4

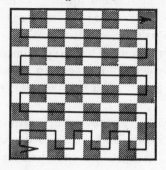

Did you give up? The stipulation clearly specifies that the Rook *enters every square* in the course of his travels. This necessarily includes the square on which he stands originally.

As a sop to the frustrated, be it known that the exception is he who is *not* stumped by this verbal devil. Sad to relate, your authors may be counted among its prey.

5. ANOTHER QUEEN'S TOUR

Diagram S-5

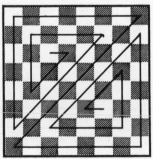

6. Hodgepodge

a. 772
b. 444

7. All Roads Lead to . . .

Diagram S-7a

Diagram S-7b

Diagram S-7c

If the task does not clearly specify that the mating positions must be *distinguishable*, we can have an absurdity such as illustrated in Diagram S-7a (total of 3 pieces), with an identical key move (1 K-N6 in the set position) and an identical mating position from each of the 4 sides of the board. (Obviously enough, turns of the board merely change the designations of the squares, not the identity of play.) It follows that if the solutions do not depend on Pawns, who move forward only and whose role necessarily changes when the board is turned, the task cannot be accomplished. (See, for example, E. M. Hassberg's magnificent Pawnless 2-mover, at beginning of Chapter 9, in which the identically intended solution operates from any side of the board.)

In Diagram S-7*b* the task is *apparently* accomplished with a total of 4 pieces. But we have 2 pairs of identical keys leading to identical mates. In the set position *and* when the board is given a quarter turn to the right, so that the White King is again on B6, the *common* solution is 1 K-N6 followed by 2 P-N8(R or Q) mate. When the board is turned twice more, the White King is on B3, in each case, and again we have the common solution 1 P-N8(Q) and 2 Q-N2 mate. Therefore, S-7*b* does not answer the required stipulations.

The actual task *is* fulfilled in S-7*c*, where the four mating positions are distinct:

Set position	1 P-B8(R) K-B4	2 R-B5 mate
Quarter turn to right (WK on K1)	1 P-B8(R) K-K3	2 R-K8 mate
Quarter turn again (WK on QR4)	1 P-N8(R) K-B5	2 R-N4 mate
Quarter turn again (WK on Q8)	1 P-N8(Q) K-Q6	2 Q-Q5 mate

A total of 7 pieces appears to be the minimum required for demonstrating the task. If, however, it is more stringently specified that the key moves (whether or not made by different pieces) must be absolutely distinguishable—for you will note that 1 P-B8(R) solves both the set position and the one that follows—a greater force is required. Perhaps the more exacting stipulation will invite your fancy. . . .

8. DETECTIVE WORK

Since a Knight moves from a square of one color to that of another, it is obvious that if he is stationed on a square of the same color as his home square, he has necessarily made an *even* number of moves; if not, he has made an *odd* number of moves. (This accounts for the well-known principle in Chess that the *Knight cannot gain or lose a move.* In other words, a Knight can reach a specified destination square in an even *or* odd number of moves, with no option available to him. Such option *is* available to other pieces. The King, for example, can travel from KR1 square to KN2 in an odd or even number of moves, as he wishes.) In each of the three positions, our task is to determine whether each piece which could conceivably have moved has made an odd or even number of moves, and the totals spell out the conclusions.

a. In Diagram 8*a*, it can be conclusively determined that it is Black to move.

It is obvious that Black has made an even number of moves. The Knights and Rooks (only) could possibly have moved. If each Knight is on his home square, then each has necessarily made an even number of moves. If they have interchanged, then each has made an odd number of moves (adding up to even). No more than one free square (N1) could possibly have been available to each of the Rooks. Each is now in his home square, and each could have shuffled between N1 and R1, only in an even number of moves.

White, on the other hand, has made an odd number of moves. The two Knights, two Pawns (which have moved) and R on KR1 account for an even number of moves; R on N1 must necessarily have made an odd number of moves. We have even plus odd adding to odd. Black must be a move behind and it is now Black's turn to move.

b. In Diagram 8*b,* which *appears* to be an open-and-shut case (even for White and even for Black), there is a catch. It cannot be determined whether White or Black is on the move.

Although White has definitely made an even number of moves, Black *could* have made an even *or* odd number of moves. Note that the White Knight could have conceivably captured the Black Bishop long before the set position arose, and he could have moved out of the square (White's KB8) on which the Bishop was captured. In such case, after Black's King's Knight has moved, Black's King's Rook could have had *two* squares available to him on the first rank, thus being able to return to the R1 square in an odd *or* even number of moves. Therefore, Black could have made an odd or even number of moves, and we do not know whose move it is in the set position. A likely sequence of moves for each possibility follows:

1	N-KB3	N-KB3
2	N-N5	N-N1
3	N-K6	N-KB3
4	NxB	N-N1
	White to move	

1	N-KB3	N-KB3
2	N-N5	R-N1
3	N-K6	R-R1
4	NxB	R-N1
5	N-K6	R-B1
6	N-N5	R-R1
7	N-K6	N-N1
8	N-B8	
	Black to move	

c. In Diagram 8*c,* we can again be hastily led to the conclusion that White and Black have each made an even number of moves, but that is not so. Hence, it is not possible to determine who is on the move.

Clearly, Black has made an even number of moves. But the missing White Rook could have been captured on one of *two* squares, White's QR1 or QN1. If the Rook was captured on

QR1, White has made an even number of moves, and it is now White's turn; if on QN1, White has made an odd number of moves, and it is now Black's turn. As in the preceding position, a likely sequence of moves for each possibility follows:

1	N-QB3	N-QB3	1	N-QB3	N-KB3
2	N-N1	N-R4	2	R-N1	N-Q4
3	N-QB3	N-N6	3	N-R4	N-B6
4	N-N1	NxR	4	N-B5	NxR
5	N-QB3	N-N6	5	N-R4	N-B6
6	N-N1	N-R4	6	N-B5	N-Q4
7	N-QB3	N-QB3	7	N-R4	N-KB3
8	N-N1	N-N1	8	N-QB3	N-N1
	White to move		9	N-N1	
				Black to move	

You are now a certified Chess sleuth, and we extend our congratulations. If you are brave, there are many astonishing retrograde positions available, the creations of great analytical minds. One of the earliest (and best!) examples is entitled "Spectrum Analysis." The composer? Sam Loyd, of course.

9a. YOU ARE DRAUGHTED

Solution to *Byers' Gem* (also frequently referred to as *Byers' Brilliancy*) follows: 22–17, 21–25, 17–21* (A), 10–14 (B), 18–9* (C), 25–30, 21–25* (D), 30–21, 9–6, becoming a King on the next move, capturing Black's man on 11 and winning easily.

A. If 17–13, hoping Black will play 25–30, allowing a quick win by 18–14, 10–17, 13–22, Black, instead, plays 10–14, followed by 18–9, 25–30, winning the White man on 19 and drawing easily. [Incidentally, the asterisk (*) in the notation of moves in checkers denotes the *only move* to accomplish the desired end (win or draw) and *no other*.]

B. A lovely trap offering an *apparent* choice, but . . .

C. If 21–30, 14–23 clearly leads to a draw; therefore, 18–9 is forced, and now Black gets his man back—or does he??

D. An exquisite sacrifice, the effect of which is quite remindful of the Roman theme in Chess problems.

Such an abundance of riches in a position of such limited forces is truly amazing. *Byers' Gem* has been selected on its absolute merits, but also in connection with a delightful experience, directly related to the Byers' *opus,* dating back a number of years.

One of your authors (PLR) was casually observing the progress of an uneventful game of checkers in which the stronger participant was Clement Crawford of New York City, a crack player in master class. Suddenly, the table was surrounded by eager kibitzers. The absolutely precise Byers position was reached, with Crawford, playing White, on the move. Crawford sensed a telepathy of a sort; the setting was completely novel to him, but the observers *and* his opponent were familiar with it. He looked up bemusedly, returned to a study of the setting, consuming no extraordinary length of time in the process, and moved. And then Crawford moved again and again, finding each time the precise maneuver called for in the solution of the setting. His opponent, it is pleasant to relate, shared the thrill of the audience. Then Crawford, with characteristic diffidence, remarked: "Without you guys becoming excited, I don't know whether I would have seen it." (The *telepathy* aspect is not as fantastic as it may seem. It is the contention of Chessmaster Horowitz and other experts that kibitzers, without saying so much as one word, *can* betray something in the Chess position that may escape the player. This, most frequently, is attributable to uncontrolled excitement of the observers. Barring an audience from proximity to the Chessboard in a critical match is, therefore, quite understandable.)

9*b*. KING DEFLATED

Diagram S-9*b*

Black

White

The *King Deflated* task is depicted above.

If the White piece on 21 is a King, White *must* lose:

a. If 21–17, 27–31 wins at once.

b. If 30–25, 22–29, 21–17, 29–25, 17–14, 25–22, 14–9 (or 14–10) (if White instead plays 14–18, then 8–11 or 6–10 wins), 22–18 wins.

c. If any other sacrifice, White must remain one piece behind and lose.

d. But if White piece on 21 is a man, White simply moves 21–17, capturing Black man on 6 and winning.

Feature of this paradox is that the backward jump of the King in checkers, compulsory when a capture is available, proves fatal.

10. STILL ANOTHER QUEEN'S TOUR

Diagram S-10*a*

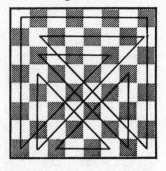

This lovely discovery by Loyd can begin and end in exactly 14 moves on any square of the Chessboard except those noted in Diagram S-10*b*.

Diagram S-10*b*

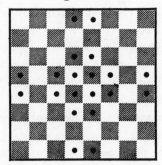

Black and White make identical moves until mate (of Black) do them part. . . .

Solutions

11. FLATTERY

a.
1 P-K4
2 Q-R5
3 K-K2
4 K-B3
5 B-K2
6 Q-B5 Mate

Diagram S-11a

Final Position

b.
1 P-QR4
2 P-QN4
3 PxRP
4 P-R6
5 P-QB4
6 P-Q4
7 K-Q2
8 K-B3
9 K-N3
10 KxP
11 PxBP
12 P-K4
13 P-KB4
14 PxKP
15 P-K6
16 P-K7
17 PxQ(N)
18 K-N4 Mate

Diagram S-11b

Final Position

12. PAWN ARRAY

Diagram S-12

13. DECONTROL

Diagram S-13

Three Queens have been transferred from K1, KB1, and KN1 to QB2, KN2, and KN3. The 11 dotted squares, no longer guarded, have been *decontrolled*.

14. KING'S MAGIC TOUR

Diagram S-14

61	62	63	64	1	2	3	4
60	11	58	57	8	7	54	5
12	59	10	9	56	55	6	53
13	14	15	16	49	50	51	52
20	19	18	17	48	47	46	45
21	38	23	24	41	42	27	44
37	22	39	40	25	26	43	28
36	35	34	33	32	31	30	29

This may well rank as the most difficult Chessboard stunt of its type.

15. QUO VADIS, KING?

Place the Black King on Black's indicated square in each of the following, as noted:

a. KR8

b. K6

c. QR1

d. KN2 (as explained below)

The King must stand on N2 (or the corresponding N7) of the *same* color as the square on which the Bishop is situated. It is then impossible for King, Queen, and Bishop to deliver mate. In Loyd's setting, the Black King cannot stand on QN7 because the White King is situated in a contiguous square. Hence, KN2 (only) is the desired square.

16. LONESOME TWOSOME

Play as follows: 7–15, 8–16, 8–7, 2–10, 1–9, 1–2, 5–13, 3–4, 6–3, 11–1, 14–8, 6–12, 5–6, 5–11, 31–23, 32–24, 32–31, 26–18, 25–17, 25–26, 22–32, 14–22, 29–21, 14–29, 27–28, 30–27, 25–14, 30–20, 25–30, 25–5.

25 and 19 (which has never been moved) are left; both, of course, are from the same side of the board. The *Lonesome Twosome* remain on (White's) QB2 and QB5. A precise sequence cannot be forced, and it is believed that it is not possible to maneuver the pieces so that one piece (only) is left.

17. LOYDOWN ON STALEMATES

a.			Diagram S-17a
1	P-K3	P-QR4	
2	Q-R5	R-R3	
3	QxQRP	P-R4	
4	QxBP	QR-R3	
5	P-KR4	P-KB3	
6	QxP ch	K-B2	
7	QxNP	Q-Q6	
8	QxN	Q-R2	
9	QxB	K-N3	
10	Q-K6	Stalemate	

Final Position

Except that White's KRP need not be moved precisely on the 5th turn, it is remarkable that the sequence of moves is forced and completely accurate.

b.	1	P-Q4	P-K4
	2	Q-Q2	P-K5
	3	P-QR4	P-QR4
	4	Q-B4	P-KB4
	5	P-R3	Q-R5
	6	Q-R2	B-N5 ch
	7	N-Q2	P-Q3
	8	R-R3	B-K3
	9	R-KN3	B-N6
	10	P-QB4	P-B4
	11	P-B3	P-B5
	12	P-Q5	P-K6
		Stalemate	

Diagram S-17*b*

Final Position

This incredible accomplishment of Loyd's is quite remindful of the exclamation by a man who saw the skeleton of a 35-foot fish exhibited in a museum: "The man who caught this fish is a liar."

18. PERMUTATIONAL PICNIC

a.	359,800	f.	483
b.	28,008	g.	400
c.	1,568	h.	156
d.	392	i.	44
e.	296		

19. COVER THE WORLD

Diagram S-19a

Diagram S-19b

Diagram S-19c

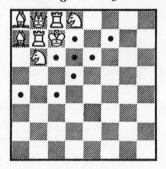

a. 63 squares are guarded, all except the indicated square (White's K2). That has been found to be the maximum. The given solution is *not* unique. There are over 80 different patterns, in none of which, however, it has been found possible to leave a corner square unguarded.

b. All 64 squares are guarded, with the two Bishops on squares of the *same* color. Except for possibility of interchange of King and Queen, the pattern is unique and completely symmetrical.

c. Sixteen squares are guarded: the 8 marked and the 8 on which the pieces stand. That has been determined to be the minimum.

20. CORNUCOPIA

Diagram S-20a

Diagram S-20b

a. Play B-N4 and you have presented Black a gift of 32 moves!! Each of the Black pieces (except the King) is given maximum mobility: Rook, 14 moves; Bishop, 13; QP, 4 (each of 4 possible promotions being counted as a move, of course); RP, 1.

b. Play B-B5 and you have increased Black's mobility by 47 moves!!! All Black pieces (except the King) gain the indicated number of moves, as follows: Queen, 22; Rook (R6), 4; Rook (Q8), 5; Bishop (K4), 13; Bishop (N8), 2; Pawn, 1. Black's mobility is increased from 13 to 60 moves!

It dawns on us, by the way, that if the "aid and comfort to the enemy," implicit in the above tasks, strikes you as treason, you may contemplate the positions *after* the designated move has been made in each. You may then *retract* the move, and you will have converted *cornucopia* into *famine*, thus giving the enemy his traditional due. . . .

21. MAXIMA & MINIMA

Diagram S-21a by S. H. Hall and W. H. Reilly
Fairy Chess Review, 1937

a. 220 moves.

Diagram S-21c by S. A. Shinkman
Golden Argosy, 1929

c. 158 moves.

Diagram S-21b by W. H. Reilly
Fairy Chess Review, 1937

b. 312 moves.

Diagram S-21d by L. Lowenton
Hamburg Correspondent, 1924

d. 173 moves.

Diagram S-21e by K. Fabel
Ultimate Themes, 1938

e. 119 moves.

Diagram S-21g by
M. Bezzel
Schachzeitung, 1848

(see next page)

Diagram S-21f by
H. F. L. Meyer
Groydon Guardian, 1880

f. 143 moves.

Diagram S-21g
(supplement)

(see next page)

g. 100 moves, 5 short of *theoretical* maximum. Bezzel's position has been proved to be unique [but for possibility of placement of Rook (N5) on QR5] and showing the absolute maximum. We have appended Diagram S-21g (supplement) as a curio. All Black pieces, including, necessarily, two promoted men, can be added to the Bezzel position, with White's 100-move mobility fully maintained.

Diagram S-21*h* by
T. R. Dawson
Chess Amateur, 1923

Diagram S-21*i* by
E. Fielder
British Chess Magazine,
1938

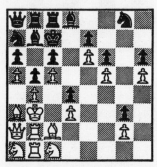

h. 2 moves: B-Q1 and N-K2.

i. Yes. The White Queen (only) is able to move in diagramed position consisting of all 32 pieces.

**Diagram S-21*j* by
G. R. Reichelm
Brentano, 1882**

**Diagram S-21*k* by
T. R. Dawson
Problemist, 1935**

j. Total of 30 pieces is maximum in a double stalemate position.

k. 10 moves.

All the wonderful task compositions listed above appear in T. R. Dawson's authoritative *Ultimate Themes* (1938). They speak eloquently for the fantastic range of mobility in Chess positions. Except for 21*g* (and *possibly* some of the others), there is no *proof* that the ultimate has been attained. On the other hand, the records that have remained unchallenged over a period of many years (such as, for example, Meyer's 21*f*, dating back to 1880) appear to be reasonably safe.

2 2 . KING IN THE CORNER

The reason why a routine count will not do is the fact that when the Black King is stationed on (Black's) QR8 or KR8, there are *two more* mates in each case than is possible to deliver when the Black King is stationed in either of the other corners. See accompanying diagram.

Diagram S-22

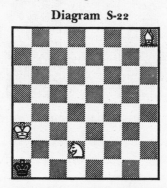

You will note that the illustrated mate is perfectly legal, the Bishop having reached KR8 by *promotion*. Turn the position around and that becomes impossible. Hence, we have the mate in diagramed position, and a companion mate with White King on QB1 (instead of QR3) and White Knight on QN4 (instead of Q2); obviously, two corresponding mates are possible when the Black King is in the other lower corner (Black's KR8). We thus have a total of *four* mates accomplished by promoting Pawn to Bishop. Since 62 mating positions are otherwise possible for each corner, there is a total of 252.

For good measure, we are giving you the count for *all* possible K-B-N vs. K mates: 460; 64 mates are possible when the King is stationed on N1 (or any of the other 7 corresponding squares (R2, R7, etc.); 144 mating positions account for the King's standing on the remaining 16 squares on the edges of the board.

23. FINALE: DUDENEY MASTERPIECE

Diagram S-23

The man who plays first must win!

The solution of this brilliancy relates entirely to an elementary consideration of the symmetrical features in a *regular* geometric plane, such as a perfectly constructed Chessboard. It is, of course, basic that for every point or subdivision of the plane there is necessarily a counter-point or counter-subdivision, each symmetrically complementing the other. Thus, with relation to the very center of the Chessboard, White's KR1 square is counter-symmetrized by White's QR8 square, KN3 by QN6, K1 by Q8, etc. Have we, then, succeeded in showing that the *second* man can *always* find a counter-point of symmetry for every Pawn placed on the board by the first man, and that he, the second man, must inevitably be able to make the last play and win? Good grief, what has happened to the answer given at the very outset of the solution? We did say that the first man *must* win. Be assured that that is correct!

There is one point on the Chessboard (and one only) for which there is no counter-point of symmetry. That is the *center* of the board. All the first player need do is occupy the center (the intersection of squares K4-K5-Q5-Q4) and his opponent cannot match it. The first man then proceeds to counter-symmetrize every one of his opponent's moves. See diagram. Move 1, in the very center of the board, cannot be countered; second player's move 2 is countered by II—always in the precisely corresponding area; 3 is followed by III; IV comes after 4, and so on, until the first player is last to fill the board.

Dudeney's masterpiece, which has appeared in a variety of garb, has been adapted to the Chessboard as the greatest common-sense challenge in existence. In the simplicity of its eloquence, it is a living monument to Emerson's "eloquence in simplicity."

15

Paul Morphy

TRAGEDY AND TRIUMPH

A publisher's blurb on *Morphy's Games of Chess* reads, in part: "—— by the greatest chess player of all time. . . ."

No exaggeration!

True, the history of Chess has seen Grandmasters who—*in their own time,* obviously—played better Chess than Morphy; knew vastly more about the complex intricacies of the various stages of the game: opening, middle, ending; enriched Chess annals with brilliancies that fairly eclipse Morphy's accomplishments. But none of these giants of the Chessboard—Steinitz, Lasker, Capablanca, Alekhine, Euwe, Botvinnik, Tarrasch, Nimzovich, Tchigorin, Fine, Marshall, Reshevsky, Rubinstein, Reti—has escaped defeat in critical matches and tournaments.

Morphy is the only Chessmaster to remain undefeated in key encounters with *all* contemporaries with whom he locked horns.

It is, of course, freely conceded that Morphy's Chess genius surpassed that of all who preceded him in the entire history of Chess. It is also conceded that Morphy's genius developed, incredibly, from his own brain, almost completely unaided by existing studies and analyses. Granted also is the fact that the past century has brought forth more tenacious and scholarly work on Chess than ever before, and that the Grandmasters who have graced the Chess scene since Morphy's time, while their superb skill is fully recognized, have indeed had the benefit of existing literature on Chess, the *sine qua non* to the serious Chess student.

And yet, there are even responsible writers on Chess who, blind apparently to the most basic considerations, tend to compare Morphy's games with those by Grandmasters played a century later and to conclude that Morphy was the *lesser* player. This, to be sure, amounts to a denigration of Galileo or Newton for not having the basic resourcefulness to use an IBM calculator.

The term "greatest" can indeed play havoc. Just what do we mean by so endowing an individual, in any field of endeavor? Once we establish basic criteria, however, we are in a position to pass reasonable judgment. In a word, the person who accomplishes the optimum, with the resources available to him, is the greatest—and so he must remain, no matter how insignificant the resources and the accomplishments become in the face of future developments. Marconi's crude experiments in wireless are now child's play to an RCA junior engineer; Marconi is still the genius! A remote button is pressed, setting off hours of music on an LP disc; Edison is still the greatest of all! If we deny the pioneer his genius, we, in effect, announce smugly that we are able to reach the top rung of the ladder in one stride.

Morphy attained an optimum—escaping defeat in Chess!—defeating, among others, the great Adolph Anderssen, considered the leading player in the world up to the time of his encounter with Morphy.

As a rule, a detailed account of the personal life of a Chess-master can prove to be a colossal bore. Of what interest, pray, are the activities of an individual unrelated to his genius? The classical biographies and autobiographies that have held our attention are essentially concerned with persons the *totality* of whose existence offers a magnetic configuration. Let us in support of this point but consider the autobiographies of Cellini and Lincoln Steffens, Boswell's *Johnson,* Beveridge's *Marshall,* Tarlé's *Bonaparte.* Little is of interest about most Chessmasters beyond their special gift and, to the student of Chess, their individual style and lessons derived from their power of analysis. There are, however, two outstanding exceptions, one of whom is Morphy; the other, Alekhine (see Chapter 16). Morphy, not unlike Alekhine but along entirely different lines of personality development, was not only a Chess phenomenon but a complex human phenomenon as well.

Paul Charles Morphy, one of four siblings, was born on June 22, 1837, in New Orleans, Louisiana, the son of Judge Alonzo Morphy of the High Court of Louisiana. The father was of Spanish-Irish stock; the mother, of French Creole extraction. The boy was reared in an economically comfortable home and after early schooling at the Jefferson Academy in New Orleans he entered, at the age of thirteen, St. Joseph's College, a Jesuit institution, in Spring Hill (near Mobile), Alabama. At St. Joseph's he decided to follow the legal profession, and remained there for a year after graduation, until 1855, pursuing studies in law and mathematics. He completed the study of law at the University of Louisiana. In April 1857, when he was not quite twenty years of age, he was admitted to the bar.

Paul Morphy learned the game of Chess at the age of ten. Both his father and uncle were enthusiastic players. In no time, Morphy beat all comers, including Johann Loewenthal, a leading European Master who visited the United States when the boy was twelve years of age, and thereafter remained a staunch admirer of his.

The boy Morphy quickly absorbed the limited literature on Chess then available, and it was his habit as quickly to part with the material—to be unhampered, as it were, by the meager text aids. While attending school he gave limited attention to Chess, as much apparently through his own restraint as on the insistence of his parents that he shun distractions from his studies. He was too young to practice law when admitted to the bar, and as the beneficiary of a sizable patrimony (his father having died while he was attending the University of Louisiana), he devoted his time to travel and Chess. It is at this point that Morphy's Chess career actually begins.

Young Morphy was a meticulously groomed person of exquisite mannerisms, at and away from the Chess table. Never was he known to show even so much as a trace of impatience at an opponent's slowness in making moves, nor did any other manifestations of his demeanor reflect anything but gentleness, gentlemanliness, calm, and taciturnity. (Time limitation on moves was not in effect in Morphy's time.) As a rule, he remained seated until the game was over, lest his rising and returning to the chair cause distraction to his opponent. For the same reason, he was also wont to avoid gazing at an adversary until such time as the latter's defeat became inevitable. Eyewitness accounts of this characteristic gesture of Morphy's present a picture of a quiet, calm, absorbed young man, so completely devoted to proprieties, so effortlessly determined to abstain from doing anything offensive, and allowing himself, finally, the luxury of looking up straight at an opponent who was facing inevitable defeat, but doing so with steadfast gentleness and not a trace of arrogance.

Morphy's resounding triumphs immediately fired the world of Chess. His first accomplishment was to win the U.S. Championship in New York City (the First American Chess Congress) in 1857, outdistancing Louis Paulsen along with 14 lesser competitors. Morphy played much offhand Chess during the tournament, finding one and all easy prey. So tremendous was his success that after the tournament was over he offered Pawn and move to all members of the New York City Chess Club. (A blanket offer of such odds to leading players in this country is *now* inconceivable!) The great, genial Louis Paulsen, who was responsible for Morphy's sole defeat in the tournament, regarded Morphy strong enough to give him (Paulsen) such odds!

At the end of 1857 Morphy returned home with a record of:

	WINS	LOSSES
Level games (i.e., no odds)	95	5
Odds games (Knight mostly)	128	32
Over-all	223	37

Chess enthusiasts throughout the country, and particularly in New Orleans, acclaimed the young Chess gladiator, who was beset with importunities to visit Europe to compete with its leading Chessmasters: Anderssen, Staunton, Harrwitz, Bird, et al. It was then that the taunts of Howard Staunton began and proved eventually to be the basis of the irreparable wounds in Morphy's life.

England can look back to a long honorable history of gentlemen with unflinching devotion to the principle of fair play. Definitely not to be counted among them is Howard Staunton who somehow—with no convincing record to substantiate it —gained for himself, in his own day, a name of eminence in the Chess world. His principal *forte,* presumably, was his expertness as a Shakespearean scholar. Were it worth while to invest time in conducting research on this person, it would not surprise us to discover that Iago was his favorite character. It is certain, as we shall see, that one of the most tragic chapters of shame in the history of Chess is Staunton's gross, shabby, arrogant treatment of a highly sensitive young Chess genius, generally regarded by his contemporaries (in the words of Augustus Mongredien, President of the London Chess Club) as a "most splendid and chivalrous player." Philip W. Sergeant, biographer of and greatest authority on Morphy, suggests with characteristic restraint that Staunton's "scandalous abuse . . . tells heavily against him when we attempt to explain his attitude now."

Staunton initiated his campaign of perfidy in his December 24, 1857 column in the *London Illustrated News,* commenting on a general challenge issued by the American Chess Association to any European Chessmaster to play Morphy for stakes from $2,000 to $5,000. Staunton wrote: "No doubt an European champion could be found who would play the match in London or Paris, but the best players in Europe are not chess professionals, but have other and more serious occupations, the interest of which forbid such an expenditure of time as is required for a voyage to the United States and back again."

The New Orleans Chess Club then issued a personal challenge to Staunton to come to New Orleans and to play for stakes of $5,000 of which $1,000 was to go to Staunton if he lost. Staunton declined, in a civil manner, but he noted in his column:

"If Mr. Morphy—for whose skill we entertain the liveliest admiration—be desirous to win his spurs among the chess chivalry of Europe, he must take advantage of his purposed visit next year; he will then meet in this country, in France, in Germany, and in Russia, many champions whose names must be as household words to him, ready to test and do honour to his prowess."

Morphy's family voiced firm objections to his traveling alone in Europe at the age of twenty, but finally succumbed—more so at the insistence of Morphy's admirers than in response to pressure exerted by himself. The New Orleans Chess Club offered sufficient money to cover all expenses but Morphy refused to accept a single copper, stating that he did not wish to travel as a professional Chessplayer. This insistence on maintaining a name untainted by monetary gain was in evidence throughout Morphy's Chess career. Money prizes awarded him in Europe were given to his defeated opponents (or to other Chess personalities). In one case, Morphy added his own money to a cash prize, and presented the total to Loewenthal to enable the latter to buy articles of furniture for a new home.

It is well to keep in mind that although Morphy's unmistakable desire was to prove that he was the best Chessplayer in the world, he was never tempted to employ any but the most scrupulous and ethical measures in attaining this goal. It was rather an obsession with him to guard against accusations of "professionalism" or desire for material gain. Upon his return from his tragi-triumphant trip in Europe, he was presented a Chess set consisting of a Chessboard with mother of pearl and ebony squares, and gold and silver pieces then—in 1859— valued at $1,700. He also received a gold watch, designed with Chess pieces for numerals. The chairman of the reception committee, Colonel Charles Mead, delivered a warm welcoming address, but made an unfortunate allusion to Chess as a profession. Morphy protested violently, and the embarrassed Colonel withdrew from further participation.

Morphy arrived in Europe on June 21, 1858, on the eve of his twenty-first birthday, and remained there until April 30, 1859. In effect, less than one year of concentrated Chess activity in Europe, added to the aforementioned several months of serious Chess in New York City during the latter part of 1857, is the sum total of Morphy's Chess career.

He won his matches in Europe against the specified opponents as follows:

	WINS	LOSSES	DRAWS
Johann Loewenthal	9	3	2
*Rev. John Owen	5	0	2
Daniel Harrwitz	5	2	2
Adolf Anderssen	7	2	2
Augustus Mongredien	7	0	0

* Pawn and Move odds.

Morphy, in addition, played some 67 level games, against Barnes, Bird, Boden, Loewenthal, Anderssen, Harrwitz, winning 48, losing 12, and drawing 7. He also played 91 Pawn and move odds games, winning 65, losing 18, and drawing 8.

The match with Harrwitz, who was known as the "King of the Régence," was never finished. (The Régence Cafe was the leading gathering place for Chess enthusiasts in Paris.) The stipulation called for the first 7 victories. Herr Harrwitz, apparently, was vying with Staunton for the title of prime scamp. As prospects for Harrwitz were beginning to appear worse and worse, he kept on claiming one physical indisposition after another, while shamelessly appearing at the Régence and playing with opponents other than Morphy, until he finally refused, arbitrarily, to finish the match. Morphy, characteristically enough, was deeply hurt.

In the meantime, the Shakespearean scholar, the man of culture, Howard Staunton, carried on dilatory tactics with a firm resolve, born of a craven soul, never to face *alone* an inevitable drubbing at the hands of the young American genius. (The wily savant, along with the Rev. John Owen, had twice faced Morphy and Barnes in consultation games, shortly after Morphy's arrival in Europe, and had twice been beaten. This was a "test run" for the Englishman.) Staunton stated at first, upon being approached for a match with Morphy, that he needed about a month to "brush up on my openings and endings." About a month later, in August 1858, he asked for an extension of a "few weeks." This was in answer to Morphy's letter, the quintessence of gentlemanliness, reading as follows:

Dear Sir: As we are now approaching the Birmingham meeting, at the termination of which you have fixed our match to commence, I think it would be advisable to settle the preliminaries during this week. Would you be good enough to state some early period when your seconds can meet mine, so that a contest which I have so much at heart, and which from your eminent position excites so much interest in the chess world, may be looked upon as a *fait accompli?*

I am, dear sir,
Yours very respectfully,
Paul Morphy.

(Staunton, incidentally, did participate in the Birmingham tournament to which allusion is made in the Morphy letter. Staunton was knocked out by Loewenthal 2–0. It is doubtful whether this offered any pleasure to Morphy, who was not at all attracted by gratifications born out of vindictiveness.)

Staunton then saw fit to refer to the contemplated match between him and Morphy as "bunkum," stating that Morphy had come to Britain unprovided with representatives to arrange for terms and stakes. Moreover, Staunton began to ridicule Morphy mercilessly when Harrwitz won the first two games of the (unfinished) match. When the tide turned, Staunton was, of course, forced to change his tune. When he failed to fix a date for November, as promised, Morphy, deeply wounded, wrote a letter to Staunton (on October 6), reading in part, as follows:

Permit me to repeat what I have invariably declared in every chess community I have had the honour of entering, that I am not a professional player—that I never wished to make any skill I possess the means of pecuniary advancement—and that my earnest desire is never to play for any stake but honour. My friends in New Orleans, however, subscribed to a certain sum, without any countenance from me, and that sum has been ready for you a considerable time past. Since my arrival in

Paris I have been assured by numerous gentlemen that the value of those stakes can be immediately increased to any amount; but, for myself personally, reputation is the only incentive I recognize.

Finally, Staunton replied on October 9, withdrawing any promise to play a match.

Surprisingly, the one person of standing who has come to Staunton's defense is H. J. R. Murray, famed Chess historian. In an article in *Chess Magazine,* December, 1908, Murray justifies Staunton's stand on the ground of his "arduous literary occupations." It is to be hoped that Murray's conclusions in his *History of Chess* are based on more firm ground than is his preposterous *apologia* in behalf of the unspeakable Howard Staunton.

Says Philip W. Sergeant in reviewing the melancholy Staunton (and Harrwitz) episodes: "Morphy sickened by Chess tactics off the board. Is there any wonder?" Yes, this delicate human being was mortally wounded, for in his own mind he had failed to accomplish his purpose, and he was not at all impressed with the overwhelming evidence that Staunton had run away, cravenly, in virtual disgrace.

Morphy returned to the United States to face warm plaudits and genuine admiration for him as a Chessmaster and a noble personality. To no avail. Basically, Morphy was a beaten man. The prelude to his inevitable resolve (of some ten years later) not to have anything to do with Chess was an announcement that he would face nobody in the United States at less than Knight odds and nobody in the world at less than Pawn and move odds. He settled in New Orleans. Chess activity, almost entirely limited to Knight odds games with a personal friend, Charles A. Maurian, stopped altogether in 1869.

Attempts to practice law met with failure. Legal circles looked at Morphy as a great Chessplayer. Interest in a young lady met with failure, for, it was reported to him, she scorned the idea of marrying a "mere chess-player." In his own mind, he had failed to reach one shore, the ultimate in Chess in defeat of Staunton and (conclusive) defeat of Harrwitz, and had been peremptorily pushed away from the other, a professional career, marriage, adjustment to normal life. The mental disturbance was inevitable.

Paul Morphy developed illusions of persecution. He initiated groundless litigations against a relative whom he accused of plotting to deprive him of the inheritance left him by his father. His program of activity, consisting mostly of leisurely walks and visits at the opera, made for more and more seclusion, and a conviction that he himself was a nonentity. In reply to a request for data about himself to sponsors of a project for biographies of famous Louisianans, he wrote angrily that his father had left him "$146,162.54 c." and since he himself followed no profession, there was no biography. He added that he had a "lawyer's diploma." This was in 1882. In 1883 the great Steinitz was in New Orleans. He expressed a wish to see Morphy, who declined at first, but finally acceded, on condition that nothing be said about Chess. They spent an agonized ten minutes together: Morphy's very last known *symbolic* exposure to Chess.

Nine years earlier, on June 22, 1874, Morphy's thirty-seventh birthday, death had come to Howard Staunton.

On July 10, 1884, Paul Charles Morphy died, in his mother's house, Royal Street, New Orleans. He had taken a long walk; the shock of cold water on his overheated body caused a congestion of the brain.

Paul Morphy's astounding skills as a Chessplayer have been confirmed by no lesser Chessmasters than Steinitz and Emanuel Lasker. Steinitz says:

Morphy's career marks a grand epoch in the history of our pastime, and a careful study of his games will always be essential for the purpose of acquiring a complete knowledge of the direct attack against the King, which forms a most important element in mastering our science. . . . If Morphy were alive and were to be the leading spirit of our day, as he was the superior of his own, he would of necessity cultivate and extend the system which has been developed since his time. He would probably have been the very first to make improvements or to perceive and acknowledge them in the practice of others, instead of reverting to the methods of the old school, as maintained by some critics.

There are clear indications in his match-style of that steady pressure and studious regard for the balance of position which requires an almost instinctive judgment in its application, and which has been cultivated and trained to a much higher degree since the Morphy period.

. . . It appears that Morphy, as far as his match-play is concerned, has received credit and praise for faults which he did not possess (such as creating positions, against his strongest opponents, in which sacrifices formed a distinct feature), while his really admirable qualities have been almost ignored.

Lasker minimizes the "intuition" frequently attributed to Morphy, while stressing Morphy's genius in applying logical principles scientifically.

Adolf Anderssen, his greatest Chess contemporary, had an ungrudging admiration for Morphy. The hulky mathematics professor at the University of Breslau had a love for the game that was the *only* prize that lured him. His match with Morphy involved no stakes. Reminded by an admirer that he, Anderssen, had not played as well against Morphy as he had against other leading opponents, the genial Teuton remarked: "Morphy won't let me."

It is, then, relatively simple to assess Morphy as a Chessplayer. He was the greatest of all time, within the limitations specified at the beginning of this chapter. Far more complicated is an analysis of the disintegration of Morphy as a human being, following his return from Europe in 1859, when he was not quite twenty-two years of age, and by choice at the end of his Chess career. Let us turn to an incisive analysis of Morphy by the late eminent psychiatrist, Dr. Ernest Jones.

PSYCHIATRIC ASSESSMENT

First, Dr. Jones (in a paper delivered in 1930 before the British Psychoanalytical Society) indicates that Morphy, upon his return from Europe, was of the type "wrecked by success" (*Die am Erfolge sheitern,* in the words of Freud). Dr. Jones stresses particularly the wild acclaim of Morphy at the Régence Cafe in the fall of 1858, when 8 simultaneous blindfold games resulted in 6 wins for Morphy and 2 draws. The adulation that awaited him upon his return to New York imposed still another "severe strain on his mental integrity." Basically, Dr. Jones points out, Morphy had failed to find a fulfillment of three conditions in his relation to Chess: (1) that the act be received in a friendly manner, as it had *not* been by his two leading adversaries, Staunton and Harrwitz; (2) that the act be ascribed to worthy motives, as it had *not* been by Staunton; and (3) that it be regarded as a serious, grown-up endeavor, as it had *not* been by Staunton.

The young Chess genius found himself ground between the impact of idolization and his inner conviction of failure. The unattained—and never to be reached—goals operated as an obsession. His estimate of his own *limited* accomplishments as a Chessplayer was being constantly challenged by persons with whom he was hungrily seeking a par status. To members of the legal profession and to the aforementioned young woman he remained a "great" Chessplayer. This spelled out persecution and led, tragically, to a paranoiac pattern of behavior.

It is idle to contemplate what Morphy as a Chessplayer could have accomplished one hundred years later. We wonder, however, what the Chess genius in Morphy would have brought forth but for the wounds inflicted by Staunton, which led to terrible developments in the life of a remarkable person.

16

Alexander Alekhine

TRIUMPH AND TRAGEDY

If you can imagine, painfully, an obscenity scratched on a Michelangelo masterpiece; or a boogie-woogie coda to a Brahms symphony; or a profanity at the end of the Declaration of Independence—only then can you grasp the ugliness of a footnote to the brilliant accomplishments of a giant in the world of Chess, Alexander Alekhine.

A panegyric on Alekhine, the Chess genius, is automatic. Linking this amazing Chess brain with Alekhine, the man, is an aching experience.

Dr. Alexander Alekhine (1892–1946), a Russian expatriate, made France his home after the 1917 Revolution. He devoted full time to Chess, and held the title of Chess Champion of the World from 1927 to 1930 and from 1937 to the time of his death in 1946. The "Dr." was a degree in jurisprudence. His recorded Chess career began in 1908, when he was sixteen years of age. An attempt to describe his astonishing achievements as a Chessmaster entails the task of finding an adequate number of superlatives. We shall let his record speak for itself. It appears below, along with significant breakdowns which your authors have compiled. In the explanatory notes you will find incredible facts which the bare statistical tables, howsoever impressive, fail to reveal.

Alexander Alekhine's Record

Tournaments and Matches

TOURNAMENTS[a]		GAMES				POINTS		
Number	When	Won	Lost	Drew	Ratio[b]	Won	Lost	%[c]
61 (total)	1908–39	455	73	237	6 to 1	563.5	191.5	73.6
[50 (part)	1914–39	372	37	207	10 to 1	475.5	140.5	77.0]
Matches[d]								
9 (total)	1908–37	62	31	81	2 to 1	102.5	71.5	58.8

Grand Total (Tournaments and Matches)

70	1908–39	517	104	318	5 to 1	676	263	72.0

[a] Alekhine had a minus score in one tournament only: Vilna, 1912 (won 7, lost 8); he was then twenty years of age. He had an even won-lost score in one tournament only: Avro, 1938 (won 3, lost 3); he was then forty-six years of age. In the 59 remaining tournaments, he had a plus score throughout.
In all, Alekhine won:

First Prize	29 times	in 47.5%	(of tournaments)
First & 2d shared	5 "		
First, 2d, 3d shared	1 "	in 23.0%	"
Second	6 "		
Second & 3d shared	2 "		
Second Prize or *better*	43 "	in 70.5%	"

In fifty tournaments (1920–39), Alekhine was *undefeated* 28 times, in 56% of the events! He won 214 games and drew 91. There were no draws at all in three tournaments, all victories (Birmingham, 1926; Hamburg, 1930; Montivideo, 1936). In two tournaments, Alekhine won and drew an identical number of games: Kecskemet, 1927 (won 8, drew 8); Buenos Aires, 1939 (won 5, drew 5). In four tournaments, he drew more games than he won: Hastings, 1933–34 (won 4, drew 5); Warsaw, 1935 (won 7, drew 10); Bad Nauheim, 1936 (won 4, drew 5); Podebrad, 1936 (won 8, drew 9). (It is interesting to note that most of the listed tournaments in which Alekhine drew more games than he won took place during the 1935–37 interval when Dr. Euwe held the world championship.) In the twenty-two remaining tournaments, Alekhine won more games than he drew. He won eighteen firsts and figured in three ties for first and second, spelling out first place rank three out of four times!—and he placed second four times. (The precise rankings in the remaining three tournaments are not available.)

   b The ratio is of *games won* to *games lost*.

   c The percentage is for total *points* earned, including drawn games.

   d Alekhine had an even won-lost score in one match only: Teichmann, 1921 (won 2, lost 2, drew 2). He had a minus score in one match only (won 8, lost 9, drew 13), when Euwe defeated him for the world championship in 1935. Two years later Alekhine regained the title, at the age of forty-five, winning 10 (!), losing 4, and drawing 11. The 30-game match was terminated at the indicated point when it became a mathematical impossibility for Euwe to win.

Never during his lifetime did Alekhine, as a human being, invite affection. His devotion to his ego, possibly rivaled only by his love for Chess, constantly spurred circulation of dark tales about this or that manifestation of contemptible behavior. Much was in form of rumor, bald and unsubstantiated; the undisputed incidents, however, were alarmingly symbolic of twisted tendencies.

The late Oscar Tenner, an American Chessmaster, presented proof at one time to one of your authors (IAH) of an incredible bit of skulduggery. Alekhine and Tenner had played a game of Chess resulting in a draw. Analysis revealed that had Tenner followed a different line of play, Alekhine would have won by an unusually sparkling combination. Much to Tenner's astonishment, he discovered, months later, that Alekhine had submitted the score of the game to a Chess periodical, incorporating the *unplayed* combination as an actuality.

Dr. Reuben Fine in a psychological study of Alekhine (see Bibliography at end of book) cites a number of ugly incidents, including the conversion of a Chess hall into a latrine, within the sight of all present, while in a state of intoxication.

In the interest of separating the man from his genius, however, it appears to be fitting to be charitable enough to overlook the strange behavior. Surely, of no consequence are Dostoyevski's mania for gambling, O. Henry's addiction to drink, or the profligacies of Poe, Heine, Goldsmith, and Wilde. We are interested (if at all) *only* in the creative genius of each. Does not this forebearance, however, reach logical limits? What if the artist turns into an actual *Volksfeind?*

When it was discovered that a number of vicious, Nazi-inspired articles appeared in a European periodical in 1941, under the byline of Alexander Alekhine, the forgive-and-forget formula was applied at once and it has been hotly fostered ever since. (A certified translation of these articles is included in this chapter, along with a disclaimer of authorship by Dr. Alekhine, issued shortly before he died, some five years after the articles were written. We have conducted a reasonably careful search, and we find that no English translation of the articles has ever been published. The disclaimer, however, was given prompt recognition. It appeared sixteen years ago!)

CERTIFIED TRANSLATIONS

Following is a certified translation of three articles that appeared respectively in the April, May, and June issues of the *Deutsche Schachzeitung.* Each is presented as a reprint, and there is no indication whether the articles had appeared originally in a language other than German. Given as the original source for the first is *Deutsche Zeitung in den Niederlanden* (German News in the Netherlands); for the second and third, *Pariser Zeitung* (Paris Journal). Strangely, a Paris date line heads the second *and* first articles; there is no date line for the third.

We are indebted to Mr. Arthur Rath, eminent linguist and member of the staff of the Queens (New York) Public Library, for the certified translation. Mr. Rath tells us, quite in confirmation of your authors' estimate on the basis of a comparatively limited acquaintanceship with German, that the articles are "vitriolic," "hysterically incoherent," and, generally, remindful of the solecisms and panicky screechings in A. Hitler's *Mein Kampf*. Mr. Rath adds that it is almost impossible to catch the calumny and vindictiveness in translated form, incorporated as they are in a web of *nonsequiturs*. In short, whatever is found to be coherent in the translation tends to elevate the tone of the original. Rath has found no evidence pointing to the possibility that the articles were written by more than one person.

JEWISH AND ARYAN CHESS

A psychological study which—based on the experiences at the chess board—demonstrates the Jewish lack of courage and creative power.

By World Chess Champion Dr. Alekhine in *German News in the Netherlands*.

Paris, March 22, 1941

Can we hope that with Lasker's death, the death of the second and probably the last Jewish World Chess Champion—Aryan Chess, misguided so long by Jewish defensive thinking, will find its way to the top? It is incumbent upon me not to be too optimistic, for Lasker has created a school and has left disciples behind who can, conceivably, do much harm to chess. Lasker's great offense as a leading Chess Master—I can't speak about him as man and philosopher—was manifold. After Lasker, on the strength of his tactical skills, defeated Steinitz, 30 years Lasker's senior, he never contemplated to offer the chess world a creative thought of his own, but merely published a series of talks he had given in Liverpool entitled, "Common Sense in Chess." It was "edifying," by the way, to observe these two adept tacticians, Lasker and Steinitz, strain to tell the world that they were great strategists and innovators.

LASKER PLAGIARIZED THE GREAT MORPHY

In these talks, Lasker plagiarized the great Morphy appropriating the latter's ideas on the "struggle for the center" and on the "concept of attack." To Lasker the idea of attack as a gratifying experience was altogether foreign, and in this respect he was a natural successor to Steinitz, the most grotesque player in chess history.

What is actually Jewish Chess, the Jewish concept of chess? This question is not difficult to answer. 1. Material gain at all costs. 2. Opportunism in the extreme, which seeks to eliminate every shadow of possible danger and, as a result, gives rise to an idea (if one can call it an idea), "defense *per se*." In the last analysis, this "idea" of Jewish chess, amounting as it does to suicide in every form of struggle, has dug its own grave. For by mere defense one can occasionally (and not too often) avoid loss—but how does one win with it? One possible answer would be: through an error of the opponent. But what if this error does not materialize? Then the "defender *à tout prix*" has nothing left but tearful complaints about his opponent's stubborn refusal to blunder.

The question of how the concept of defense gained a following is not so easy to answer. Between the spirited La Bourdonnais–MacDonald matches and the appearance of Anderssen and Morphy, a period of stagnation, of which the high point was the Staunton–St. Amant match, settled on European chess. The latter event ended with Staunton's victory, assuring the Englishman a legitimate claim to a place of eminence in the chess history of the 19th century. While I am writing this, I have before my eyes a book by Staunton dealing with the first world tournament held in London in 1851 and won by the brilliant German Master Adolf Anderssen. This tournament which in fact marked a breakthrough for our * aggressive,

---

* I.e. Aryan; wherever *our* appears hereinafter in similar context it denotes "Aryan." [Translator's note.]

fighting chess against the English-Jewish concept (Anderssen annihilated the Polish Jew Kieseritzky * in the first round of the tournament) has been considered by the theoretician Staunton as a pure coincidence. Staunton claimed that he had not been feeling well, being overburdened with numerous chores in connection with the event, etc.; in essence, the familiar alibis. But Staunton's defeat by Anderssen was far more than a decision between two chess masters; it was actually the defeat of the Anglo-Jewish concept of defense and a triumph for the German-European idea of fighting chess.

EUROPE'S CHESS DRAMA

Anderssen's victory set the stage for Europe's chess drama: one genius was opposed by an even greater genius from New Orleans. This, however, would not have been such a calamity, because Morphy's game was chess in the truest sense of the word. It turned out to be a catastrophe, for Morphy lost his mind shortly after his defeat of Anderssen and thus was lost to chess; and because Anderssen never recovered from this defeat and, with no will to win, defaulted the title to the Jew Steinitz in 1866. In order to clarify the question who Steinitz really was and why he was successful in playing a prominent role in chess, one must first look into the status of professional chess. In any art (and chess, notwithstanding its competitive character, is a creative art), there exist two categories of professionals—those who devote themselves compulsively and exclusively to the one chosen field, and show no interest whatever in any other line of endeavor. These "victims of the art" can by no means be reproached for trying to earn their living only in their chosen profession, for they bring esthetic and spiritual pleasures to their fellow men. The same criteria can, however, not be applied to the second category, namely the "Eastern Jewish" type of professional chess player. Steinitz, a Jew born in Prague, was probably the first representative of this type, and he promptly set a pattern.

Do the Jews as a race show talent for chess? After 30 years' experience in chess I would like to suggest this answer: Yes, indeed. The Jews are extremely talented in the exploitation of chess for the gain it offers. But up to this day there has never

---

* Was Kieseritzky really a Jew? Schlechter, whom the world champion also considers to be Jewish, certainly was not. [*Deutsche Schachzeitung* Editor's note.]

been a real Jewish chess artist. By contrast, I would like to name the following representatives of creative Aryan chess, men of top calibre: Philidor, La Bourdonnais, Anderssen, Morphy, Tchigorin, Pillsbury, Marshall, Capablanca, Bogoljubow, Euwe, Eliskases, Keres. During the same period, on the other hand, the "Jewish crop" turned out to be rather mediocre. Besides those of Steinitz and Lasker, the "achievements" of the following group (in chronological order) warrant closer examination.

1. In the period of decadence marked by Lasker's predominance (1900–1921) two of his nearest Jewish rivals—Janowski and Rubinstein—do, in some respects, merit attention.

"BRILLIANT MATCHES" (*Glanzpartien*)
AGAINST WEAKER OPPONENTS

The Polish Jew Janowski, as a resident of Paris, was probably the most typical representative of this group. He succeeded in becoming the protégé of another Jew in the French capital, the Dutch "artist" Leo Nardus, on whom Janowski kept a firm grip for 25 years. Someone in America demonstrated before Nardus a number of Morphy games featured by sacrifices. Nardus was so carried away by Morphy's style that he demanded from his protégé Janowski nothing but so-called beautiful games. Janowski created "brilliant games," *nolens volens,* but as it soon turned out, only against weaker opponents. When he played real masters, his style was as unimaginative, dry, and materialistic as the style of 99 out of 100 of his jew brethren. Janowski never was a serious threat to Lasker, who easily beat him in their matches. In this connection, we would like to point out one of the typical attributes of Lasker's "talent," avoiding the most dangerous opponents while in their prime. He took them on only when they were handicapped by old age, illness, or lack of preparation. Numerous examples of this tactic can be cited; for example, his dodging matches against Pillsbury, Maroczy, and Tarrasch, while accepting Tarrasch's challenge (1908) when the latter was no longer a serious contender for the title; and finally the brief matches against Schlechter (Vienna, 1910), ending in a tie, which were set up as a decoy for the staging of an impressive and, needless to say, profitable championship tournament.

Reared in hate against the "Goyim" (Gentiles), the second of Lasker's Jewish rivals was the Master from Lodz, Akiba

Rubinstein. Strictly (Hebrew) orthodox, steeped in Talmudic hatred against the "Goyim," he saw himself, at the very beginning of his chess career, charged with fulfilling a sort of "mission." He therefore started, as a young man, to study the theory of chess with the same ardor with which he had, in his childhood, tried to absorb the Talmud. This happened in a period of decadence of chess when the so-called Viennese School reigned supreme on the world chess stage. Founded by the Jew Max Weiss, and fostered later on by the Jews Kaufmann and Fahndrich, this School saw the secret of success not in winning, but in not-losing.

Small wonder that Rubinstein who had his openings consistently better prepared during this period than his opponents, scored impressive victories shortly after his first appearance in international tournaments. His most important success perhaps was a share in the first prize with Lasker in St. Petersburg (1909), a memorable tournament which I attended at the age of 16. After this climax, Rubinstein's star began to fade, first imperceptibly, then rapidly. No doubt he studied tirelessly, scoring occasional victories, yet one could feel that this effort was too much for a brain showing a talent for chess but otherwise altogether mediocre. When I returned to Berlin after 4 years in the Soviet Union, I found Rubinstein disintegrating both as a grandmaster and as a human being. His intellectual capacity was impaired; partly by megalomania, partly by a persecution complex. The following episode may serve as an illustration: At the end of the same year (1921), Bogoljubov arranged a small tournament in Triberg in which Rubinstein also took part. As usual, there were *post-mortem* analyses by the participants. On one such occasion I (the tournament director) asked Rubinstein: "Why did you make this opening move? This one is certainly not as strong as the move which enabled me to beat Bogoljubov a few months ago, and which we analyzed together as most effective."

HE WANTED TO ESCAPE THE OPPONENT'S INFLUENCE

"True," answered Rubinstein, "still it is somebody else's move." In short, *his* chess and only *his* chess was meaningful to him during this period. In the last 10 years of his activity (1920–30), he undoubtedly played some good games, scored partial successes, but the symptoms of his persecution complex became more obvious. In the last 2 or 3 years of his public appearances, he used to run away from the chess board every time he had completed his move, sit in a corner of the tournament room, and return only after his opponent had countered his move. This he did "in order not to have to submit to the evil influence of the opponent's ego." Right now Rubinstein is somewhere in Belgium, forever eliminated from chess.

The Jew from Riga, Aaron Nimzowitsch, belongs to the Capablanca rather than the Lasker period. His instinctive, anti-Aryan chess concept was, in a strange way—subconsciously and in spite of himself—influenced by the Slavic-Russian concept of attack (Tchigorin!). I say "subconsciously," because he violently hated us Russians and Slavs. Never will I forget a brief conversation we had at the end of the New York tournament in 1927. Nimzowitsch had been overtaken by me in the standings and had been beaten in several single games by the Yugoslav Grandmaster, Prof. Vidmar. Incensed at his poor showing, he did not dare to assail us directly, but instead he turned the conversation to Soviet Russia. Turning toward me he remarked: "Who says Slav, says slave" to which I replied: "But who says Jew has surely nothing more to add."

In certain circles Nimzowitsch gained the reputation of a "deep thinker," mainly through the publication of two books entitled "My System" and "The Praxis of My System." Yet I am fully convinced that this whole "Nimzowitsch system" is based on wrong premises (apart from the fact that it lacks originality). For Nimzowitsch not only makes the mistake of attempting to proceed from an analytical beginning to a synthetical end, but he compounds his error by basing his analysis exclusively on his own practical experience, while offering the results of this analysis to the chess world as the supreme synthetical truth. Certainly there are bits of truth, traces of correct thinking in Nimzowitsch's teachings. These ideas, however, did not originate in his own brain, but were borrowed from both old and contemporary masters and were consciously or unconsciously plagiarized. His correct ideas: 1. The fight for the center, a Morphy concept illustrated both by the best achievements of Tchigorin and the Pillsbury–Charousek matches. 2. and 3. The obvious fact that it is advantageous to occupy the seventh rank; and finally, that it is more profitable to exploit two weaknesses of the opponent than just one. And with such petty tricks ("niaiseries") Nimzowitsch succeeded in building up his reputation as a chess authority in England and in New York (not America, because this city of Jewry is, thank heaven, not at all representative of America).

Those were the few elements of truth which Nimzowitsch expounded in his books, alongside much that was wrong, reflecting his basic attitude toward chess. His half-original ideas were contaminated; they were a negation of the creative spirit. For example: 1. His idea of "manoeuvring" is nothing but a variation of the old Steinitz–Lasker theme of waiting until the opponent makes a mistake. 2. The idea of overprotection (the premature defense of supposedly weak positions) again is a clearly Jewish idea contrary to the concept of fight. In other words: Fear of the fight, doubts about its spiritual qualities— a sad picture indeed of intellectual self-degradation! Leaving this pitiful chess legacy behind him, Nimzowitsch died lamented by few disciples and even fewer friends (except for some Jews).

Richard Reti of Pressburg has earned the "gratitude" of the chess world by carrying Nimzowitsch's overprotection theory *ad absurdum*. He applies the theory of guarding one's weak positions in the openings, regardless of how the opponent builds up *his* position. He thought he could attain his objective by the double flank of the bishops. This manoeuvre was called the "double-hole game" by the German Grandmaster Richard Teichmann, a man of unusually fine chess instinct.

A united front of purely destructive Jewish chess tacticians (Steinitz–Lasker–Rubinstein–Nimzowitsch–Reti) began to shape up, destined to hamper, for half a century, the logical evolution of our fighting chess.

(to be continued)

JEWISH AND ARYAN CHESS

By World Chess Champion Dr. Alekhine in the *Pariser Zeitung*.

Herewith the reprinting of the World Champion's comments is continued. These would have been more convincing several years ago. But at the outbreak of war in 1939, Dr. Alekhine joined forces with Tartakover (who is today a lieutenant in the army of a traitor, General De Gaulle), in the masters' tournament in Buenos Aires, and together they aided the Palestine team, all Jews, in an effort to demoralize the German team and to prevent its victory. Compare Becker's letter, *Deutsche Schachzeitung*, 1940, page 1.

By the way, as we already suspected, Kieseritzky was not a

Jew. G. Jirikoff points out that Kieseritzky was born in Dorpat (Livonia, not Poland!) which was among the Russian cities in which no Jews were permitted to live. Besides, Kieseritzky is a highly regarded Baltic-German name and many of its bearers probably live in Greater Germany today. See also *Deutsches Wochenschach* 1912, p. 353.

(Editor's Comment; M.B.)

THE AGGRESSIVE JEWISH PLAYER BOTVINNIK AND CAPABLANCA, WHO STRONGLY BELIEVED IN THE DEFENSE CONCEPT, WERE EXCEPTIONS TO THE RULE.

PARIS, MARCH 28, 1941

Just as Nimzowitsch with his "System," so did Reti with his tract, "The New Ideas in Chess," earn the warm applause of the majority of the Anglo-Jewish pseudo-intellectuals. These people were particularly impressed by the absurd slogan which Reti invented: "We, the young players (he was already 34 at that time) are not interested in the rules, but in the exceptions." If this statement makes any sense at all, it is supposed to mean: "We (really I) know the rules which govern chess only too well; to explore them further shall from now on be the task of the general chess community. I, however, the great master, shall devote myself exclusively to the finer "filigree" work and demonstrate before a spellbound chess world brilliant exceptions accompanied by lucid explanations." This cheap bluff, this shameless self-advertisement was swallowed hook, line, and sinker by the chess world that had been poisoned by Jewish journalists. Jews and their friends triumphantly chanted: "Long live Reti, long live ultramodern, neoromantic chess!"

THE "DOUBLE HOLE IDEA" DIED BEFORE RETI

Reti died young, at the age of 40. But his "double hole idea" had already before him died a quiet, inglorious death. Today's representatives of Jewish chess theory do not follow him, but prefer to imitate older exponents (Steinitz and Rubinstein).

Thus, Solomon Flohr of Prague is a product partly of Steinitz's timorous concept of defense, partly of Rubinstein's "religious" faith in the intensive study of openings and endings. There is, however, one difference: Flohr, in contrast to Rubinstein, is sound of body and mind, and will therefore probably maintain his standing for some time to come.

Reuben Fine, a New Yorker of Eastern European Jewish descent, is undoubtedly more intelligent than Flohr. Educated in a Communist school maintained by a Jewish community, he is perhaps not under the influence of Russian chess, but certainly under the political influence of the ideas of today's Russia. For this reason, he is more aggressive than the other Jewish masters, in his personality as well as in his chess. His general chess attitude, however, is nevertheless purely traditional: Don't risk anything. He tries to accomplish this in a relatively novel manner: not by mere waiting tactics or pure defense, but through intensive study of modern opening variations, enabling him to improve his chances in the game. For example, he undertook to modernize the old English textbook by Griffith and White. In doing so, he had to study thousands of opening variations and because of his superior knowledge of modern theory, he shared top honors at the AVRO tournament of 1938, to everyone's surprise, a success unlikely to be duplicated.

POOR AMERICAN CHESS

Two more of the present Jewish masters are to be mentioned; Reshevsky and Botvinnik. The East European Jewish ex-*wunderkind* (there have been so many child prodigies of this race in all branches of the arts—why not one in chess?) Reshevsky was systematically exploited by his Jewish managers ever since he was 5 years old. Of course, in that period (1919–1922) there was enough money in circulation to satisfy all appetites in democratic countries intoxicated with war profits. No wonder that Reshevsky, now about 30 years of age, Americanized and holder of the U.S. Championship, is the possessor of a fortune, the interest of which permits him to play chess (to which he really owes everything) as a pure amateur.* To the surprise of all, however, when he returned to Europe as a grown man, he showed that he represented the worst type of

---

* Amateur, in the sense of economically secure; hence, not in need of financial return from Chess. [Translator's note.]

chess professional, resorting to the shabbiest tricks. If Reshevsky, as it is claimed, really represents American Chess of today, one can only say "Poor American Chess."

The Soviet Champion Mikhail Botvinnik probably owes the development of his style, in even greater measure than the American Jew Reuben Fine, to the influence of the young Russian school. Instinctively leaning toward "safety first" chess, he slowly developed into a master who uses his offensive weapons to great advantage. But the way in which he reached this stage is strange and typical at the same time; not through the concept of attack, and, if necessary, of sacrifice, but—paradoxically as it may seem—through the idea of gaining additional security by attacking. Only through exact knowledge, and through extremely intense study of (1) new opening possibilities, and (2) the technique of attack and sacrifice as developed by the old masters, did Botvinnik perfect his original style and develop an ostensible versatility. That he is strong today, even very strong, is not to be doubted. How else could he have won the championship of Russia 5 or 6 times in succession, despite the high level of chess in that country? This obvious superiority can only be compared with the series of convincing victories gained by the German Master Eliskases, at home and abroad, during the last few years. Yet, most of Botvinnik's games leave a dry uninspired impression. This is not really so strange because in the realm of art a copy, no matter how perfect, can never generate the same feeling as the original, and Botvinnik's chess, as far as attack is concerned, is only a very fine copy of the old masters. All the same, Botvinnik can be called an exception to all others referred to.

(to be continued)

THE ARYAN CONCEPT OF ATTACK

By World Chess Champion Dr. Alekhine in *Pariser Zeitung*.

THE CHESS PHENOMENON CAPABLANCA

The case of Ex-World Champion Capablanca is highly informative. Idolized as a type of a wonder child in his native

Havana, where he won the Cuban Championship at the age of 12; admired at the beginning of his career as a fiery aggressor with Morphy-like ideas, Capablanca would have become not only the God of the Latin chess world—a role he actually held for a long time—but the idol of the whole chess world, had he not been sent to Columbia University, in New York, and in that Jewish capital had not acquired the professional methods of the chess-Yankees. Suppressing tremendous tactical gifts, Capablanca prevailed upon himself, at the early age of 18, to look upon chess not as an end in itself but as a means of making money; and to develop the Jewish "safety-first" principle to its extreme.

But his natural gift for chess was so great that for a certain time he was able to maintain a leading position even as a master in the art of defense; and he was clever enough to make half-hearted attempts to justify the negative principle of defensive chess in various articles, by means of pseudo-strategic concepts. At times, though, fiery flashes of genius occurred even during the period when Capablanca was World Champion, but essentially these were brilliant exceptions, probably subconscious reactions to his stifled chess temperament. Today, however, he produces such brilliancies less and less frequently.

Thus it happened that the Latin Capablanca and the Jew Botvinnik found each other on the same mental and spiritual path (*Wege*) or rather, bypath (*Abwege*). Their existence is no doubt useful for our art and for the fight against the concept of defense, because they are the exceptions confirming the rule. Exceptions? Yes, truly exceptions. Unfortunately there are also false exceptions in *our* chess, phony artists, who exploit the Aryan idea of attack to satisfy their professional lust for money. The most typical representatives of this tendency are probably the Viennese Jew Rudolph Spielmann, who at present lives in Stockholm, and the Leipzig Jew Jacques Mieses whose home is now London. Spielmann, who is unquestionably gifted for tactical chess, realized at an early stage of his career that he had the best chance to drain money from the large chess public if he succeeded in making a name for himself as a "brilliant sacrificial player." And just as Fine and Botvinnik, a quarter of a century later, studied the openings and the principles of attack, Spielmann concentrated on the much simpler problem of the technique of sacrifices. One must admit that after long years of practice he succeeded in gaining a number of successes in his chosen field. In 1935 he even published a little book with the attractive title, "How to Make Correct Sacrifices." In it he analyzed every possible type of sacrifice, except the one that characterizes the real artist—the intuitive sacrifice.

Just as remote from the true concept of sacrifice are the ideas of the chessmaster and journalist Mieses who years ago flooded the German Press with releases of his "brilliant achievements." Mieses furnished convincing proof of this in an article written for *Chess,* a journal edited by the Jew Baruch Wood in Birmingham, in which he published as the best game of his career the one against Von Bardeleben for which he had been awarded a prize (Barmen 1905).

Up to now I have said much about the Jewish concept of defense and little about the Aryan concept of attack. I would like to clarify this concept by giving a literary source which typifies the complex misconception regarding the game of chess. In the 30's and 40's of the past century, after the meteoric rise of Mahé De La Bourdonnais, the game of chess suffered a definite eclipse. At that time the Englishman Howard Staunton was—justifiably, perhaps—considered the most formidable chess player in the world. His game, which unfortunately had some influence on his contemporaries, was so monotonous and unimaginative that one need not be surprised at Edgar Poe's devastating critique of chess art in his *Murders in the Rue Morgue.* Right at the beginning of his mystery, Poe writes, actually without inner conviction: "Yet to calculate is not in itself to analyze. A chessplayer, for example, does the one without effort at the other. It follows that the game of chess, in its effects upon mental character, is greatly misunderstood. I am not now writing a treatise, but simply prefacing a somewhat peculiar narrative by observations very much at random: I will, therefore, take occasion to assert that the higher powers of the reflective intellect are more decidedly and more usefully tasked by the unostentatious game of draughts than by all the elaborate frivolity of chess. In this latter, where the pieces have different and bizarre motions, with various and variable values, what is only complex is mistaken (a not unusual error) for what is profound. The attention is here called powerfully into play. If it flag for an instant, an oversight is committed, resulting in injury or defeat. The possible moves being not only manifold, but involute, the chances of such oversights are multiplied; and in nine cases out of ten it is the more concentrative rather than the more acute player who conquers."

AND NOW THE POSITIVE SIDE

"In draughts, on the contrary, where the moves are unique and have but little variation, the probabilities of inadvertence are diminished." And later on Poe continues: "Whist has long been noted for its influence upon what is termed the calculating power; and men of the highest order of intellect have been known to take an apparently unaccountable delight in it, while eschewing chess as frivolous. Beyond doubt there is nothing of a similar nature so greatly tasking the faculty of analysis. The best chessplayer in Christendom may be little more than the best player of chess; but proficiency in whist implies capacity for success in all those more important undertakings where mind struggles with mind."

THE CONCEPT OF CHECKMATE IS ALL-IMPORTANT

Enough of Poe! These quotations prove beyond doubt that the illustrious creator of "The Raven," the captivating author of "Eureka" and "Dialogue between Monos and Una," committed, in this particular instance, a monumental error of judgment or, for reasons unknown, he deliberately misled his readers. The game of chess cannot be compared with any other board game on account of one basic element which elevates chess to an art. The absence of this element in other board games, while not necessarily rendering them inferior, places them in another category. While other games aim at conquest or "territorial gains," chess is distinguished by the unique concept of checkmate. It is true that the initial phases of a chess match are characterized by moves designed to gain "territorial and material" advantage. However, as soon as checkmate, that is, the idea of doing in the opponent's King, is envisioned, neither time, nor territory, nor material is spared in pursuit of this objective. What makes chess so constructive and appealing is the fact that it answers a human yearning—if often only present in the subconscious—for an ideal; a joyful self-sacrifice for a cause. And because the deeper spirit of chess generates in us the creative power of self-sacrifice, it gratifies, by the same token, our aesthetic needs.

What other game even remotely embodies such virtues? No, not even the genius Edgar Poe could detect, let alone prove, these superb qualities in other games. Poe's comparison with whist is even less tenable because this card game stimulates a mental process entirely different from that involved in playing chess. Chess is a war game of the moment and of the future; a move once completed no longer requires the player's attention. In bridge, by contrast (to name only the most modern card game), a good player is expected not only to recall each trick played but also each card in it. And as to the alleged "analysis," it is hard to see how it can be practically applied, since too many imponderables are here involved. Consequently, the attack on chess launched by the American poet fizzles out. Still as a typical voice of the past, he deserves a hearing.

Following is Alekhine's disclaimer preceded by a piece entitled "Alekhine's Defence!" Both appeared in *Chess World* [Australia], on March 1, 1946. The prefatory remarks are by Chessmaster C. J. S. Purdy, editor of *Chess World*.

ALEKHINE'S DEFENCE!

Dr. Alekhine, chess champion of the world, sent an open letter to Mr. Hatton-Ward, organiser of the masters' tourney held in London in January. It was in reply to a letter in which Mr. Hatton-Ward had evidently spoken of the United States Chess Federation as having sent him an "ultimatum." Apparently the U.S.C.F. had stated that the U.S.A. would not be represented if Alekhine played; the U.S.C.F. now denies that it sent an "ultimatum"—meaning of course, that it does not want it called that.

We publish Alekhine's letter in full. We also quote a sentence in a letter from a correspondent to *Chess*.

"If Alekhine had committed any offence it would have been dealt with by the War Crimes Commission—it is their job to dispense justice."

Very true—and let us give no more weight to hearsay accusations than a court of justice gives, i.e. nil. For instance, Dr. Bernstein, writing in *Chess*, accused Alekhine of failing to intervene to save the life of the Jewish master Przepiorka, who died in a concentration camp in Poland. Alekhine's answer to that was given in a short letter to *Chess*. He wrote:—

"As for Dr. Bernstein's information. I can only state that my friend D. Przepiorka was murdered before the end of 1939 (I heard the narrative of this from an eye-witness) and it is known that I played in Germany and Poland only from the end of

1941. What connection could I have with this tragical event?"

The Dutch player, Dr. Oskam, in the November *Chess* descends to vulgar abuse. He calls Alekhine "this small-minded drunkard." This harks back to a rumor (afterwards proven false) spread by Dutch newspapermen whom Alekhine had annoyed during his 1935 match with Euwe; it was part of a general campaign of vilification against him by the Dutch press at that time. See our books, *How Euwe Won,* page 7, and *The Return of Alekhine,* page 31. Oskam's letter in *Chess* is merely impassioned (not to say scurrilous) rhetoric, and contains not a word of direct evidence.

As a victim of Nazi brutality, Dr. Oskam commands all our sympathy, but we must not be swayed by purely emotional verbiage. His whole letter is based on acceptance of Alekhine's complete authorship of the notorious anti-Jewish articles, which Alekhine denies.

Chess World, March 1, 1946

ALEKHINE'S OPEN LETTER

Dear Mr. Hatton-Ward,

I received your letter on my return from the Canaries on November 28th. Before I knew what you now tell me, it was evidently impossible for me to undertake anything for I had no idea of the exact motives which had induced you to cancel your invitation. Now I can and must speak not because you are organising a tournament, whatever purely chess interest it might have for me—but above all because of the motives you give.

Firstly, you tell me that in certain circles people have lodged objections based on my alleged sympathies during the war. But any disinterested person must realise what must have been my real feelings towards the people who robbed me of everything which gives life meaning; the people who destroyed my home, robbed my wife's chateau (and eventually everything I possess) and finally stole my very name!

Having devoted my life to chess, I have never been concerned in anything not concerned with my profession. But unfortunately for me, throughout my life—and especially since I gained the world title—people have sought to present me in an absolutely fantastic political light. For more than twenty years I was labeled a "White Russian." This was particularly damaging as it made impossible contact with my native country, which I have never ceased to love and admire. In 1938–39 I had hoped as a result of negotiations and correspondence with the champion of U.S.S.R., Botvinnik, to have put an end to this absurd legend, for a match between us and the U.S.S.R. had practically been fixed. [The "us" must mean France.—Ed.]. But . . . the war came—and after its termination here I am a "pro-Nazi," accused of collaboration, etc., etc. Far from thinking ill of you, I am grateful to you for having brought this accusation to a head—the uncertain situation in which I have lived for the last two years has been morally intolerable.

That Dr. Euwe protested does not surprise me—it would have been far more surprising if he had not. Among the heap of monstrosities published by the *Pariser Zeitung* appeared insults against the members of the Committee which organised the 1937 match; and the Dutch Chess Federation even lodged a protest on this matter with *Post*. At that time I was powerless to do the one thing which would have clarified the situation, to declare that the articles had not been written by me. Dr. Euwe was so convinced of my influence with the Nazis that he wrote me two letters asking me to take steps to alleviate the lot of poor Landau and my friend Dr. Oskam . . . but in Germany and the occupied countries we were under constant surveillance and threat of the concentration camp from the Gestapo. Therefore Dr. Euwe's reaction to my invitation is very natural; but like so many others, he is badly mistaken.

Your principal reason for withdrawing your invitation is the "ultimatum" (as you call it) of the U.S. Chess Federation. This is very serious, for these men have evidently taken this decision and given reasons which in their opinion justify it. I cannot know these at the moment but it seems reasonable to suppose that it is a question of collaboration with the Nazis. The charge "collaboration" is generally directed against those who fell in with the Vichy Government. But I never had anything to do with either that government or its officials. I played in Germany and the occupied countries because that was not only our means of subsistence but also the price of my wife's liberty, and going back in memory to the situation in which I found myself four years ago, I maintain that today I should act in exactly the same way. My wife would in normal circumstances have the ability and means to look after herself. But not in wartime, and in the hands of the Nazis. I repeat, if the charge of "collaboration" is based on my forced sojourn in Germany, I have nothing to add—my conscience is clear.

It is another thing entirely if I am accused of fabrications and in particular the articles which appeared in the *Pariser Zeitung*.

Against this I must formally protest. For three years, until Paris was liberated, I had to keep silent. But from the first opportunity I tried in interviews to show up the facts in their true light. Of the articles which appeared in 1941 during my stay in Portugal and which I learned about in Germany through their being reproduced in the *Deutsche Schachzeitung, nothing was actually written by me.* I had submitted material dealing with the necessary reconstruction of the F.I.D.E. (the International Chess Federation) and a critique, written well before 1938, of the theories of Steinitz and Lasker. I was surprised when I received letters from Messrs. Helms and Sturgis at the reaction which these articles—purely technical—had provoked in America, and I replied to Mr. Helms accordingly. Only when I knew what incomparably stupid lucubrations had been created in a spirit imbued with Nazi ideas did I realise what it was all about. But I was then a prisoner of the Nazis and our only hope of preservation was to keep silent. Those years ruined my health and my nerves and I am even surprised that I can still play chess.

My devotion to my art, the esteem that I have always shown for the skill of my colleagues, and the whole of my pre-war professional life should have made people realise that the articles were spurious. And I am particularly sorry not to be able to come to London and speak for myself.

Let's get to the point. *Was* Dr. Alekhine the author of the fantastic balderdash? He issued a disclaimer, some ten months after the Nazis were defeated. This denial came from a man who, under the most favorable conditions, had failed to endear himself to the world of Chess.

Respectable evidence in support of Dr. Alekhine's denial would offer all his Chess admirers much joy. In the meantime, we ask:

1. Since Dr. Alekhine lived in Nazi-occupied Europe throughout the war, and since a burning interest in Chess was always an integral part of him, is it not logical to assume that the publication of the articles had come to his attention long before he issued the disclaimer?

2. Why did not Alekhine, an excellent logician and a holder of a degree in jurisprudence, write an immediate denial? In

the absence of a possibility of smuggling a letter out of Nazi territory to a trusted source in the free world, why did not Alekhine somehow arrange to safeguard a timely disclaimer until such time as he would be able to present it to the free world as reasonable proof of his innocence? (It would appear that if he had immediately jotted down a few convincing words on, say, the blank portions of a current newspaper, that would have been impressive.)

3. Or is it possible—and we are continuing to base our questions on no assumption that the articles were necessarily his—that he believed that the Nazis would win the war, and why bother?

4. If that is so, is it not logical to conclude that the articles failed to arouse indignation in Alekhine, and that his eventual disclaimer, offered close to a year after the war was over, was a necessary self-serving step in the light of world opinion?

5. What conclusions, if any, can be drawn from the fact that Alekhine's devotion to the German cause is being questioned by the editor of *Deutsche Schachzeitung* (introduction to second article)? What was the purpose of the editor in pointing an accusing finger at the *purported* (let us say) author of a feature in his magazine? Was it—in the spirit of the vogue of that dark era in Germany—to out-Nazi his neighbors? Or does the editor's castigation operate in favor of Alekhine?

6. If the articles were not Alekhine's but, as is implicit in pro-Alekhine claims, either rewritten by others (after Alekhine had submitted different material in good faith) or written by others (on the basis of source material obtained from Alekhine and deliberately distorted), what is the origin of some of Alekhine's personal experiences related in the articles, such as the snide interchange with Nimzovich?

7. Finally, is it not strange that in the course of all the years since 1941, not one person has come foreward with *evidence* in support of Dr. Alekhine?

17

Honor Roll

MASTERS' MASTERPIECES

In practically every field of activity there are those who have failed to reach the top; yet, they may be better known than those who have. Were you asked to identify H. Clay, D. Webster, and R. B. Hayes, chances are good that you would at once recognize the first two as personalities in American history. It may not dawn on you as quickly that the third was the nineteenth President of the United States.

So in Chess. Akiba Rubinstein, Aaron Nimzovich, Siegbert Tarrasch, Richard Reti, Rudolph Spielmann, Salo Flohr, Reuben Fine, S. Tartakover, Miguel Najdorf, E. Bogolubov, and others of pre-eminent standing have never won the world championship (or even, in some cases, significant sectional crowns); yet, the name of each is fairly synonymous with Chess.

In presenting two honor rolls, one consisting of World Chess Champions and the other of Champions of the United States, we necessarily include those only who have actually earned the title. But how can a United States honor roster possibly be complete without inclusion of Fine, Isaac Kashdan (who had a *co*-taste of the laurel for several months in 1942, pending loss of playoff to Reshevsky), I. A. Horowitz, Dr. Edward Lasker, Herman Helms, Althur W. Dake, Alexander Kevitz, A. C. Simonson, and many others? But the rules govern the roll call, "limited" as it is to the *official* best talent in Chess.

WORLD CHESS CHAMPIONS

There is no absolute unanimity of judgment of authorities on the validity of listed champions *prior* to Dr. Emanuel Lasker. Some dispute strongly the inclusion of Staunton; others, that of the great Morphy (see Chapter 15). There is, however, reasonably united agreement that in *modern* Chess, so-called, beginning in the latter part of the eighteenth century, the listed predecessors of Lasker were the strongest players of their day. After Philidor, time intervals between one date and the following are continuous, except for 1946–1948.

Steinitz defeated Anderssen, laid claim to the title, and successfully defended it in formal matches with Blackburne, Zuckertort, Tchigorin (twice) and Gunsberg before he was dethroned by Lasker. Strangely, Steinitz has not been included consistently in the official list of champions.

After the death of Alekhine (1946) a tournament settled the succession (1948), which has since then been determined by match play under the sponsorship of the International Chess Federation (FIDE: *Federation Internationale des Echecs*).

The roster follows:

FRANÇOIS PHILIDOR	France	(1747)–1795
ALEXANDRE DESCHAPELLES	France	1815
LOUIS DE LA BOURDONNAIS	France	1820
PIERRE DE SAINT-AMANT	France	1840
HOWARD STAUNTON	England	1843

ADOLPH ANDERSSEN	Germany	1851
PAUL MORPHY	United States	1858
ADOLPH ANDERSSEN (again)		1859
WILHELM STEINITZ	Austria	1866
DR. EMANUEL LASKER	Germany	1894
JOSE R. CAPABLANCA	Cuba	1921
DR. ALEXANDER ALEKHINE	France	1927
DR. MAX EUWE	Holland	1935
DR. ALEXANDER ALEKHINE (again)		1937
MIKHAIL BOTVINNIK	Russia	1948
VASSILY SMYSLOV	Russia	1957
MIKHAIL BOTVINNIK (again)		1958
MIKHAIL TAL	Russia	1960
MIKHAIL BOTVINNIK (again)*		1961

* Lost title to Soviet Grandmaster Tigran Petrosian, May, 1963.

CHESS CHAMPIONS OF THE UNITED STATES

The winner of the Grand Tournament of the First American Chess Congress, Paul Morphy, became the first *official* United States Chess Champion and is considered to have held the title until the Second American Congress (1871) in which he firmly refused to participate. After Lipschuetz, the time intervals between one date and the following are continuous, but his date and that of his predecessor, Max Judd, are not certain.

Marshall won the title in match play, and retired, after some twenty-seven years, in favor of (initially) biennial championship tournaments sponsored by the United States Chess Federation. These became triennial in 1948, and have taken place annually since 1957. Reshevsky has participated in all the tournaments since 1936 except 1944, 1948, 1954, and 1961. In 1942, Reshevsky won playoff with Kashdan who had tied him for first. Fischer did not participate in 1961. His first try was in 1957, when he won the championship at the age of fourteen!

Chess Champions of the United States

The roster follows:

PAUL MORPHY	New Orleans, La.	1857
GEORGE H. MACKENZIE	New York, New York	1871
MAX JUDD	St. Louis, Missouri	1887
SIMON LIPSCHUETZ	New York, New York	1894
JACKSON W. SHOWALTER	Georgetown, Ky.	1894
ALBERT B. HODGES	New York, New York	1894
JACKSON W. SHOWALTER (again)		1894
HARRY NELSON PILLSBURY	Boston, Massachusetts	1897
JACKSON W. SHOWALTER (again)		1906
FRANK JAMES MARSHALL	Brooklyn, New York	1909
SAMUEL J. RESHEVSKY	Brooklyn, New York	1936–1938–1940–1942
ARNOLD S. DENKER	New York, New York	1944
SAMUEL J. RESHEVSKY (again)		1946
HERMAN STEINER	Los Angeles, Calif.	1948
LARRY EVANS	New York, New York	1951
ARTHUR B. BISGUIER	New York, New York	1954
ROBERT J. FISCHER	Brooklyn, New York	1957–1958–1959–1960
LARRY EVANS (again) *		1961

* In the very last round of the 1962 United States Chess Championship tournament (January 3, 1963), Fischer faced Bisguier in a dead tie; the latter had gone undefeated up to that point. A colossal blunder by Bisguier, at a stage in the game when his prospects were *at least* as good as Fischer's, gave Fischer the coveted title. Bisguier earned second place, obviously; tied for third were Evans, Reshevsky and William Addison (of Los Angeles, California). Such are the fortunes of Chesswar.

DESIGNATIONS OF MASTER
AND GRANDMASTER

In the United States, the title of Master is awarded by the U. S. Chess Federation on the basis of achievement in leading national and interzonal tournaments and other significant competitions. Substantially the same criteria govern selections in other countries, where authorized central bodies maintain rating systems. There are dozens of United States Chessplayers who have earned the title of Master.

The designation of Grandmaster is decided upon by FIDE, which maintains its headquarters in Stockholm, Sweden, on the basis of achievement in international Chess competition. As a rule, the title of Grandmaster must be applied for. At present there are seven active United States Grandmasters: Pal Benko, Arthur B. Bisguier, Larry Evans, Robert J. Fischer, William Lombardy, Samuel J. Reshevsky, Nicholas Rossolimo; two are inactive: Dr. Reuben Fine and Isaac Kashdan.

THE AGE FACTOR IN
MASTER CHESS

Recent events of a national character have called unusual attention to the prevalence of the age factor in human affairs. I refer to the recent political contest in the United States; the ages of the principal protagonists were a "young 43" and an "old 47" years. In the world of primarily physical sports most participants are retired from active competition before age 40. Ted Williams, the well-known baseball player, retired this fall at the advanced sport age of 42. Few athletes in baseball, basketball, football, soccer, boxing or track, to mention a few sports, reach their fortieth birthday on the active list.

A demographic examination of these sports would probably reveal interesting and significant differentials of average retirement ages. I would guess that these ages are about 30 years in football, 35 years in boxing and 38 years in baseball. In billiards and golf, sports in which there is a more equal balance between physical and mental exertion, the average retirement age of professionals is probably closer to 50 years. What can be said of the age factor in a purely mental sport such as master chess? [1]

The age spectrum of master chess play covers the biblical three-score and ten years. There are records of master players who were not in their teens and of players who engaged in active play until their mid-seventies. Paul Morphy (1837–1884), Jose R. Capablanca (1888–1942), Samuel Reshevsky (1911———) and Bobby Fischer (1943———), the current U.S. champion and international grandmaster, are a few of the players who exhibited remarkable chess power as children. James H. Blackbourne (1842–1924) at 72, played in the great St. Petersburg tournament of 1914; Emanuel Lasker was 68 when he retired from active competition in 1936. In this discussion, I am considering primarily the "aging" aspect, i.e., as the chess player ages, what can be said about the quality of his performance. Is master chess a young man's game?

I have used various statistical approaches to develop measurable results. First, I considered the ages of all world champions and of their successful challengers at the time of the critical match. Second, I examined the tournament performances of two players, Emanuel Lasker and Jose R. Capablanca, for the period of their chess careers. Third, I obtained rank correlation co-efficients between age and final standing of contestants in a number of international tournaments.

[1] Current chess rules for master tournaments require that each player make 40 moves in 2 hours or 50 moves in 2½ hours on his stop clock. Failure to satisfy this condition results in automatic forfeiture of the game at the time this breach, overstepping the time limit, has been committed. [*Ed.*—for world championship matches, the time is usually 30 moves in 2 hours.]

Earlier this year, Mikhail Tahl, 23, defeated Mikhail Botvin-nik, 49, for the chess championship of the world. Table 1 gives the relevant age data for the world champions and the success-ful challengers for the period, 1858–1960. The arithmetic mean ages of champions and challengers are respectively, 44.7 and 32.8 years. The *t* distribution was used to test whether these means differ significantly; the result obtained was *P* < .01, that is, this difference of means is extremely signif-icant.[2] At the highest level of chess, the age factor is quite discernible. It will be observed (Table 1) that in only two in-stances did an ex-champion regain the title.

The chess history of selected masters does not constitute a valid sample or a basis for generalization. These data are presented as suggestive rather than as conclusive evidence re-garding the relationship between chess performance and aging. Between 1889 and 1936, Emanuel Lasker[3] participated in 21 international tournaments. He scored 239½ out of 321 points for a life tournament average of .746. Jose R. Capablanca's[4] tournament career covers three decades, 1910–39. During this period, Capablanca participated in 37 major tournaments, scoring 366½ out of 481 points, a life average of .762. Tables 2 and 3 give the age distribution of their performances by per-centage points scored and by tournament standing.

The data in Table 2 show a very marked trend in the case of Capablanca, that is, as he became older, his percentage score decreased perceptibly. Although there is a percentage im-provement for Lasker between the two age groups, 20–29 and 30–39, this difference may be more illusory than real. The

[2] Briefly, the calculation is $t = \dfrac{44.7 - 32.8}{3.7} = 3.2+$ for 18 degrees of free-dom.

[3] Lasker was born in 1868 in Germany and died in New York City in 1941.

[4] Capablanca was born in 1888 in Cuba and died in New York City in 1942.

number of games played by Lasker in the age group, 30–39, is substantially less than the number played in the younger age group, 20–29; consequently, the percentage improvement may reflect the smaller sample size in the later age period. It is also likely that each player has an individual rate of aging curve, with variations around different peak periods. The last four decades of Lasker's chess career also indicate successive declines in scoring.

Although somewhat more difficult to interpret, the data on tournament standings given in Table 3 are also indicative of declines associated with increasing age. For the comparable periods of their careers, i.e., 20–59 years, Lasker appears to do better than Capablanca in both tournament standing and percentage scores; it is not until Lasker is in his 60's that he finishes below 3rd place and that his percentage score falls substantially.

Another aspect of the aging effect in tournament play may be detected in the movement of the ratio, games drawn to total games played. In effect, the advantage that White is conceived to have (by virtue of the first move) is not fully exploited by older players. It would seem that older players draw more frequently than younger players. The data showing the trends in draws for Lasker and Capablanca are presented in Table 4.

Rank correlation co-efficients between age and tournament standing were computed for a dozen international tournaments (held between 1894 and 1958). These co-efficients range between .2 and .8 and were in all instances positive. Although not statistically significant, these results do not contradict the other findings presented in the foregoing discussion. The use of rank correlation is not appropriate to detailed analysis; slight changes in age (a year or two) result in ranking differences, although such age differences do not affect performance.

The results I have obtained suggest some tentative answers

to the questions posed at the outset. The statistical data that I have selected and analyzed indicate definite relationships between aging and chess performance.[5] More extensive research may serve to confirm (or deny) the conjecture that increases beyond a certain average age (perhaps 40 years) decrease the quality of tournament chess play definitively.[6]

Table 1

World Chess Champions and Successful Challengers by Age at Time of Critical Match: 1858–1960 [7]

DATE OF MATCH	WORLD CHAMPION	AGE AT MATCH	SUCCESSFUL CHALLENGER	AGE AT MATCH
1858	A. Anderssen	40	P. Morphy	21
1866	A. Anderssen	48	W. Steinitz	30
1894	W. Steinitz	58	E. Lasker	26
1921	E. Lasker	53	J. R. Capablanca	33
1927	J. R. Capablanca	39	A. A. Alekhine	35
1935	A. A. Alekhine	43	M. Euwe	34
1937	M. Euwe	36	A. A. Alekhine	45
1957	M. Botvinnik	45	V. Smyslov	35
1958	V. Smyslov	36	M. Botvinnik	46
1960	M. Botvinnik	49	M. Tahl	23

[5] Of interest regarding some of the casual aspects of aging is the discussion in Chapter 3, "What is 'Aging,' " and Chapter 4, "The Abilities of the Old," in *Longer Life* by George Soule (Viking Press. N.Y., 1958).

[6] From "Questions and Answers," edited by Ernest Rubin, U.S. Department of Commerce and American University. Address correspondence to Dr. E. Rubin, A.S.A., 810 18th St., NW, Washington 6, D.C.

[7] Source: *The World Almanac: 1959 (N.Y. World-Telegram* and the *Sun,* 1959), p. 854. *New York Times,* May 14, 1960.

Table 2

Tournament Scores of Lasker and Capablanca, by Age [8]

	LASKER			CAPABLANCA		
AGE GROUP	GAMES PLAYED	POINTS SCORED	%	GAMES PLAYED	POINTS SCORED	%
20–29	102	79½	.779	133	111	.835
30–39	58	48	.828	106	82	.774
40–49	36	28	.778	199	145	.729
50–59	59	45	.763	43	28½	.663
60–69	66	39	.591	—	—	—
Total	321	239½	.746	481	366½	.762

[8] Sources: *Emanuel Lasker: The Life of a Chess Master*, by J. Hannak (Simon and Schuster, N.Y., 1959) and *Capablanca's Hundred Best Games of Chess*, by H. Golombek (Harcourt, Brace, N.Y., 1947).

Table 3

Tournament Standings of Lasker and Capablanca, by Age [8]

	LASKER'S STANDING [9]				CAPABLANCA'S STANDING [9]			
AGE GROUP	LASKER'S GAMES				GAMES			
	1ST	2ND	3RD	OTHER	1ST	2ND	3RD	OTHER
20–29	5	1	2	0	7	3	0	0
30–39	2	½	½	0	5	1	1	0
40–49	1½	½	0	0	7½	5	1	2½
50–59	3	1	0	0	2	½	½	1
60–69	0	0	1	3	—	—	—	—

[9] When a tie results in a chess tournament, two or more contestants share the ranking. A tie by two players for the first place, e.g., means that each player will receive one-half of the first and one-half of the second prize money.

Table 4

Proportion of Games Drawn by Lasker and Capablanca in Tournaments, by Age [8]

AGE GROUP	LASKER GAMES			CAPABLANCA GAMES		
	PLAYED	DRAWN	%	PLAYED	DRAWN	%
20–29	102	23	.225	133	28	.211
30–39	58	12	.207	106	42	.396
40–49	36	10	.278	199	86	.432
50–59	59	22	.373	43	21	.488
60–69	66	36	.545	—	—	—
Total	321	103	.311	481	177	.368

Ernest Ruben, *The American Statistician*, December, 1960 *

MASTERS' MASTERPIECES

Selection of *Masters' Masterpieces* is an extraordinary challenge, for basic is the problem of not omitting games that clearly merit inclusion. The task resolves itself into a reconciliation of rigid objective standards with personal predilections. Where unique excellence allows for no alternative but selection—Anderssen's *Immortal Game* and *Evergreen Game* (Nos. 14 and 15); Fischer's *Game of the Century* (No. 12); Marshall's *Shower of Gold* (No. 6); Steinitz's *Gem* (No. 9); and others in the zenith class—there is, happily, no problem. But where there is a question of assessing the precise points of excellence that distinguish one gigantic performance from another, the job is an unenviable one. (Reaching for a *ready*

* For a related discussion on chess in this section, see *The American Statistician* of June 1957, "The Significance of the Initiative in Chess."

compilation could be an easy way out; in one case, a blurb on some 600 collected games announces merrily that *all* of them are "outstanding Chess masterpieces. . . .") We advisedly hesitate categorically to designate the forty selections as representing *all* the best in the game of Chess. It is, however, safe to note that they are superb. (You will note that some of the games have won brilliancy prizes. That fact alone does not necessarily spell out extraordinary merit as against the quality of others, which may well have taken place in Chess events where no prizes were awarded.)

Of one-thing we are certain: that we shall hear from an outraged partisan, "How come that you dopes have omitted the greatest (half-blindfold) Chess game of all, that of Cyclops vs. Vulcan (Olympus, Ides of March, 2345 B.C.)?" And we reply now: "Sorry, sir, to have overlooked the famed 'Cyclops Cynosure,' but we do hope that you will prepare an anthology of your own and rectify our aberration."

The selections follow.

(1) NEUHAUSEN, 1953

Early Losses Presage Future Gains

KING'S INDIAN
DEFENSE

M. Euwe	M. Najdorf
White	Black

	White	Black
1	P-Q4	N-KB3
2	P-QB4	P-KN3
3	P-KN3	B-N2
4	B-N2	O-O
5	N-QB3	P-B4
6	P-Q5	P-K4
7	B-N5	P-KR3
8	BxN	QxB
9	P-Q6!	N-B3
10	P-K3	P-N3
11	B-Q5	K-R1
12	N-K4	Q-Q1
13	P-KR4	P-B4
14	N-N5	B-N2!
15	P-KN4	P-K5
16	N-K2	BxP
17	N-B4	Q-B3

(*Continued*)

	White	Black
18	PxP	BxR
19	NxP ch	K-N2
20	NxP	B-B6 ch
21	K-B1	QxBP

	White	Black
22	N-B4	K-R1
23	NxB	QR-K1
24	N/3-K2	R-KN1
25	P-R5	R-N4
26	N-N3	RxN
27	PxR	RxP
28	K-B2	R-K1
29	R-K1	RxR
30	QxR	K-N2
31	Q-K8	Q-B7 ch
32	K-N1	Q-Q8 ch
33	K-R2	Q-B7 ch
34	N-N2	Q-B4
35	Q-N8 ch	K-B3
36	Q-R8 ch	K-N4
37	Q-N7 ch	Resigns

(2) NEW YORK, 1933

Pyrotechnics

QUEEN'S GAMBIT DEC.

	N.
R. Fine	**Grossman**
White	*Black*

	White	Black
1	P-Q4	N-KB3
2	P-QB4	P-K3
3	N-QB3	P-Q4
4	B-N5	B-N5
5	P-K3	P-B3
6	Q-N3	BxN ch
7	PxB	QN-Q2
8	PxP	BPxP
9	B-Q3	O-O
10	N-K2	Q-R4
11	P-B3	P-QN3
12	O-O	B-R3
13	Q-B2	BxB
14	QxB	KR-B1
15	B-R4	P-QN4
16	P-K4	R-B5
17	P-K5	N-K1
18	P-B4	P-N3
19	P-N4	Q-N3
20	K-R1	N-N2
21	P-B5	KPxP
22	PxP	NxKP
23	Q-R3	N-B3
24	B-B6	N-R4
25	PxP	RPxP

(*See diagram at right*)

26	N-B4	NxB

Position after 25 ... RPxP

	White	Black
27	NxNP	K-N2
28	R-KN1	PxN
29	RxP ch	KxR
30	Q-K6	NxP
31	R-N1 ch	K-R3
32	Q-K3 ch	K-R2
33	Q-K7 ch	K-R3
34	Q-N7 ch	Resigns

(3) COPENHAGEN, 1923

The Evergreen
Zugzwang Game

QUEEN'S INDIAN
DEFENSE

	A.
F. Saemisch	**Nimzovich**
White	*Black*

	White	Black
1	P-Q4	N-KB3
2	P-QB4	P-K3
3	N-KB3	P-QN3
4	P-KN3	B-N2

	White	Black
5	B-N2	B-K2
6	N-B3	O-O
7	O-O	P-Q4
8	N-K5	P-B3
9	PxP	BPxP
10	B-B4	P-QR3
11	R-B1	P-QN4
12	Q-N3	N-B3
13	NxN	BxN
14	P-KR3	Q-Q2
15	K-R2	N-R4!
16	B-Q2	P-B4
17	Q-Q1	P-N5
18	N-N1	B-QN4
19	R-N1	B-Q3
20	P-K4	BPxP
21	QxN	RxP
22	Q-N5	QR-KB1
23	K-R1	QR-B4
24	Q-K3	B-Q6
25	QR-K1	P-R3
	Resigns	

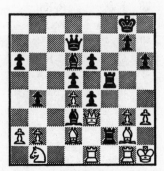

Final Position

(4) NEW YORK, 1918

The Trapper Trapped

RUY LÓPEZ

J. R. Capa-
blanca   **Fonaroff**
White   *Black*

	White	Black
1	P-K4	P-K4
2	N-KB3	N-QB3
3	B-N5	N-B3
4	O-O	P-Q3
5	P-Q4	B-Q2
6	N-B3	B-K2
7	R-K1	PxP
8	NxP	NxN
9	QxN	BxB
10	NxB	O-O
11	Q-B3	P-B3
12	N-Q4	N-Q2
13	N-B5	B-B3
14	Q-KN3	N-K4
15	B-B4	Q-B2
16	QR-Q1	QR-Q1

	White	Black
17	RxP	RxR
18	BxN	R-Q8
19	RxR	BxB
20	N-R6 ch	K-R1
21	QxB	QxQ
22	NxP ch	Resigns

(5) NEW YORK, 1915

Sacrificio con Amore

DUTCH DEFENSE

Smyth   **H. Helms**
White   *Black*

	White	Black
1	P-Q4	P-KB4
2	N-KB3	N-KB3
3	P-B4	P-K3
4	N-B3	P-QN3
5	P-K3	B-N2
6	B-Q3	B-Q3
7	P-QR3	P-QR4
8	O-O	O-O
9	Q-B2	N-B3
10	P-K4?	PxP
11	NxP	NxN
12	BxN	NxP
13	BxP ch	K-R1
14	NxN	Q-R5
15	P-KN3	QxN
16	B-Q3	R-B6
17	B-K3	Q-K4
18	QR-K1	QR-KB1
19	BxP	Q-R4
20	B-K3	Q-R6
21	B-K4	QR-B4

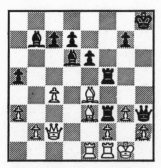

Position after 21 ... QR-B4

White	Black
22 BxQR	Q-N7 ch
23 KxQ	RxNP mate

(6) BRESLAU, 1912

Shower of Gold

(Marshall was *not* showered with gold coins, as is generally believed.)

FRENCH DEFENSE

S. Lewitzky	F. J. Marshall
White	Black
1 P-Q4	P-K3
2 P-K4	P-Q4
3 N-QB3	P-QB4
4 N-B3	N-QB3
5 KPxP	KPxP
6 B-K2	N-B3

White	Black
7 O-O	B-K2
8 B-KN5	O-O
9 PxP	B-K3
10 N-Q4	BxP
11 NxB	PxN
12 B-N4	Q-Q3
13 B-R3	QR-K1
14 Q-Q2	B-N5
15 BxN	RxB
16 QR-Q1	Q-B4
17 Q-K2	BxN
18 PxB	QxP
19 RxP	N-Q5
20 Q-R5	QR-KB1
21 R-K5	R-R3
22 Q-N5	RxB

23 R-QB5	Q-KN6!
Resigns	

(7) LONDON, 1912
Fatal King's Tour
DUTCH DEFENSE

	Ed. Lasker	Sir George Thomas
	White	*Black*
1	P-Q4	P-KB4
2	N-QB3	N-KB3
3	N-B3	P-K3
4	B-N5	B-K2
5	BxN	BxB
6	P-K4	PxP
7	NxP	P-QN3
8	N-K5	O-O
9	B-Q3	B-N2?
10	Q-R5!	Q-K2

11	QxP ch	KxQ
12	NxB ch	K-R3
13	N/5-N4 ch	K-N4
14	P-R4 ch	K-B5
15	P-N3 ch	K-B6
16	B-K2 ch	K-N7

	White	*Black*
17	R-R2 ch	K-N8
18	K-Q2 Mate	

(8) LODZ, 1907
Rubinstein's Immortal Game
QUEEN'S GAMBIT DECLINED

	G. Rotlewi	A. Rubin-stein
	White	*Black*
1	P-Q4	P-Q4
2	N-KB3	P-K3
3	P-K3	P-QB4
4	P-B4	N-QB3
5	N-B3	N-B3
6	PxBP	BxP
7	P-QR3	P-QR3
8	P-QN4	B-Q3
9	B-N2	O-O
10	Q-Q2	Q-K2
11	B-Q3	PxP
12	BxP	P-QN4
13	B-Q3	R-Q1
14	Q-K2	B-N2
15	O-O	N-K4
16	NxN	BxN
17	P-B4	B-B2
18	P-K4?	QR-B1
19	P-K5	B-N3 ch
20	K-R1	N-N5!
21	B-K4	Q-R5

Position after 21 ... Q-R5

	White	Black
22	P-N3	RxN!!
23	PxQ	R-Q7
24	QxR	BxB ch
25	Q-N2	R-R6!
	Resigns	

(9) HASTINGS, 1895

Steinitz's Gem
First Brilliancy Prize
GIUOCO PIANO

W. Steinitz
White

C. Von Bardeleben
Black

	White	Black
1	P-K4	P-K4
2	N-KB3	N-QB3
3	B-B4	B-B4
4	P-B3	N-B3
5	P-Q4	PxP
6	PxP	B-N5 ch
7	N-B3	P-Q4

	White	Black
8	PxP	KNxP
9	O-O	B-K3
10	B-KN5	B-K2
11	BxN	QBxB
12	NxB	QxN
13	BxB	NxB
14	R-K1	P-KB3
15	Q-K2	Q-Q2
16	QR-B1	P-B3
17	P-Q5!	PxP
18	N-Q4	K-B2
19	N-K6	KR-QB1
20	Q-N4	P-KN3
21	N-N5 ch	K-K1

	White	Black
22	RxN ch	K-B1
23	R-B7 ch	K-N1
24	R-N7 ch	K-R1
25	RxP ch	Resigns
		(*Continued*)

Steinitz gives this brilliant finish:

	White	Black
25	. . .	K-N1
26	R-N7 ch	K-R1
27	Q-R4 ch	KxR
28	Q-R7 ch	K-B1
29	Q-R8 ch	K-K2
30	Q-N7 ch	K-K1
31	Q-N8 ch	K-K2
32	Q-B7 ch	K-Q1
33	Q-B8 ch	Q-K1
34	N-B7 ch	K-Q2
35	Q-Q6 Mate	

(10) LONDON, 1858

Morphy's Masterpiece

PHILIDOR DEFENSE

H. E. Bird   **P. Morphy**

	White	Black
1	P-K4	P-K4
2	N-KB3	P-Q3
3	P-Q4	P-KB4
4	N-B3	PxKP
5	QNxP	P-Q4
6	N-N3	P-K5
7	N-K5	N-KB3
8	B-KN5	B-Q3
9	N-R5	O-O

	White	Black
10	Q-Q2	Q-K1
11	P-KN4	NxP
12	NxN	QxN
13	N-K5	N-B3
14	B-K2	Q-R6
15	NxN	PxN
16	B-K3	R-N1

	White	Black
17	O-O-O	RxBP
18	BxR	Q-R6!
19	P-B3	QxP
20	P-N4	Q-R8 ch
21	K-B2	Q-R5 ch
22	K-N2?	BxNP
23	PxB	RxP ch
24	QxR	QxQ ch
25	K-B2	P-K6
26	BxP	B-B4 ch
27	R-Q3	Q-B5 ch
28	K-Q2	Q-R7 ch
29	K-Q1	Q-N8 ch
	Resigns	

(11) U.S.S.R.–U.S.A., NEW YORK, 1954

Impetuous Invasion Repelled

KING'S INDIAN DEFENSE

M. Taimanov — L. Evans

	White	Black
1	P-QB4	N-KB3
2	N-KB3	P-KN3
3	N-B3	B-N2
4	P-K4	O-O
5	P-Q4	P-Q3
6	B-K2	P-K4
7	O-O	N-B3
8	P-Q5	N-K2
9	N-K1	N-Q2
10	N-Q3	P-KB4
11	P-B3	P-B5
12	B-Q2	P-KN4
13	R-B1	R-B3
14	P-B5	NxBP
15	NxN	PxN
16	N-R4	P-N3
17	P-QN4	PxP
18	BxNP	B-B1

(See diagram at right)

19	RxP?	N-B4!
20	BxB	QxR
21	B-R3	N-K6
22	Q-B1	Q-KN2
23	R-B2	B-Q2
24	N-B3	P-N5
25	B-N2	P-N6
26	PxP	QxP
27	B-B1	R-QB1
28	Q-K1	P-N4
29	N-K2	Q-R5
30	P-N3	PxP
31	NxP	NxB
32	N-B5	R-N3 ch
33	KxN	Q-R8 ch
34	K-K2	R-B7 ch
35	K-Q1	QxQ ch
36	KxQ	R-N8 ch
	Resigns	

Position after 18 ... B-B1

(12) U.S. CHAMPION-SHIP, NEW YORK, 1956

Game of the Century

GRUENFELD DEFENSE

D. Byrne	R. Fischer
White	*Black*
1 N-KB3	N-KB3
2 P-B4	P-KN3
3 N-B3	B-N2
4 P-Q4	O-O
5 B-B4	P-Q4
6 Q-N3	PxP
7 QxBP	P-B3
8 P-K4	QN-Q2
9 R-Q1	N-N3
10 Q-B5	B-N5
11 B-KN5	N-R5!
12 Q-R3	NxN
13 PxN	NxP
14 BxP	Q-N3
15 B-B4	NxQBP
16 B-B5	KR-K1 ch
17 K-B1	B-K3!!

(See diagram at right)

18 BxQ	BxB ch
19 K-N1	N-K7 ch
20 K-B1	NxP ch
21 K-N1	N-K7 ch
22 K-B1	N-B6 ch

	White	*Black*
23	K-N1	PxB
24	Q-N4	R-R5
25	QxP	NxR
26	P-KR3	RxP
27	K-R2	NxP
28	R-K1	RxR
29	Q-Q8 ch	B-B1
30	NxR	B-Q4
31	N-B3	N-K5
32	Q-N8	P-QN4
33	P-R4	P-R4
34	N-K5	K-N2
35	K-N1	B-B4 ch
36	K-B1	N-N6 ch
37	K-K1	B-N5 ch
38	K-Q1	B-N6 ch
39	K-B1	N-K7 ch
40	K-N1	N-B6 ch
41	K-B1	R-QB7 Mate

Position after 17 ... B-K3!!

(13) **WARSAW, 1935**

The Polish Immortal

DUTCH DEFENSE

Glucksberg   **M. Najdorf**
White   *Black*

	White	Black
1	P-Q4	P-KB4
2	P-QB4	N-KB3
3	N-QB3	P-K3
4	N-B3	P-Q4
5	P-K3?	P-B3
6	B-Q3	B-Q3
7	O-O	O-O
8	N-K2	QN-Q2
9	N-N5?	BxP ch
10	K-R1	N-N5
11	P-B4	Q-K1
12	P-KN3	Q-R4
13	K-N2	B-N8
14	NxB	Q-R7 ch
15	K-B3	P-K4

16	QPxP	QNxP ch
17	PxN	NxP ch
18	K-B4	N-N3 ch

	White	Black
19	K-B3	P-B5!
20	KPxP	B-N5 ch
21	KxB	N-K4 ch
22	PxN	P-R4 Mate

(14) **LONDON, 1851**

The Immortal Game

KING'S BISHOP
GAMBIT

A.   **L.**
Anderssen   **Kieseritzky**
White   *Black*

	White	Black
1	P-K4	P-K4
2	P-KB4	PxP
3	B-B4	P-QN4
4	BxP	Q-R5 ch
5	K-B1	N-KB3
6	N-KB3	Q-R3
7	P-Q3	N-R4
8	N-R4	P-QB3
9	N-B5	Q-N4
10	P-KN4	N-B3
11	R-N1	PxB
12	P-KR4	Q-N3
13	P-R5	Q-N4
14	Q-B3	N-N1
15	BxP	Q-B3
16	N-B3	B-B4
17	N-Q5	QxP
18	B-Q6!	BxR
19	P-K5	QxR ch
20	K-K2	N-QR3
		(Continued)

Position after 20 ... N-QR3

White	Black
21 NxP ch	K-Q1
22 Q-B6 ch	NxQ
23 B-K7 Mate	

(15) BERLIN, 1853

The Evergreen Game

EVANS GAMBIT

**A.
Anderssen**
White

J. Dufresne
Black

White	Black
1 P-K4	P-K4
2 N-KB3	N-QB3
3 B-B4	B-B4
4 P-QN4	BxP
5 P-B3	B-R4
6 P-Q4	PxP
7 O-O	P-Q6

	White	Black
8	Q-N3	Q-B3
9	P-K5	Q-N3
10	R-K1	KN-K2
11	B-R3	P-N4
12	QxP	R-QN1
13	Q-R4	B-N3
14	QN-Q2	B-N2
15	N-K4	Q-B4
16	BxP	Q-R4
17	N-B6 ch	PxN
18	PxP	R-N1

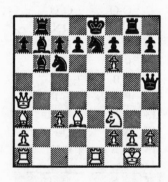

19 QR-Q1	QxN
20 RxN ch	NxR
21 QxP ch!!	KxQ
22 B-B5 ch	K-K1
23 B-Q7 ch	K-Q1
24 BxN Mate	

(16) U.S. CHAMPIONSHIP, NEW YORK, 1938

Sudden Collapse
First Brilliancy Prize

QUEEN'S GAMBIT
DECLINED

S. Reshevsky White	A. C. Simonson Black
1 P-Q4	P-Q4
2 P-QB4	P-QB3
3 N-KB3	N-KB3
4 N-B3	PxP
5 P-K3	B-B4
6 BxP	P-K3
7 O-O	QN-Q2
8 P-KR3	B-Q3
9 Q-K2	N-K5
10 N-Q2	QN-B3
11 KNxN	NxN
12 B-Q3	NxN
13 PxN	BxB
14 QxB	O-O
15 R-N1	Q-K2
16 P-KB4	KR-Q1
17 P-K4	Q-Q2
18 P-K5	B-B1
19 P-B5	PxP
20 RxP	P-QN3
21 B-N5	B-K2

White	Black
22 QR-KB1	BxB
23 RxB	R-K1
24 Q-N3	P-N3
25 R/5-B5	R-K2
26 R/5-B4	R-Q1
27 Q-N5	Q-K1
28 R-R4	Q-B1
29 R/1-B4	R/1-Q2
30 R-B6	R-K3
31 R/4-B4	Q-R6?
32 K-R2!	RxR
33 QxR	QxRP

34 P-Q5!!	R-N2
35 PxP	R-N1
36 P-B4	Q-K7
37 QxBP ch	K-R1
38 P-B7	R-QB1
39 Q-B6 ch	Resigns

(17) BLED, 1931

Bishop Pawn
Murder Case

QUEEN'S PAWN
OPENING

	E. Colle	I. Kashdan
	White	*Black*
1	P-Q4	P-Q4
2	N-KB3	N-KB3
3	P-K3	P-B4
4	P-B3	P-K3
5	QN-Q2	N-B3
6	B-Q3	B-Q3
7	O-O	O-O
8	PxP	BxP
9	P-K4	Q-B2
10	PxP	PxP
11	N-N3	B-N3
12	Q-B2	R-K1
13	B-KN5	N-K5
14	QR-K1	B-KB4
15	B-K3	B-N3

| 16 | N-R4 | NxKBP! |

	White	*Black*
17	BxN	BxB ch
18	KxB	Q-N3 ch
19	K-N3	R-K6 ch
20	RxR	QxR ch
21	R-B3	Q-N4 ch
22	K-R3	N-K4
23	R-N3	Q-R3
24	B-B5?	R-K1
25	N-Q4	B-R4
26	Q-B2	P-KN4
27	BxP ch	K-B1
28	B-B5	PxN
29	R-K3	R-K2
30	R-K1	B-N5 ch
31	BxB	N-Q6
32	QxRP	N-B5 ch
33	K-N3	QxQ ch
34	KxQ	NxP ch
35	K-N5	RxR
36	P-KR4	N-K6
37	B-B3	N-B5
38	N-B5	R-N8 ch
39	K-B4	R-KB8
40	N-K3	R-B7
41	N-Q1	R-R7
42	P-R5	NxP
43	N-K3	N-Q6 ch
44	K-N3	RxQRP
45	BxP	R-QN7
46	P-R6	N-K4
47	K-B4	N-N3 ch
48	K-K4	P-N3
49	N-B5	N-K2
	Resigns	

(18) NEW YORK, 1924

Profundity and
Exactitude

QUEEN'S GAMBIT
DECLINED

	A. Alekhine *White*	**Emanuel Lasker** *Black*
1	P-Q4	P-Q4
2	P-QB4	P-K3
3	N-KB3	N-KB3
4	N-B3	QN-Q2
5	PxP	PxP
6	B-B4	P-B3
7	P-K3	N-R4
8	B-Q3	NxB
9	PxN	B-Q3
10	P-KN3	O-O
11	O-O	R-K1
12	Q-B2	N-B1
13	N-Q1	P-B3
14	N-K3	B-K3
15	N-R4	B-QB2
16	P-QN4	B-N3
17	N-B3	B-KB2
18	P-N5	B-KR4
19	P-N4	B-KB2
20	PxP	R-B1

	White	Black
21	Q-N2	PxP
22	P-B5	Q-Q3

23	N-N2	B-B2
24	KR-K1	P-KR4
25	P-KR3	N-R2
26	RxR ch	RxR
27	R-K1	R-N1
28	Q-B1	N-N4
29	N-K5	PxN
30	QxN	P-K5
31	P-B6	P-N3
32	P-B4	RPxP
33	B-K2	PxP
34	B-R5	R-N7
35	N-R4	QxP/5
36	QxQ	BxQ
	Resigns	

(19) U.S.A.–U.S.S.R. RADIO MATCH, 1945

Flohr's Fatal Gift of a Bishop

QUEEN'S GAMBIT
ACCEPTED

	I. A.
S. Flohr	**Horowitz**
White	*Black*

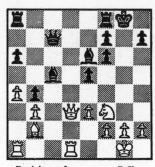

Position after 17 ... B-K3

	White	Black
1	P-Q4	P-Q4
2	P-QB4	PxP
3	N-KB3	N-KB3
4	P-K3	P-K3
5	BxP	P-B4
6	O-O	P-QR3
7	Q-K2	N-B3
8	R-Q1	P-QN4
9	PxP	Q-B2
10	B-Q3	BxP
11	P-QR4	P-N5
12	QN-Q2	O-O
13	P-QN3	N-K4
14	N-K4	NxB
15	NxN ch	PxN
16	QxN	P-K4
17	B-N2	B-K3

(See diagram at right)

18	BxP	PxB
19	N-N5	K-N2
20	QxP ch	K-B3
21	N-K4 ch	K-K2
22	Q-R4 ch	P-B3
23	KR-QB1	QR-B1

	White	Black
24	RxB	Q-N1
25	P-B4	RxR
26	NxR	Q-N3
27	NxB	QxP ch
28	K-R1	KxN
29	PxP	PxP
30	Q-N4 ch	R-B4
31	Q-N6 ch	R-B3
32	Q-K8 ch	K-B4
33	R-B1 ch	Resigns

(20) MOSCOW, 1957

Go, Bishop, Go

QUEEN'S GAMBIT
DECLINED

P. Keres	**M. Tal**
White	*Black*

	White	Black
1	P-Q4	N-KB3
2	P-QB4	P-K3
3	N-KB3	P-B4
4	P-K3	P-Q4
5	P-QR3	BPxP
6	KPxP	B-K2

	White	Black
7	N-B3	O-O
8	B-B4	N-B3
9	R-B1	N-K5
10	B-Q3	NxN
11	RxN	PxP
12	RxP	Q-R4 ch
13	B-Q2	Q-Q4
14	Q-B2	P-B4
15	O-O	B-Q2
16	R-Q1	QR-B1
17	B-K3	N-R4
18	RxR	RxR
19	Q-K2	B-Q3
20	N-K5	B-R5
21	R-K1	BxN
22	PxB	R-Q1
23	P-QN4	B-B3
24	P-B3	QxB
25	QxQ	RxQ
26	PxN	RxP
27	BxP	RxRP
28	B-Q4	R-R7
29	R-N1	R-Q7
30	B-K3	R-QB7
31	B-Q4	K-B2
32	P-R4	K-N3
33	R-N4	P-R3
34	R-N2	RxR
35	BxR	K-R4
36	B-R3	KxP
37	B-B8	K-N6
38	BxP	P-R4
39	B-R6	

	White	Black
39	. . .	BxP
40	PxB	KxP
41	K-B1	P-N4
42	B-Q2	P-R5
43	B-N4	P-R6
44	K-N1	K-K7
	Resigns	

(21) VIENNA, 1929

A Perfectly Coordinated Attack à la Spielmann

CARO-KANN DEFENSE

	Spielmann White	Honlinger Black
1	P-K4	P-QB3
2	P-Q4	P-Q4
3	N-QB3	PxP
4	NxP	N-B3
5	N-N3	P-K3
6	N-B3	P-B4
		(*Continued*)

	White	Black
7	B-Q3	N-B3
8	PxP	BxP
9	P-QR3	O-O
10	O-O	P-QN3
11	P-N4	B-K2
12	B-N2	Q-B2
13	P-N5	N-QR4
14	N-K5	B-N2
15	N-N4	Q-Q1
16	N-K3	N-Q4
17	Q-R5	P-N3

18	N-N4	B-KB3
19	NxB ch	NxN
20	Q-R6	R-B1
21	QR-Q1	Q-K2
22	KR-K1	N-K1
23	N-B5	Q-B4
24	R-K5	B-Q4
25	N-K7 ch	Resigns!

(22) WARSAW TEAM TOURNAMENT, 1935

Elimination of Obstacles
in Grand Style

SICILIAN DEFENSE

	P. Keres	W. Winter
	White	*Black*
1	P-K4	P-QB4
2	N-KB3	N-KB3
3	P-K5	N-Q4
4	N-B3	P-K3
5	NxN	PxN
6	P-Q4	P-Q3
7	B-KN5	Q-R4 ch
8	P-B3	PxQP
9	B-Q3	PxBP
10	O-O	PxNP
11	R-N1	PxP
12	NxP	B-Q3

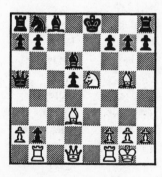

13	NxP	KxN
14	Q-R5 ch	P-N3

White	Black		White	Black
15 BxP ch	PxB		16 B-Q3	KR-B1
16 QxR	B-KB4		17 QR-K1	R-B2
17 KR-K1	B-K5		18 P-K4	QR-B1
18 RxB	PxR		19 P-K5	N-K1
19 Q-B6 ch	Resigns		20 P-B4	P-N3
			21 R-K3	P-B4
			22 PxP e.p.	NxP
			23 P-B5	N-K5
			24 BxN	PxB
			25 PxNP	R-B7
			26 PxP ch	K-R1

(23) LONDON, 1883

White's Fantastic
28th Move

QUEEN'S GAMBIT
DECLINED

J. Zukertort   Blackburne
White   Black

	White	Black
1	P-QB4	P-K3
2	P-K3	N-KB3
3	N-KB3	P-QN3
4	B-K2	B-N2
5	O-O	P-Q4
6	P-Q4	B-Q3
7	N-B3	O-O
8	P-QN3	QN-Q2
9	B-N2	Q-K2
10	N-QN5	N-K5
11	NxB	PxN
12	N-Q2	QN-B3
13	P-B3	NxN
14	QxN	PxP
15	BxP	P-Q4

	White	Black
27	P-Q5 ch	P-K4
28	Q-N4!	R/1-B4
29	R-B8 ch	KxP
30	QxP ch	K-N2
31	BxP ch	KxR
32	B-N7 ch	K-N1
33	QxQ	Resigns

297

(24) VIENNA, 1898

Deployment
par Excellence

PETROFF'S
DEFENSE

S. Tarrasch	G. Marco
White	*Black*
1 P-K4	P-K4
2 N-KB3	N-KB3
3 NxP	P-Q3
4 N-KB3	NxP
5 P-Q4	B-K2
6 B-Q3	N-KB3
7 O-O	O-O
8 P-KR3	B-K3
9 P-B4	P-B3
10 N-N5!	N-R3
11 N-QB3	N-B2
12 P-B4	P-KR3
13 N-B3	Q-B1
14 Q-B2	R-N1
15 P-KB5	B-Q2
16 B-B4	P-QN4
17 P-QN3	P-B4
18 P-Q5	P-N5
19 N-K2	P-QR4
20 P-N4	N-R2
21 P-KR4	Q-Q1
22 B-N3	P-R5
23 K-R1	R-R1
24 QR-K1	N-K1
25 N-B4	B-KB3

White	Black
26 N-K6	PxP
27 PxP	Q-N3
28 NxR	KxN
29 P-N5	PxP
30 PxP	NxP
31 Q-KR2	K-N1
32 NxN	BxN
33 P-B6!	P-N3
34 BxNP	Resigns

(25) AVRO TOURNA-MENT, HOLLAND, 1938

12-Move Deep
Combination

NIMZOINDIAN
DEFENSE

M. Botvinnik	J. R. Capablanca
White	*Black*
1 P-Q4	N-KB3
2 P-QB4	P-K3
3 N-QB3	B-N5

White	Black
4 P-K3	P-Q4
5 P-QR3	BxN ch
6 PxB	P-B4
7 BPxP	KPxP
8 B-Q3	O-O
9 N-K2	P-QN3
10 O-O	B-R3
11 BxB	NxB
12 B-N2	Q-Q2
13 P-QR4	KR-K1
14 Q-Q3	P-B5
15 Q-B2	N-N1
16 QR-K1	N-B3
17 N-N3	N-QR4
18 P-B3	N-N6
19 P-K4	QxP
20 P-K5	N-Q2
21 Q-B2	P-N3
22 P-B4	P-B4
23 PxP e.p.	NxBP
24 P-B5	RxR
25 RxR	R-K1
26 R-K6	RxR
27 PxR	K-N2
28 Q-B4!	Q-K1
29 Q-K5	Q-K2

(See diagram at right)

30 B-R3	QxB
31 N-R5 ch	PxN
32 Q-N5 ch	K-B1
33 QxN ch	K-N1
34 P-K7	Q-B8 ch

Position after 29 ... Q-K2

White	Black
35 K-B2	Q-B7 ch
36 K-N3	Q-Q6 ch
37 K-R4	Q-K5 ch
38 KxP	Q-K7 ch
39 K-R4	Q-K5 ch
40 P-N4	Q-K8 ch
41 K-R5	Resigns

(26) MOSCOW, 1943

Quick Change of Pace

SICILIAN DEFENSE

V. Smyslov	A. Kotov
White	Black

1 P-K4	P-QB4
2 N-QB3	N-QB3
3 P-KN3	P-KN3
4 B-N2	B-N2
5 P-Q3	P-Q3
6 N-B3	P-K3
	(Continued)

	White	Black		White	Black
7	B-N5	KN-K2	27	R-N6	R-B2
8	Q-Q2	P-KR3	28	QR-N1	K-N1
9	B-K3	P-K4	29	RxRP	K-B1
10	O-O	B-K3	30	R-R7	K-K2
11	N-K1	Q-Q2	31	Q-R5	K-Q3
12	P-QR3	B-R6	32	B-B4 ch	N-K4
13	P-B4	N-Q5	33	BxN ch	PxB
14	R-N1	PxP	34	P-B6!	NxP
15	BxP	BxB	35	QxP ch	K-B3
16	QxB	O-O	36	R/7B	K-N4
17	P-KN4	QR-Q1	37	NxP ch	K-N3
18	K-R1	N-K3	38	P-N4	R-QB1
19	B-Q2	P-Q4	39	RxR	QxR
20	N-B3	P-Q5	40	Q-Q6 ch	R-B3
21	N-K2	N-B3	41	NxR	NxP
22	Q-R3	K-R2	42	PxP ch	Resigns
23	N-N3	P-B3			

24	N-B5	PxN
25	NPxP	N-B2
26	R-N1	N-K1

(27) MOSCOW, 1951

Homer Nods

NIMZOINDIAN
DEFENSE

**M.
Botvinnik** **Bronstein**
White *Black*

1	P-Q4	N-KB3
2	P-QB4	P-K3
3	N-QB3	B-N5
4	P-K3	P-QN3
5	N-K2	B-R3
6	P-QR3	B-K2

White	Black
7 N-N3	P-Q4
8 PxP	BxB
9 NxB	PxP
10 N-N3	Q-Q2
11 Q-B3	N-B3
12 O-O	P-N3
13 B-Q2	O-O
14 N/B-K2	P-KR4
15 KR-QB1	P-R5
16 N-B1	N-K5
17 N-B4	P-R4
18 R-B2	B-Q1
19 B-K1	N-K2
20 Q-K2	N-Q3
21 P-B3	P-KN4
22 N-Q3	Q-K3
23 P-R4	N-N3
24 P-R3	P-KB4
25 B-B3	B-B3
26 R-K1	R/R1-K1
27 Q-Q1	R-B2
28 P-QN3	R/2-K2
29 B-N2	P-B5!
(See diagram at right)	
30 N-K5	BxN
31 PxB	N-B2
32 PxP	NxBP
33 N-R2	P-B4
34 N-N4	P-Q5
35 N-B6 ch??	QxN
Resigns	

Position after 29 ... P-B5!

(28) U.S. CHAMPIONSHIP, NEW YORK, 1944

On the Road to the United States Championship

NIMZOINDIAN DEFENSE

A. Denker	R. Fine
White	*Black*
1 P-Q4	N-KB3
2 P-QB4	P-K3
3 N-QB3	B-N5
4 P-K3	P-QN3
5 B-Q3	B-N2
6 N-B3	N-K5
7 O-O	NxN
8 PxN	BxP
9 R-N1	B-R4
	(*Continued*)

White	Black
10	B-R3	P-Q3
11	P-B5!	O-O
12	PxQP	PxP
13	P-K4	R-K1
14	P-K5	PxP
15	NxP	Q-N4?
16	P-N3	P-N3
17	Q-R4	Q-Q1
18	KR-B1	P-QN4
19	BxQNP	Q-Q4
20	P-B3	B-N3

(29) NEW YORK, 1942

A Raging Battle
to the End

RUY LÓPEZ

I. Kashdan	H. Steiner
White	*Black*

	White	Black
1	P-K4	P-K4
2	N-KB3	N-QB3
3	B-N5	P-QR3
4	B-R4	N-B3
5	O-O	P-QN4
6	B-N3	B-K2
7	P-QR4	R-QN1
8	PxP	PxP
9	Q-K2	O-O
10	P-B3	P-Q4!
11	P-Q3	P-Q5
12	PxP	B-KN5
13	P-Q5	N-Q5
14	Q-Q1	N-R4
15	B-K3	NxN ch
16	PxN	B-KR6
17	R-K1	B-QN5
18	N-B3	N-B5
19	BxN	PxB
20	K-R1	R-N3
21	R-KN1	BxN

	White	Black
21	R-B5!	BxR
22	BxB	R-KB1
23	B-B4	B-B3
24	BxQ	BxQ
25	BxQR	Resigns

	White	Black
22	PxB	Q-R5
23	R-N2	R-KR3
24	Q-KN1	BxR ch
25	QxB	R-KN3
26	Q-B1	Q-R4!
27	B-Q1	R-B1?
28	R-R5!	P-QB3
29	PxP	R/3xP
30	P-B4	R-B4
31	P-Q4	R-N4
32	P-B5	P-R3
33	RxP	R-R1
34	R-N1	R-R3
35	P-Q5	R/3-N3

	White	Black
36	P-B6?	Q-R6!
37	B-K2	R-N7
38	Q-N1	RxQ ch
39	RxR	RxR ch
40	KxR	Q-B1
41	B-N5	Q-B2
	Resigns	

(30) U.S.A.–U.S.S.R. 1945
RADIO MATCH

Asphyxiating Attack

(Brilliancy Prize)

CARO-KANN
DEFENSE

I. A.

Horowitz	S. Flohr
White	*Black*
1 P-K4	P-QB3
2 P-Q4	P-Q4
3 N-QB3	PxP
4 NxP	N-B3
5 NxN ch	NPxN
6 N-K2	B-B4
7 N-N3	B-N3
8 P-KR4	P-KR3
9 P-R5	B-R2
10 P-QB3	Q-N3
11 B-QB4	N-Q2
12 P-R4	P-R4
13 Q-B3	P-K3
14 O-O	B-B7
15 B-B4	B-N6
16 B-Q3	P-K4
17 B-K3	B-Q4
18 B-K4	Q-N6
19 PxP	PxP
20 QR-Q1	BxB
21 QxB	Q-K3
22 R-Q2	N-B3
23 Q-B3	R-KN1
	(Continued)

White	Black
24 KR-Q1	R-N5
25 N-B5!	P-K5

26	B-N6!	RxP ch
27	QxR	QxN
28	R-Q8 ch	RxR
29	RxR ch	K-K2
30	Q-N3!	N-Q2
31	B-B7	Q-Q4
32	P-QB4	Q-KN4
33	QxQ ch	PxQ
34	R-R8	K-K3
35	BxP	P-KB4
36	B-B3	P-B5
37	P-R5	P-N5
38	P-N4	P-B6
39	B-Q2	K-B2
40	R-R7	P-N6
41	RxP	Resigns

(31) NEW YORK, 1924

The Stranger
in Between

(First Brilliancy Prize)

RETI OPENING

	R. Reti *White*	E. Bogolubov *Black*
1	N-KB3	N-KB3
2	P-B4	P-K3
3	P-KN3	P-Q4
4	B-N2	B-Q3
5	O-O	O-O
6	P-N3	R-K1
7	B-N2	QN-Q2
8	P-Q4!	P-B3
9	QN-Q2	N-K5
10	NxN	PxN
11	N-K5	P-KB4
12	P-B3	PxP
13	BxP	Q-B2
14	NxN	BxN
15	P-K4!	P-K4
16	P-B5	B-KB1
17	Q-B2!	PxQP
18	PxP	QR-Q1
19	B-R5!	R-K4
20	BxP	RxKBP
21	RxR	BxR

White	Black		White	Black
22 QxB	RxB		10 Q-B3	P-K4
23 R-KB1	R-Q1		11 P-K3	P-QR4
			12 P-N3	Q-K1
			13 P-QR3	Q-R4
			14 P-KR4	N-KN5
			15 N-N5	B-Q2
			16 P-B3	N-B3
			17 P-B4	P-K5
			18 KR-Q1	P-R3
			19 N-R3	P-Q4

White	Black		White	Black
			20 N-B1	N-K2
			21 P-R4	N-B3
			22 R-Q2	N-QN5
			23 B-R1	Q-K1
24 B-B7 ch	K-R1		24 R-KN2	PxP
25 B-K8	Resigns		25 PxP	BxP
			26 N-B2	B-Q2
			27 N-Q2	P-QN4
			28 N-Q1	N-Q6
			29 RxP	P-N5!
			30 RxR	PxQ

(32) HASTINGS, 1922

Combinative Classic

DUTCH DEFENSE

E.
Bogolubov   **A. Alekhine**
   White   *Black*

1	P-Q4	P-KB4
2	P-QB4	N-KB3
3	P-KN3	P-K3
4	B-N2	B-N5 ch
5	B-Q2	BxB ch
6	NxB	N-B3
7	KN-B3	O-O
8	O-O	P-Q3
9	Q-N3	K-R1

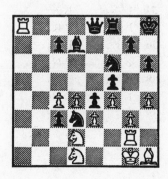

(Continued)

	White	Black
31	RxQ	P-B7!
32	RxR ch	K-R2
33	N-B2	P-B8/Q ch
34	N-B1	N-K8
35	R-R2	QxBP
36	R-QN8	B-N4
37	RxB	QxR
38	P-N4	N-B6 ch
39	BxN	PxB
40	PxP	Q-K7
41	P-Q5	K-N1
42	P-R5	K-R2
43	P-K4	NxKP
44	NxN	QxN
45	P-Q6	PxP
46	P-B6	PxP
47	R-Q2	Q-K7
48	RxQ	PxR
49	K-B2	PxN/Q ch
50	KxQ	K-N2
51	K-B2	K-B2
52	K-K3	K-K3
53	K-K4	P-Q4 ch
	Resigns	

(33) CAMBRIDGE SPRINGS, 1904

Price of Safety is Eternal Vigilance

(First Brilliancy Prize)

QUEEN'S GAMBIT DECLINED

	C. Schlechter	Emanuel Lasker
	White	Black
1	P-Q4	P-Q4
2	P-QB4	P-K3
3	N-QB3	N-KB3
4	B-N5	B-K2
5	P-K3	O-O
6	N-B3	P-QN3
7	B-Q3	B-N2
8	PxP	PxP
9	N-K5	P-B4
10	QR-B1	N-B3
11	O-O	NxN
12	PxN	N-K1
13	B-KB4	P-B4
14	Q-B2!	P-KN4
15	B-N3	P-KB5?

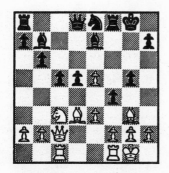

Vindication of

Pillsbury's Opening

QUEEN'S GAMBIT
DECLINED

H. N. Pillsbury	Emanuel Lasker
White	*Black*

	White	Black
1	P-Q4	P-Q4
2	P-QB4	P-K3
3	N-QB3	N-KB3
4	N-B3	P-B4
5	B-N5	PxQP
6	QxP	N-B3
7	BxN	PxB
8	Q-R4	PxP
9	R-Q1	B-Q2
10	P-K3	N-K4
11	NxN	PxN
12	QxBP	Q-N3
13	B-K2	QxNP
14	O-O	R-B1
15	Q-Q3!	R-B2
16	N-K4	B-K2
17	N-Q6 ch	K-B1
18	N-B4	Q-N4
19	P-B4	PxP
20	Q-Q4	P-B3
21	QxP/B4	Q-QB4
22	N-K5	B-K1

	White	Black
16	BxP ch	K-R1
17	Q-N6	N-B3
18	PxN	RxP
19	Q-R5	K-N2
20	QxP ch	KxB
21	BxP	R-N3
22	Q-R5 ch	K-N2
23	KR-Q1	P-Q5
24	B-N3	R-N4
25	B-K5 ch	K-N1
26	Q-R8 ch	K-B2
27	Q-R7 ch	K-K3
28	B-N3	PxN
29	RxQ	PxP
30	R/8-Q1	PxR/Q
31	RxQ	R-Q1
32	P-B4	R/4-Q4
33	P-K4	R-Q8 ch
34	RxR	RxR ch
35	K-B2	R-Q5
36	P-B5 ch	K-Q2
37	P-K5	Resigns

(Continued)

White	Black		White	Black
23 N-N4	P-B4		7 B-N3	O-O
24 Q-R6 ch	K-B2		8 P-B3	P-Q4
25 B-B4	R-B3		9 P-Q3	PxP
			10 PxP	P-R3
			11 R-Q1	B-Q3
			12 QN-Q2	B-Q2
			13 N-B1	R-K1
			14 N-N3	N-K2
			15 N-R4	P-N4

26 RxP ch	QxR
27 R-KB1	QxR ch
28 KxQ	B-Q2
29 Q-R5 ch	K-N1
30 N-K5	Resigns

(35) NEW YORK, 1945

Brilliant Opening Attack

RUY LÓPEZ

A. **Bisguier**	D. **Byrne**
White	Black

1 P-K4	P-K4
2 N-KB3	N-QB3
3 B-N5	P-QR3
4 B-R4	N-B3
5 O-O	B-K2
6 Q-K2	P-QN4

16 N-R5	N-R2
17 Q-B3	R-KB1
18 N-B6 ch	K-R1
19 NxN	KxN
20 Q-R5	N-N3?
21 N-B5	BxN
22 PxB	N-R1
23 R-Q3	Q-B3
24 R-R3	B-K2
25 B-B2	R-KN1
26 P-R4	P-QN5
27 B-K3	QR-Q1
28 B-K4	PxP

	White	Black		White	Black
29	PxP	P-B4	4	P-K4	P-Q3
30	R-N1	R-Q2	5	P-B3	O-O
31	K-B1	K-N2	6	B-K3	P-K4
32	P-R5	B-Q1	7	KN-K2!	P-N3
33	R-N8	Q-Q3	8	Q-Q2	N-B3
34	BxBP	Q-Q8 ch	9	P-Q5	N-K2
35	QxQ	RxQ ch	10	P-KN4	N-Q2
36	K-K2	R-QR8	11	R-KN1	P-QR4
37	B-N6	BxB	12	O-O-O	N-QB4
38	RxR ch	KxR	13	N-N3	B-Q2
39	PxB	R-R7 ch	14	P-KR4	P-R5
40	K-Q1	R-N7	15	P-R5	Q-N1
41	P-N7	P-B3	16	B-R6	Q-R2
42	K-B1	R-N3	17	BxB	KxB
43	P-QB4	N-B2			
44	P-B5	R-N5			
45	B-Q5	Resigns			

(36) LONDON CONGRESS, 1932

Frailty, Thy Name Is Not Vera Menchik

INDIAN DEFENSE

	Mrs. V. Menchik Stevenson	Sir G. A. Thomas			
	White	Black			
1	P-Q4	N-KB3	18	N-B5 ch	NxN
2	P-QB4	P-KN3	19	NPxN	P-R6
3	N-QB3	B-N2	20	P-B6 ch!	K-R1
			21	Q-R6	PxP ch
			22	K-N1	R-KN1
			23	PxP	PxP
			24	QxP ch!	Resigns

(37) MAGDEBURG, 1927

L'Hermet Outspieled

FRENCH DEFENSE

	R. Spielmann *White*	R. L'Hermet *Black*
1	P-K4	P-K3
2	P-Q4	P-Q4
3	N-Q2	PxP
4	NxP	N-Q2
5	N-KB3	KN-B3
6	NxN ch	NxN
7	B-Q3	P-KR3?
8	Q-K2	B-Q3
9	B-Q2	O-O
10	O-O-O	B-Q2
11	N-K5	P-B4
12	PxP!	BxN
13	QxB	B-B3
14	B-KB4!	Q-K2
15	Q-Q4	KR-Q1
16	B-Q6	Q-K1
17	KR-N1	P-QN3
18	Q-KR4	PxP
19	B-K5	Q-K2
20	P-KN4!	P-B5
21	P-N5!	N-Q2

(See diagram at right)

22	QxP!	PxQ
23	PxP ch	K-B1
24	R-N8 ch	KxR
25	P-R7 ch	K-B1
26	P-R8/Q Mate	

Position after 21 ... N-Q2

(38) BERLIN, 1926

Colle's Cool Combination

QUEEN'S PAWN GAME

	E. Colle *White*	E. Gruenfeld *Black*
1	P-Q4	N-KB3
2	N-KB3	P-K3
3	P-K3	P-QN3
4	B-Q3	B-N2
5	QN-Q2	P-B4
6	O-O	B-K2
7	P-QN3	PxP
8	PxP	P-Q3
9	B-N2	QN-Q2
10	P-B4	O-O
11	R-B1	R-K1
12	R-K1	Q-B2
13	Q-K2	QR-B1
14	N-B1	Q-N1
15	N-N3	Q-R1
16	N-N5	P-N3
17	NxBP	KxN

White	Black		White	Black
18 QxP ch	K-N2		4 P-K3	P-K3
19 P-Q5	N-B4		5 BxP	P-QR3
			6 O-O	P-B4
			7 Q-K2	P-QN4
			8 B-Q3	B-N2
			9 P-QR4	P-B5
			10 B-B2	QN-Q2
			11 P-K4	Q-B2
			12 PxP	PxP
			13 RxR ch	BxR
			14 B-N5	B-K2
			15 QN-Q2	P-K4
			16 PxP	NxP/4

White	Black		White	Black
20 N-B5 ch	K-B1		17 N-Q4!	Q-B4
21 Q-K3	PxN		18 N-B5	O-O
22 Q-R6 ch	K-B2		19 K-R1	P-R3
23 BxP	BxP		20 B-K3	Q-N5
24 RxB ch!	RxR		21 P-B4	N-N3
25 QxN ch	K-K1		22 B-Q4	R-Q1
26 Q-R8 ch	K-B2		23 P-K5	N-K1
27 BxR	Resigns		24 P-K6	B-Q4
			25 N-K4!	Q-R4
			26 PxP ch	BxP

(39) ARGENTINA, 1961, SANTA FE INTERNATIONAL

A Strategic Brilliancy

QUEEN'S GAMBIT

Robert Byrne	Hector Rossetto
White	Black

White	Black
1 P-Q4	P-Q4
2 P-QB4	PxP
3 N-KB3	N-KB3

(Continued)

	White	Black		White	Black
27	BxP!	NxB	6	BxN	BxB
28	NxP ch	K-B1	7	N-B3	N-B3
29	NxB	KxN	8	O-O	B-K2
30	N-N5 ch!	K-N1	9	N-Q5	BxN
31	BxN	B-B3	10	PxB	O-O
32	N-B7	R-Q7	11	B-N5	P-B3
33	Q-K3	R-Q4	12	P-B4	PxP
34	Q-KR3	K-B1	13	PxP	R-K1
35	Q-B8 ch!	K-K2	14	KR-K1	P-QR4
36	N-K5	Q-N3	15	R-K2	R-QB1
37	N-B6 ch	K-Q3	16	QR-K1!	Q-Q2
38	Q-B8 ch!	KxN	17	BxN!	BxB
39	QxB ch	Resigns			

(40) NEW ORLEANS, 1925

Merry Chase of the Queen

PHILIDOR DEFENSE

E. Z. Adams — **C. Torre**

	White	Black
	White	Black
1	P-K4	P-K4
2	N-KB3	P-Q3
3	P-Q4	PxP
4	QxP	N-QB3
5	B-QN5	B-Q2

	White	Black
18	Q-KN4!	Q-N4
19	Q-QB4!	Q-Q2
20	Q-B7!	Q-N4
21	P-QR4!	QxRP
22	R-K4!!	Q-N4
23	QxNP!	Resigns

18

Amaurosis Schacchistica

MASTERS' MISTAKES

When Homer nods, mere mortals are less pained by their fallibility. When Chessmasters err, ordinary woodpushers tend to derive a measure of satisfaction, if not actual glee.

In the pages that follow, there is an impressive roster of Masters' mistakes. These may be attributed to a variety of aberrations, all necessarily traceable to *amaurosis schacchistica:* Chess blindness. In many of the positions the "mistakes" are far from obvious to the casual player, but implicit in earning the title of Chessmaster is no license to overlook *anything.* Thus, *amaurosis schacchistica* it is, and nobody is exempt, not even I. A. Horowitz. A bobble of his *is* included in the compilation.

Clearly, the option is yours. You may sympathize or you may gloat or you may take a stand somewhere in between. But, before reading the text, do allow yourself the fun of determining whether you would have done better.

41 EXAMPLES WITH CRITICAL
DIAGRAMS

(1) **LONDON, 1932**

Milner-Barry

Kashdan

Black to play and win

Actual play here was 1
. . . NxP? 2 PxN QxP ch
3 K-B2, etc., after which
Kashdan reached a winning
endgame by trading Rooks
and returning his extra
piece at a propitious mo-
ment.

According to Dr. Ale-
khine, Black should win as
follows:

| 1 | . . . | Q-R3! |
| 2 | K-R2? | QxP ch |

White mates next move.
Or . . .

2	BxN	QxP
3	Q-K2	Q-N6 ch
	(or Q2)	

The rest is easy. Or . . .

2	RxN	PxR
3	QxP	QxQ ch
4	BxQ	R-B6
5	B-B2	RxP
6	K-N2	R-QN6
7	B-N3	P-B3

(2) **BAD SLIAC, 1932**

Spielmann

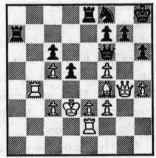

Bogolubov

White to play and win

Bogolubov played 1 B-Q6? and eventually lost. An amateur pointed out a brilliant win for him as follows:

1	B-N5	PxB
2	PxP	Q-K4
3	P-KB4	Q-B2
		(or K2)

Now White wins by playing Queen and Rook to the King Rook file. Or . . .

1	. . .	Q-K4
2	P-KB4	Q-B2
3	BxP	PxB
4	R-KN2	N-N3
5	PxN	. . .

Now if 5 . . . Q-R4 6 PxP, Q-R3 ch 7 K-B2, Q-R7 ch 8 R-QN2, Q-R5 ch 9 K-Q2, RxBP 10 Q-N6, etc. Or if 5 . . . Q-K2 6 R-KN3, P-Q5 7 Q-B5!, PxKP 8 PxP, R-Q1 ch 9 R-Q4, RxR ch 10 PxR, R-R6 ch 11 K-B4, etc.

(3) BERNE, 1932

Naegeli

Alekhine

Black to play and win Prof. Naegeli played 1 . . . Q-N8, and after a few more moves the game ended in a perpetual check.

With one fell move, however, Black could end hostilities.

1	. . .	P-B4!

The threat is 2 . . . Q-N6 ch 3 QxQ, R-R4 mate. White is helpless to continue.

(4) LONDON, 1932

Tartakover

Kashdan

White to play and win

Kashdan played 1 QxQ?, and the game ended in a draw.

A more or less standard combination is in the position which wins by force.

1 B-KR6 . . .

White must now win at least the exchange, e.g.

1	. . .	N-N5
2	Q-B8 ch	K-Q2
3	B-N5 ch	K-B2
4	Q-B5 ch	K-Q1
5	Q-Q6 ch	B-Q2
6	QxB Mate	

(5) LONDON, 1932

Milner-Barry

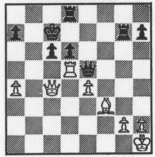

Winter

Black to play and win

Milner-Barry played 1 . . . Q-R8 ch, and after 2 R-Q1, Q-K4, White claimed a draw by threefold repetition of position, which Black had evidently overlooked.

Alekhine shows the following win:

1	. . .	R-QN1
2	P-N3	. . .

2 R-Q1 prolongs the game, but also White's suffering!

2	. . .	RxP!
3	PxR	QxNP
4	R-Q3	R-N8 ch
5	B-Q1	RxB ch

6	RxR	Q-B6 ch
7	K-R2	QxR
8	Q-B7 ch	K-N3
9	QxRP	QxP

(6) LONDON, 1932

Golombek

Jackson

White to play

White stepped into a pin with 1 N-Q4?. The game continued with 1 . . . R-Q2? 2 P-N4, B-N3 3 N-B6! and White saved his pinned piece. Ultimately, the game ended in a draw.

Black missed an immediate win:

1	. . .	RxN
2	BxR	R-Q1

Black nets two pieces for a Rook.

(7) HASTINGS, 1933

R. P. Mitchell

Sir G. A. Thomas

White to play and win

White's King Knight Pawn ought to be a deciding factor, and White should capitalize on it correctly and promptly. He played, however, 1 Q-R5 and lost after 1 . . . QxP ch 2 K-R3, Q-KB7 3 Q-B3, QxQ, reaching a winning ending for Black.

The proper play, attacking the Bishop, is as follows:

1	R-K8!	B-N1

If 1 . . . Q-B6 then 2 RxB, R-Q7 3 NxP ch, K-B1 4 P-N7 ch, K-B2 5 R-B6 ch, Queening with check!
(Continued)

2	NxP ch	KxP
3	Q-N4 ch	. . .

Mate next move.

7	Q-Q5 ch	K-N4
8	R-N7 ch	K-R5
9	Q-N3 ch	QxQ
10	RPxQ Mate	

(8) AUSTRIA, 1932

N. N.

Prof. Krejcik

(9)

Tchigorin

Schiffers

Black to move

Black should play . . . R-R2 and defend himself. Instead he grabs the tainted Queen Knight Pawn.

1	. . .	QxP

Now White forces a mate in nine.

2	Q-R3 ch	K-N1
3	N-K7 ch	K-B2
4	RxP ch!	K-K1
5	Q-R5 ch	K-Q2
6	N-B6 ch	KxN

Black to play

With a Queen for only one minor piece, Black can hardly afford inexactitudes. Yet, instead of attacking, he defends with 1 . . . P-N3. Because of his powerful position, he is able to rescue a draw.

He could have scored with a mate in five!

1	. . .	R-R8 ch
2	NxR	B-R7 ch
3	KxB	R-R1 ch

4	K-N3	N-B4 ch
5	K-B4	R-R5 Mate

Sic transit gloria mundi.

(10)

Thomas

Capablanca

White to play and win

Here Capablanca played 1 Q-R8 and Thomas resigned! Thomas' action seems to be justified as he apparently has no adequate defense against the following RxR.

But all is not what it seems. Black can emerge with at least a draw! He should have replied 1 . . . RxRP! netting a Pawn.

Curiously, Capablanca

did miss a forced win in the diagramed position.

1	RxR	QxR
2	Q-R4	. . .

The simultaneous attack on Queen and Rook nets a Rook. White's Queen is immune on account of mate.

(11) NEW YORK, 1909

Capablanca

Marshall

White to play and win

Marshall played 1 Q-N5? and eventually lost the game.

He has a clear win in the diagramed position.

1	Q-K8 ch	K-N4
2	P-B4 ch	K-B3

If 2 . . . K-N5 3 Q-K2 mate

3 Q-R8 ch . . .

White wins the Queen

(12)

Lewitsky

Alapin

White to play and win

White played 1 Q-K8?, which was tantamount to resignation, what with a piece and Pawn behind.

But White has a mate in four in the diagramed position:

1	QxR ch	KxQ
2	R/7xP ch	K-R1
3	R-N8 ch	K-R2
4	R/2-N7 Mate	

(13) CARLSBAD, 1907

Rubinstein

Wolf

Black to play and win

Rubinstein played 1 . . . B-R3 and had to be content with a draw. He could have used his Bishop to better advantage.

1	. . .	R-KR4
2	P-KR3	N-N5
3	BPxN	RxP ch

White's position falls apart.

(14) COLOGNE, 1898

Steinitz

W. Cohn

White to play and win

White played 1 B-K6 and drew. He missed a clever win.

1 R-K2!	P-N4
2 B-B7 ch	K-R3
3 Q-B6 Mate	

(15) ROGASKA-SLATINA, 1929

Takacs

Przepiorka

Black to play and win

Had Takacs won this game, he would have tied for second place with Flohr. But all he could think of was 1 . . . P-R4 ch, followed by 2 . . . Q-B7 ch (always check, it may be mate!). And so he played, and the game ended in a draw.

A forced win was in the position.

1 . . .   R-KN8

Threatening . . . RxR ch and mate. Black's Rook is immune.

2 R-N7 ch   . . .

If 2 Q-N7 ch, K-B3 and Black threatens an unavoidable mate.

If 2 R-KB4, Q-Q7 ch wins the Rook. Or if 2 Q-N8, Q-B5 ch! 3 RxQ, RxQ with a winning endgame.

2 . . .	RxR
3 QxR ch	K-B3
4 Q-N4	P-R4 ch
5 K-R4	Q-N4 Mate

(16) DEBRECEN, 1925

Mattison

P. Johner

White to play and win

White played 1 Q-N4? and mistakenly announced a mate in six. He certainly should not have lost the game. But, after many vicissitudes, he did.

White could have forced a mate.

1 R/1-N1!   N-N3

White was threatening mate in two. If 1 . . . N-R2 2 Q-Q3.

2 Q-K3   . . .

Black is helpless.

(17) LENINGRAD, 1925

Subarew

Loewenfisch

White to play and win

In time difficulties, White forced perpetual check with 1 R-R5 ch, PxR 2 QxP ch, K-B3 3 Q-R8 ch, etc.

But White has a forced win!

1 R-KR3!   . . .

The threat is 2 Q-R4 mate.

1	. . .	QxB ch
2	R-N3	P-B7
3	P-R4 ch	K-B5
4	Q-B6 ch	. . .

It is practically over.

(18) BAD KISSINGEN, 1928

Rubinstein

Marshall

White to play and win

With the game in his grasp, Marshall played 1 Q-B6 and lost.

Instead he should have won.

1 Q-R4 ...

This move is superior to Marshall's in that it keeps command of the King Rook file and it keeps KB6 open for the Knight.

1 ... B-Q4

If 1 ... Q-B4, Black is mated in three.

2 N-Q7 ...

There is no adequate defense.

(19) BRESLAU, 1889

Tarrasch

Burn

White to play and win

Burn played 1 R-B5? and lost the game many moves later.

He could win with the following brilliant sequence.

1 KR-Q1 Q-K3

Or 1 ... Q-KB4 2 BxN, RxR ch 3 RxR, NxB 4 R-Q8 ch, NxR 5 Q-K8 mate.

2 BxN NxB
3 QxN ...

White remains a piece ahead.

(20) NATIONAL CHESS FEDERATION CHAMPIONSHIP, CHICAGO, 1926

Edward Lasker

Torre

Black to play and win

In the opening stages of a game, it is rare to seek combinations. Here Lasker made a developing move and the game was eventually drawn.

Lasker can win a piece on the move, however.

1 . . .   P-B6!

No matter what White plays, he is out a piece.

(21) CARLSBAD, 1929

Yates

Tartakover

White to play and win

Tartakover played 1 N-R6 ch and after . . . K-R2 2 NxP, Q-B4 3 N-N5 ch, K-R3 4 N-B7 ch, K-R2 5 N-N5 ch, the game was drawn.

White, however, has a winning continuation.

1 BxP ch   K-R2

If 1 . . . K-B1 2 Q-R8 ch, KxB 3 N-R6 ch, K-K3 4 P-B5 ch, PxP 5 PxP ch, K-Q3 6 Q-Q4 ch, N-Q4 7 QxN mate. This combination was discovered by Tartakover . . . after the game.

Clearly 1 . . . QxB loses the Queen, and 1 . . . KxB allows mate in three: 2 N-R6 ch, K-K3 3 P-B5 ch, PxP 4 PxP mate.

2	BxR	QxB
3	N-B6 ch	NxN
4	QxN	. . .

White wins easily.

(22) BAD SLIAC, 1932

May

Rohacek

Black to play and win
Black played 1 . . . QxQ, followed by 2 . . . BxRP? and lost.

He missed a forced win!

1	. . .	R-B8!!
2	QxR	B-B6 ch
3	K-B1	BxR ch
4	KxB	QxP ch

White's Rook goes, and so does his game.

(23) HAVANA, 1921

Lasker

Capablanca

Black to play and draw.
Black played 1 . . . K-B1 and after 2 Q-N8 ch, Black resigned, for he had to lose a piece or his Queen on the following move. Thus, 2 . . . K-N2 3 Q-R8 ch or 2 . . . K-K2 3 Q-K5 ch, etc.

There was one saving move that would lead to a draw.

1	. . .	K-B3

White's exposed King reduces his winning chances to nil.

(24) WORLD CHAMPIONSHIP MATCH, 1929

Bogolubov

Alekhine

(25) KECSKEMET, 1927

Kmoch

Mueller

White to play and draw

The great Alekhine played 1 BxP and lost quickly after . . . Q-K5, simultaneously attacking Rook and Bishop.

Almost any reasonable move would lead to a draw, particularly because of the "Bishops of opposite colors."

Black to move

Here both players were in time trouble. Black naturally moved 1 . . . K-K1. White replied 2 B-R7, whereupon Black played . . . QxB ch! White's blunder cost him half a point, for he still managed to draw.

(26) NEW YORK, 1866

Zukertort

Steinitz

(27) BAD KISSINGEN, 1928

Yates

Nimzowitsch

White to move

Steinitz played 1 Nx-QBP? and the game continued . . . PxN 2 RxR, NxR, resigns. For White was out a piece. This was quite a blunder for a world championship match.

Steinitz later said that 1 B-B2, QxNP 2 B-QR4 would have given him a good game.

Black to play and win

Black played 1 . . . Q-Q8 ch 2 K-N2, Q-B7 ch? 3 K-B3, Q-Q8 ch 4 K-N2, P-R4?. White then played 5 NxP ch, and the game ended in a perpetual check.

Black could win easily.

1	. . .	Q-B8 ch
2	K-N4	Q-K7 ch
3	Q-B3	. . .

If 3 KxP, P-N4 ch 4 K-N3, B-B5 ch.

| 3 | . . . | P-B4 ch |

(28) BAD KISSINGEN, 1928

Spielmann

Tartakover

White to play and win

The game continued 1 PxN, R-B1. White still had some winning chances which he missed and they finally agreed on a draw.

Instead White has a forced win.

| 1 | RxP! | N-Q4 |
| 2 | R-N7 ch | K-R1 |

If 2 . . . K-B1 3 R/Q-B7 ch, K-K1 4 P-K6 wins.

3	RxP ch	K-N1
4	R/Q-N7 ch	K-B1
5	P-K6	R-K1
6	RxP	. . .

Black is lost.

(29) HAMBURG, 1922

Moritz

Emmrich

Black to play and win

Black played 1 . . . B-Q4 2 PxB, N-R6 ch 3 K-B1, resigns.

He has a forced mate in four!

1	. . .	QxP ch
2	KxQ	N-N5 ch
3	K-N1	N-R6 ch
4	K-B1	N-R7 mate

(30) GYOR, 1924

Nagy

Walter

White to play and win

White played 1 Q-B8 ch, Q-K1 2 QxP, RxP ch 3 KxR, Q-K3 ch 4 QxQ stalemate.

White can win easily.

1 B-N5 ...

There is no adequate defense.

(31) SYRACUSE, 1934

Horowitz

Monticelli

Black to play and win

Black had been seeking the opportunity which finally arrives. Curiously, the move he had intended to make he "entirely overlooks." Black played 1 . . . RxQ, and lost the game.

Black can win easily.

1 . . . QxR
2 QxR Q-R1 ch

It is over.

(32) GLADBECK, 1928

Euwe

Van Nuess

Black to play and win
The play was 1 . . .
QxP 2 RxP, R-K1? 3 QxR
ch, resigns.

Black could win rela-
tively easily.

1	. . .	R-K1
2	Q-B3	N-K4

(33) AACHEN, 1934

Heinrich

Carls

Black to play and win
Black played the natural
1 . . . O-O; but White's
positional superiority tri-
umphed in the end.

Black missed an immedi-
ate win.

1	. . .	P-B5

Black wins a piece.

(34) ZURICH, 1934

Stahlberg

Mueller

Black to play and win
Black played 1 . . . R-
K1 and afterward induced
his opponent to take a
draw.

Black can win brilliantly
in a couple of moves.

1	. . .	R-Q5 ch
2	QxR	Q-R7

White is lost.

(35) ZURICH, 1934
Gygli

Naegeli

White to play and win
Naegeli played 1 QxQ, drawing.

He has a clear win.

1	Q-R5!	RxN
2	BxR	QxB
3	QxB	...

The rest is technique.

(36) ZURICH, 1934
Stahlberg

H. Johner

Black to play and win
Black played 1 ... P-B7 and could not win.

A combination ought to wind up the game.

1	...	N-Q5 ch
2	NxN	BxN ch
3	KxB	PxP

There is no defense.

(37) ZURICH, 1934
Bernstein

W. Henneberger

White to move and win
White played the clever 1 Q-N4 and managed to draw.

White has a forced mate, instead.

1	B-N7 ch	RxB
2	R-B8 ch	R-N1
3	Q-N4	...

There is no way to stop mate.

(38) NEW YORK, 1924

Alekhine

Yates

(39) U.S. CHAMPIONSHIP, NEW YORK, 1942

Reshevsky

Pilnick

White to play and draw

On his previous move Reshevsky had a plethora of wins. Inadvertently, he stepped into the diagramed position.

Now White draws.

1	Q-B2	QxQ

Stalemate.

White to move and win

In his annotations to this game, Alekhine suggests that White's last move (B-Q5) loses a piece. "What follows now is sheer desperation." Alekhine then played . . . P-B3.

At this point, White has a forced win.

1	N-R4	PxB
2	QR-KB1	Q-Q1
3	N-N6 ch	K-R2
4	NxR ch	BxN
5	Q-R5	Q-K1
6	Q-N4	. . .

There is no defense.

(40) U.S. CHAMPIONSHIP, 1951

Pavey

Horowitz

(41) MATCH, NEW YORK, 1941

Reshevsky

Horowitz

Black to play

Black can win in many ways. But in previous games in this event, he had twice permitted a perpetual check, when he had an easy victory. So he determined to put an end to the haunting perpetual by simplifying with 1 . . . QxB ch 2 QxQ, R-R6. It now appears that he must recover his Queen, after which his passed Pawn decides. But . . .

3 K-R4   RxQ

Stalemate.

White to play and win

White played 1 K-N4 and after . . . K-K3 2 K-R5, K-B4 3 KxP, K-K5 4 P-N4, KxP 5 P-N5, K-B6 6 P-N7, P-Q6 8 P-N8/Q, P-Q7, he could no longer win (though the game continued to 99 moves!)

Instead the game ends abruptly with a sharper line.

1	K-R4!	K-K3
2	P-N4	K-B3
3	K-R5	K-N2
4	P-N5	PxP
5	KxP	. . .

White picks off all the remaining Pawns.

19

The Future of Chess

CHESS MACHINES

THE CHESS SCENE

In the United States, Chess has answered a dual, antipodal purpose. On the one hand, it has been the butt of banter and ridicule; on the other, it has been regarded as a symbol of gentility, gracious living, and intellectual attainment.

Still surviving, but more and more on the wane, are the "witticisms" about the slowness of the game of Chess, much in vogue during the last century and the early part of this one. Friend: "What did you do between moves?" Chessplayer: "I circled the globe." Playing Chess is frequently consigned to bearded oldsters who are supposed to symbolize superannuated codgers with nothing better to do than to play Chess. The famed Marx Brothers, in the prime of their zanyisms, contrived to inject themselves into a game of Chess (played by two elderly gentlemen)—with hilarious effects.

Much less funny, however—if not actually sad—is the flippant ridicule, so obviously born out of ignorance, that one finds in a self-styled guardian of our culture, the *New Yorker* (March 27, 1943). The late, great Geoffrey Mott-Smith had taken extraordinary pains to explain a significant phase of Chess to a beagle of this slick gazette. Upon being *approached* for the information, Mott-Smith, gentleman and scholar, had assumed that the *New Yorker* had a *bona fide* interest.

POPULAR MISCONCEPTIONS

"Joseph, my nephew, plays a marvelous game of Chess," says Mrs. Smith. The fact that Mrs. Smith knows absolutely nothing about Chess does not deter her in the least from offering an authoritative estimate of Joe's Chess skills. Hadn't she herself heard from the boy's mother, her own sister, that Joe played Chess? The listener, Mrs. Brown, exclaims: "Oh, my! He must be very smart." Within a week, all the neighbors have learned from Mrs. Brown and from one another that Joe was a "brilliant boy" and a "very great Chessplayer."

Mrs. Brown, true enough, is one and the same person who is quick to laugh at Chess *and* to regard it as the quintessence of prestige. It is the latter tendency that has been of singular interest to business concerns, ever on the lookout for ideas in advertising their products or services. There appears to be, for example, a great affinity between shirts and Chess. Two unrelated shirt manufacturers advertised recently in the same issue of *The New York Times* Sunday magazine section, each featuring a Chessboard to highlight their "superb" wares. Chess has been used as a prop by insurance companies, to stress the "ease" offered by "retirement benefits;" by manufacturers of furniture, furnishings, or materials for the manufacture of a variety of household items; and, not infrequently, by large corporations, as a symbol of respectability accompanying the "message" to the public in institutional advertisements.

The Future of Chess

Some years ago, your authors were approached by an advertising agency for a unique Chess problem. This was incorporated in a full-page advertisement in a magazine of large circulation. Prizes were offered for the first six correct solutions. Some 3,500 solutions were received, and Chess gained eminence as a solid promoter of private enterprise. The product? You guessed it. Shirts.

The paradoxical attitudes toward Chess in the United States, borne out in the discussion in the preceding paragraphs, have not affected its stability. Within the confines of its own little world, Chess is likely to continue to reign supreme as the pastime of pure skill offering the greatest intellectual challenge. But in an age facing a furious tempo of astonishing scientific developments, the "little world" of Chess is not at all immune against shrinkage. It appears that the desire for highly exciting diversions, inherent in the participation in or the viewing of "violent" body-contact sports, harmonizes more with the pace of the times than preoccupation with what is essentially a sedentary pastime, Chess. (There are dark rumors that even in the Soviet Union top Chessmasters are complaining about a lagging interest in Chess.)

Chess has never gained widespread popularity in the United States, as in Russia and in other European countries. The rise and development of this country have been intimately linked with the pioneer's interest in a practical world, in the building of the home and improving the land a century ago, in the industrial progress and technical innovations during the decades that followed. This is not to say that a cultural void has characterized the scene. Not at all. It is to say, however, that dominant interests in diversions have developed, naturally enough, along lines akin to life itself. Baseball, football, basketball are among the leading sports that have symbolized the elements of survival in a highly competitive society: physical stamina, courage, daring, blended with split-second decisions that spell out victory or ruin. It is fascinating to note how professional football and basketball have gained in popularity, as against the "traditional" interest in baseball, the slowest sport of the three.

D. W. Brogan, in *The American Character,** discusses American attitudes born of a social development which he explains cogently, as follows:

America had to be made before it could be lived in, and that making took centuries, took extraordinary energies and bred an attitude to life that is peculiarly American. It bred the temper of the pioneer, the temper of the gambler, the temper of the booster, the temper of the discounter of the future who is to some extent bound to be a disparager of the past. It took optimism to cross the Atlantic, optimism or despair and anger at the Old World from which the reluctant pioneer had come. Until this century, there was always tempting the adventurous or the unlucky the dream of a new chance a little farther on. Movement became a virtue, stability a rather contemptible attitude of mind. . . . American history has been a matter of eliminating that debatable area between the empty land and the settled land, between the desert and the town. This elimination has now been completed, but it is too early, yet, for the centuries-old habits to have changed and much too early for the attitude of mind bred by this incessant social process to have lost its power.

Mr. Brogan should have titled his deft dissertation *An Ode to Restlessness.*

The impact of a sedentary intellectual game, howsoever exciting it may be, has been destined to be limited in the United States. True enough, a clever, gimmick-geared promotional campaign can excite interest. It is not unlikely that the current extensive popularity of contract bridge, aside from other

* Reprinted from the Vintage edition by permission of Alfred A. Knopf Incorporated.

considerations covered in Chapter 13, is, to some extent, still traceable to the tremendous boost of the ingeniously conceived and highly publicized Lenz-Culberston bridge battle of some thirty years ago. In assessing the reaction of Americans to Chess, one is led to believe that nothing less than a trained seal playing blindfold Chess can stimulate a live interest in the game.

In December, 1961, an attractive young woman, Miss Lisa Lane of Philadelphia, age twenty-four, participated in a women's Chess tournament in Hastings, England. Of a sudden, while the tournament was still in progress, Miss Lane, former woman Chess champion of the United States, announced that she was withdrawing because she was "in love" and unable to concentrate on the game. Wow! The spate of publicity was unprecedented. Every big and little rag, sheet, journal, gazette, and ladies' auxiliary newsletter published Miss Lane's easy-to-look-at likeness with comments, of course, of the potency of *amor omnia vincit*. As a matter of fact, an editorial appeared in one of the leading New York newspapers (*Herald Tribune*, January 4, 1962) warmly endorsing the institution of love.

In February, 1962, Soviet Grandmasters Botvinnik and Smyslov played a game of Chess in the Lenin Stadium in Moscow using live Chess pieces: ballerinas, singers, clowns, athletes, et al. This, a stunt as ancient as Chess itself, merited first-page attention in the American press.

On November 25, 1960, the following item appeared in *The New York Times:* *

Princeton, N.J., Nov. 24—A month-old chess game that has been duplicated in the window of a Princeton jewelry store took a sharp turn this week when the black queen was captured.
The contestants are Gray Sidwell, an examination editor for

Educational Testing Service, and the Rev. David H. McAlpin Jr., assistant pastor of the Witherspoon Presbyterian Church.

The chess set was placed in the window of a jewelry store at 54 Nassau Street by Mr. McAlpin as part of a display supporting the Princeton United Community Drive in October.

Mr. Sidwell, playing the white pieces, has an *advantage of a queen and three pawns.** Each man has lost two knights.

Townspeople and students gather in front of the window to observe the match.

"It's amazing," Mr. Sidwell said. "I was just walking down the street and a woman—I didn't even know her—came up to me and shouted, 'beat him out, beat him out!' Amazing."

On March 15, 1962, the following letter, signed Reginald Matthews (of New York City), appeared in the *New York Herald Tribune:* **

I like Crosby, Lippmann, and your typography. And I've been secretly in love with Miss Peach for years. Also the critters in B.C. But chess, gentlemen, chess. An important chess tournament has been occurring in Europe. Bobby Fischer, an American chess master, was participating.

Why don't you carry chess news? With so much interest in things Russian these days, I should imagine that your readers would be interested in the fact that Fischer has been beating the Russians at their own national game. I think this affects the Russians much the same way Americans might feel if a Siberian joined the new Mets and hit 62 home runs his rookie year. If that can be done, incidentally, I'm all in favor of it. Baseball shouldn't discriminate against Siberians. And the *Herald Tribune* shouldn't discriminate against chess.

---

* Italics are ours. Nothing can possibly bring out in bolder relief the prevailing ignorance about Chess in the United States. Can you possibly imagine a raptured throng following the progress of a baseball game at a point where the score is, say, 17 to 0? And, further, can you imagine anyone apprehensive about the chances of the team leading by 17 runs? If you can—and we shall add, for good measure, that our mythical baseball game is not intended as a sandlot affair performed by tots—then the excitement of Mr. Sidwell's ebullient female fan is perfectly understandable.

** This and the two letters which follow appeared in the "Letters to the Editor" columns of the *New York Herald Tribune.* Reprinted by permission.

Came a rejoinder, signed Joseph Gancher (of Albany, New York), in the *Herald Tribune* of March 22, 1962:

The person who complained about your not printing chess news presents an interesting, entertaining argument, but I'm sure your stand is more tenable. I just do not think enough of your readers care about chess news to warrant publishing it. I dare say soccer is Russia's national game, anyway, comparable to baseball or football here. Big-time chess may be played more there than here, but that does not make it a national game. Even if it were their No. 1 pastime, why would we have to get so excited about it just because an American boy is as good as their best? A recent issue of a national magazine reported, as has been known by persons advanced in things psychological, that high proficiency in chess is not an indicator of a superb all-around mind.
I enjoyed chess when I used to play it and was improving steadily when I gave it up as a waste of time. I would not be impressed if Russia continued to have most of the world's top players even if we had none. What has their performance in chess proved? After viewing their shortages in housing, food and liberty, I might start worrying if many of our young men and women became extra-strong chess players.

And a surrejoinder, on March 26, 1962, signed Louis Burt (of New York City):

In a recent letter column my eye caught the heading, "Chess Wastes Time." I hasten to demur.
It is not essential that one be a chess player of genius in order to enjoy a hobby quietly and to one's complete satisfaction. It is sufficient that this form of recreation, although concededly it is an intellectual one, give a reasonable measure of joy and mental comfort. To the avid chess student or inveterate player, the exquisite splendors of an ingeniously conceived chess problem or setting are fully as joyful as would be the strains of Mozart or Schubert to the practiced musical ear.
The satisfactions to the dilettante are indeed quite rewarding without the austere approach that is reserved only for the dedicated and gifted chess master. We simply cannot have a world of Bobby Fischers.
That Soviet Russia enjoys a wide margin of professional ex-

cellence in contemporary chess has, in my judgment, little relation indeed to the current struggle for world power.

In contemplating the *seemingly* unrelated items in the preceding paragraphs, we do find a semblance of an attitude-index. Assuredly, the Princeton story places Chess as a *non*-integral part of the American community. The very same, in a large measure, applies to the extensive publicity received by the Smyslov-Botvinnik live-Chess-pieces game. In the romantic tale of Lisa Lane, Chess is rather incidental, although some may argue, with reason, that Chess offers a contrastive value to the newsworthiness of the affair. It is, however, conceivable that a comely young miss quitting a horseshoe pitching contest or a trapeze act, under like circumstances, can become equally newsworthy.

In the letter series of Messrs. Matthews, Gancher, and Burt we find views that squarely relate to Chess as such, and it may well be that the disparate schools of thought they represent fairly cover *all* attitudes. First, Mr. Matthews offers no clue of *his own* interest in Chess. His is the view of the bubbling, pragmatic extrovert whose complaint, on the face of it, is directed toward omission of mention of events which, in his opinion, merit recognition. To believe that there are few or many in the Matthews camp is to conjecture idly, but it *is* reasonable to assume that some Americans, whether or not they have a *personal* interest in Chess, would like to know how "our boys" measure up against others, especially the "Russian Chess wizards."

Second, we find in Mr. Gancher a loud anti-Chess attitude. If we choose to dismiss his views as emotionally motivated, for they appear to reflect active odium rather than passive in-difference, we can easily overlook the possibility that basically he may be *the* index to the shrug-of-shoulder attitude toward Chess of *most* Americans. Certain it is that the *Herald Trib*-

une, in deciding not to carry Chess news, cares little whether its readers have a dislike for Chess or just don't give a hoot.*

Third, we have Mr. Burt who, obviously, is interested in the game of Chess *and* in Chess problems, and who evaluates Chess as a pastime which need not make demands on anybody beyond his capacity, with "joy" and "comfort" to be derived on any desired level. Interestingly, the gentle tone of Mr. Burt is reflected in his careful syntax. Mildly but firmly, moreover, Mr. Burt demolishes Mr. Gancher's political and economic nonsequiturs. Does Mr. Burt represent a good portion of the Chess public? Very likely. Can we necessarily conclude that the Chess public consists of a higher intellectual level of our society? No. Our observations in the world of Chess lead us to conclude that Chess enthusiasts are as heterogeneous—culturally, socially, intellectually—as are any other groups who may have but one interest in common.

We also conclude that there are no convincing signs for the growth of interest in Chess in the United States. We do, however, believe that high-powered publicity can offer a spurt, for howsoever long or short a period, but the methods employed must be carefully calculated to relate to values that are of basic significance to the public. Stage a Chess match tomorrow, with a million-dollar purse to go to the winner; tie that up with sheafs of publicity on how Chess "helps the mind"; give numerous examples (*if* you can find them) of leaders of society endorsing Chess as a most desirable free-time activity; and you have combined in one neat package the principal elements likely to evoke an enthusiastic response: success, self-advancement, and emulation of those who have attained both. But since such a campaign is not likely ever to take place, it is

* We note (as these pages are being prepared) the designation of I. A. Horowitz as Chess Editor of *The New York Times.* His first column appeared on April 16, 1962.

reasonable to predict that the trickle of interest will continue quite unburdened by violent accretions. There are in the United States approximately 10,000 subscribers to the three leading publications, *Chess Review, American Chess Bulletin,* and *Chess Life.* That accounts for $\frac{1}{180}$ of 1% of the population.

ELECTRONIC CHESS MACHINES

Another consideration enters into an assessment of the future of Chess: the role of the electronic machines. In essence, is it likely that in the foreseeable future man will be able to program a mechanical robot to play *invincible* Chess?

There are, of course, dogmatic protagonists of the yes *and* no answer to this exciting question. The Noers claim, with passion, that no robot can return *more* than the human teaches it, but they concede that the time taken by the electronic brain to give an answer, based on the programed instruction given it, is but a tiny fraction of that needed by the human. But the Noers stress that where such rapid help is obtained from the robot, particularly in complex mathematical computations, the human has invariably given the machine *complete* instruction in the methods to be employed and in the rules to be followed. Since no human has ever mastered Chess, he is incapable of giving the electronic brain complete instruction, and it follows that no machine can be programed to cope with all the astronomical permutations in Chess. The only possibility, the Noers claim further—if, indeed, that is a possibility at all—is a machine capable, within a reasonable space of time, to compute *all* possible permutations on each turn and thus to select the *best* move. This, we are reminded, requires a consideration of approximately 1,000 moves for each turn (i.e., *circa* 30 × 30, allowing for thirty possibilities for each side), and an ultimate consideration of a figure possibly as high as 1,000⁵⁰ (1 followed by 150 zeros!!), if the calculation is to encompass all possibilities fifty moves ahead. How, in the name of common sense, ask the Noers, can such a machine be constructed? (World Champion Botvinnik, a crack engineer and mathematician, suggests the dimensions of the University of Moscow for such a robot.)

The Yessers claim, with equal passion, that the Noers are paying no attention to the absolute possibility of inclusion of *basic principles of play* in the programing of a Chess machine. They claim that these principles can be so judiciously refined that the robot would be able to "recognize" an opponent's stupid 'or inconsequential moves and pay no attention to them; that the robot would "concentrate" on reasonably relevant considerations calling for immediate attention, as does the human player. The Yessers cite success already attained by electronic brains as Chessplayers, and they claim enthusiastically that what has been shown to be possible on a limited scale can and will lend itself to any desired expansion. The Noers' argument that no human has been able to master Chess and cannot, therefore, feed the machine more than he knows is countered by the Yessers with a firm conviction that a systematized organization of all known principles of play is quite sufficient in insuring a programing of faultless play.

The American Chessmaster, Dr. Edward Lasker—also, by coincidence, a fine engineer and mathematician—appears to favor the Yessers, whereas Botvinnik, as already noted, seems to lean toward the Noers. Neither of them, however, can be considered as dogmatically addicted to one view or the other. The *apparent* disagreement of these two splendid personalities in the world of Chess serves to emphasize the reasonableness of a middle ground. In all likelihood, a robot can be "taught" to pay no attention to *palpably* stupid rejoinders, on the strength of basically fundamental programed principles. On the other hand, the inherent limitations in feeding principles are obvious. First, it appears nigh impossible to "teach" the machine a differentiation of principles at a highly critical moment. (Compare, for example, discussion of power of the Chess pieces in Chapter 5.) Second, even the inclusion of all *known* principles in the programing of a machine will not insure invincibility against the inventive, resourceful human brain which, to be sure, continues as the machine's mentor, and is as likely to discover *new* principles tomorrow just as it did yesterday. (We conjure up a scene. Chessmaster, upon discovering a brand new line of play, to mechanical monster: "You're licked, brother. I know exactly how much *you* know. . . .") That a richly endowed robot will one day be able to play a highly skillful game of Chess leaves no room for doubt. On the other hand, in the absence of a fantastic superspeed electronic brain, the Chess championship of the world is likely to be retained by humans for centuries to come.

HOW CHESS CAN HELP U.S. GOVERNMENT

Does the future hold a promise of a state subsidy for Chess, particularly in enabling leading United States masters to participate in significant tournaments throughout the world? It is doubtful; but (as citizens of this land and not at all as persons with a Chess ax to grind) we do hope that the State Department will change the stand it has taken up to now.

Regardless of one's personal reaction to Chess, it must be recognized that Chess prowess, so consistently pre-empted by the Soviet Union, continues to command much respect and admiration in many parts of the world, Europe particularly.

The United States, involved in a "cold war," is, obviously enough, eager for recognition of its *diverse* accomplishments by peoples everywhere. As yet, we have not succeeded in gaining plaudits from other lands for our Whitey Ford and Y. A. Tittle, except that the Japanese, becoming as they are more and more addicted to baseball, may be captivated by the achievements of the former. It follows, logically enough, that wherever possible we should strengthen our prestige in fields of endeavor that *do* have a meaning to others. This does not necessarily require that we must create *new* activities to please others. We are in a good position to capitalize on existing native skills of an impressive nature, in a vast variety of diversified activities, *including* Chess. (Note how cleverly the Russians time a display of their national heroes. Several years ago, Grandmaster Paul Keres staged an exhibition in Cuba at the very same time that Mikoyan visited the island.)

Curiously, the State Department has turned a deaf ear to any suggestion touching on the appropriation of a respectable subsidy for American Chessmasters who, reasonably freed from economic worries, would be in an excellent position to devote the necessary time for study and play, in constant preparation for significant Chess missions in other countries, as representatives of the United States. The price for building a good measure of good will would be small enough indeed. The argument against "professionalism," by the way, does not apply to Chess, for no distinction is drawn between amateur and professional standing.

We merely add, in addressing ourselves to the powers-to-be: "Sirs, it is your move!"

Inevitably, we return to Chapter 1. If Chess is *not* destined to remain an "everlasting challenge," it is reasonably safe to guess that the human brain will require centuries more for mastering it completely, and then not without the aid of ultra-perfect mechanical devices.

Finally, Chess, in any stage of its development, is surely destined to continue to play the role of a relentless deflater of the ego. The late Harold Morton, one-time Chess Champion of New England (and wit extraordinary), was on a Chess tour a number of years ago that brought him to a midwest community. There he faced a local luminary and won the game handily. "'Hm," the piqued native remarked, "around here I seldom if ever lose a game." "Hm," Morton countered, "where I come from I seldom if ever win one."

Envoi

Authors put the finishing touch to a book and wonder whether it is actually at an end. In our case, this disturbing thought is all the more dominant, for the writing of the preceding pages has been dominated by a desire to include *all* areas of interest relating to Chess. But *all*, in an undertaking of this sort, must necessarily fall short of the absolute totality it implies.

It remains, therefore, to ask: Has *Complete Book of Chess* offered you, the reader, a reasonably satisfactory glimpse of the Chess scene? If your answer is yes, that indeed is the ideal finishing touch.

Bibliography

The following bibliography consists of leading works on Chess; also on checkers, various other games, puzzles, mathematical recreations, and miscellaneous subjects relating to the material covered in this book, including electronic computers.

We have advisedly extended the basic bibliography from which source material for *Complete Book of Chess* was derived, in the interest of furnishing the reader a reasonably complete compilation of the various facets of Chess literature.

HISTORY OF CHESS

History of Chess, 1913; H. J. R. MURRAY
A Short History of Chess (out of print; re-appearance imminent); HENRY A. DAVIDSON

Bibliography

Handbook on Chess

The Macmillan Handbook of Chess, 1956

Chess Primers

Chess the Easy Way, 1942; Reuben Fine
Fundamentals of Chess, 1921; Jose R. Capablanca (out of print)
Manual of Chess, 1947 et seq.; Emanuel Lasker

Chess Openings

Practical Chess Openings, 1948 et seq.; Reuben Fine
Modern Chess Openings, 1957 et ante; Korn & Collins
How to Win in the Chess Openings, 1951 et ante; I. A. Horowitz
Modern Ideas in the Chess Openings, 1953; I. A. Horowitz

Middle Game of Chess

How to Win in the Middle Game of Chess, 1955; I. A. Horowitz
Middle Game of Chess (out of print; re-appearance imminent); Reuben Fine
Middle Game of Chess, 1949 et seq.; Eugene Znosko-Borovsky

Chess Endings (Practical)

Basic Chess Endings, 1941; Reuben Fine
Chess Studies and End-Games, 1889; Horwitz & Kling

Treatises on Chess (General)

Common Sense in Chess, 1946 et seq.; Emanuel Lasker
Modern Chess Strategy and the Game of Go, 1945 et seq.; Edward Lasker

Bibliography

WORKS ON CHESSMASTERS AND COMPILATIONS OF MASTERS' GAMES

Masters of the Chessboard, 1933 *et seq.;* RICHARD RETI

Meet the Masters, 1940 *et seq.;* MAX EUWE

Rubinstein's Chess Masterpieces, 1941 *et seq.;* HANS KMOCH
(translated by BARNIE F. WINKELMAN)

My Fifty Years of Chess, 1942; FRANK J. MARSHALL

Botvinnik—100 Selected Games, 1960 *et ante;* M. M. BOT-
VINNIK

My Best Games of Chess, 1908–1923; ALEXANDER ALEKHINE
(original date of publication—unavailable)

Lessons from My Games, 1958; REUBEN FINE

Emanuel Lasker, 1952; F. HANNAK

The Chess Psychologist World Champion Tal, 1961; A.
LIEPNIEKS

Bobby Fischer's Games of Chess, 1959; ROBERT J. FISCHER

Reshevsky on Chess, 1948; SAMUEL RESHEVSKY

Master Chess, 1950; LODEWIJK PRINS

Chess from Morphy to Botvinnik, 1950; IMRE KOENIG

Golden Treasury of Chess, 1961 *et ante;* I. A. HOROWITZ

UNIQUE APPROACH TO CHESS

Point Count Chess, 1960; HOROWITZ & MOTT-SMITH

CHESS INSTRUCTION (ADVANCED)

Modern Ideas in Chess, 1960 *et ante;* RICHARD RETI

Art of Chess Combination, 1959 *et ante;* EUGENE ZNOSKO-
BOROVSKY

Chess Praxis, 1936; ARON NIMZOVICH (out of print)

Bibliography

CHESS PROBLEMS

The *Alain C. White Series* (also known as the *A.C.W.* or *Christmas Series*); published annually, 1905–1936, on the principal phases of problem Chess; authored by White and other authorities, singly or in collaboration; forty-four items in all, including supplements and at least one compilation of *errata;* included in the Series: *Sam Loyd and His Chess Problems,* 1913 (favored by Alain White as *the* outstanding book; recently reprinted in the United States as a paperback); *The Chess Problem,* Weenink, 1926; *Retrograde Analysis,* Dawson and Hundsdorfer, 1915; and other classics.

Overbrook Series (limited editions), 1941–1945; eight volumes on various aspects of problem Chess; seven books authored by Alain White in collaboration with other authorities; the most beautiful Chess problem books in existence; included in the Series: *A Century of Two-Movers,* 1941; *A Sketchbook of American Chess Problematists,* 1942; *To Alain White,* 1945 (a tribute to White consisting of contributions from Chess problemists throughout the world, compiled by E. W. Allen and E. M. Hassberg).

T. R. Dawson's books on Fairy Chess, the most authoritative treatises extant on this phase of the Chess problem art:

> *Caissa's Wild Roses,* 1935
> *C. M. Fox, His Problems,* 1936
> *Caissa's Wild Roses in Clusters,* 1937
> *Ultimate Themes,* 1938 (a work on task compositions not necessarily limited to Fairy Chess)
> *Caissa's Fairy Tales,* 1947

CHESS ENDINGS (COMPOSED)

Collection of Chess Studies, 1937; A. A. TROITZKY
700 Fins de Partie, 1927; HENRI RINCK
150 Chess Endings, 1925; K. A. L. KUBBEL

Bibliography

PSYCHOLOGY OF CHESS

The Problem of Paul Morphy, a Contribution to the Psychoanalysis of Chess, 1930; ERNEST JONES

The Chess Mind, 1951; GERALD ABRAHAMS

"Psychoanalytic Observations on Chess and Chess Masters," *Journal of Psychoanaltyic Psychology,* 1956; REUBEN FINE

"On the Psychology of Chess," essay from *Centaur,* FELIX MARTI-IBANEZ

"Chess Oedipus and Mater Dolorosa," *International Journal of Psychoanalysis,* 1959. Volume 40; NORMAN REIDER

CHESS PERIODICALS

Chess Review; Volume 1 (1933) through 29 (1961)

American Chess Bulletin; random

Chess Life; random

British Chess Magazine; random

Chess (published in Britain); random

The Problemist; random

Chess Life, B.C.F., August, 1956

Fairy Chess Review (& predecessor); 1930–1958

MISCELLANEOUS ON CHESS

The Chess Reader, 1949; JEROME SALZMAN

Cabbage Heads and Chess Kings, 1960; BRUCE HAYDEN

The Adventure of Chess, 1949 et seq.; EDWARD LASKER

The Pleasures of Chess, 1960; ASSIAC

En Passant, 1937; GEORGES KOLTANOWSKI

CHECKERS

Gould's Book of Problems Critical Positions and Games—the ageless classic on the Game of Draughts (last publication date unavailable)

Lee's Guide to the Game of Draughts or Checkers, 1931 (*et seq.?*)

Bibliography

Ben Boland series, 1947 *et ante:*
  Masterpieces in the Game of Checkers
  Familiar Themes in the Scientific Game of Checkers
  Famous Positions in the Game of Checkers

GAMES (IN GENERAL)

Culbertson's Hoyle, 1950; MOREHEAD & MOTT-SMITH
Homo Ludens, 1950; JOHAN HUIZINGA (extraordinary treatise
  on "Playing Man" by the famous social historian)

PUZZLES AND RECREATIONS

Mathematical Recreations and Essays, 1944 *et ante;* W. W.
  ROUSE BALL
Mathematical Recreations, 1942 *et seq.;* MAURICE KRAITCHIK
Amusements in Mathematics, 1917 *et seq.;* HENRY ERNEST
  DUDENEY
The Canterbury Puzzles, 1932 *et seq.;* HENRY ERNEST DUDENEY
Loyd's Cyclopedia of Puzzles, 1915 (posthumous) *et ante?* (*the*
  classical compilation by the Puzzle King, SAM LOYD)

ELECTRONIC COMPUTERS

Computers and Common Sense, subtitled *The Myth of Thinking Machines,* 1961; MORTIMER TAUBE

Chess Rules

Each side has 16 men set up as shown in Diagram 1. White moves; thereafter the players alternate. A capture consists of replacement of the enemy piece (which is removed from the board) by the one taking it. Except for the Pawn (explained below), the pieces move and capture the same way as follows:

KING: one square in any direction, *provided he is not exposed to capture* on the square to which he has moved (see Diagram 2).

QUEEN: over any number of unoccupied squares in any direction, horizontally, vertically, and diagonally (see Diagram 3).

ROOK: over any number of unoccupied squares, horizontally and vertically. In the center of the board, a Rook's possible moves form a plus sign (see Diagram 4).

BISHOP: over any number of unoccupied squares, diagonally only. A Bishop starting on a light square always moves on light squares; one starting on dark squares remains on dark squares. In the center of the board, a Bishop's possible moves form an X (see Diagram 5).

KNIGHT: in any direction, *not* in a straight line, to nearest square of different color from that previously occupied, regardless of intervening pieces (see Diagram 6).

PAWN: only forward (the only piece on which such restriction exists), one square at a time, except that on the first move only it has the option of advancing one *or* two squares. The Pawn captures one square *diagonally* forward, and is the only piece which does not capture as it moves. When a Pawn reaches the top row, it *must* be replaced by a Queen, Rook, Bishop, or Knight (of its own color), regardless of the number of such pieces on the board. A Pawn can capture *en passant* under these conditions: (1) it must be on its own fifth rank (that is, it must be three squares away from its original position); (2) an enemy Pawn in an adjacent file advances two squares; (3) the capture must immediately follow the move of the enemy Pawn; otherwise the right is forfeited. The capture is made *as if the enemy Pawn had advanced only one square.* (See Diagram 7.)

CASTLING: the only move in which *two* pieces of the same color participate, King and Rook. When all the pieces between the King and Rook have moved, the King may be moved two squares toward the Rook and the Rook placed on the square passed over by the King. Castling is possible by King and either Rook, provided (1) neither the King nor the Rook has moved previously; (2) the King is not under attack by an enemy piece; (3) the King does not pass over or land on a square under attack by an enemy piece.

When the King is subjected to capture, the opponent must announce "check." One of three things must be done: (1) the King must move out of check; or (2) the checking piece must be captured; or (3) one of the King's men must be placed between the King and the checking piece. If none of these things is possible, the King is checkmated.

The object of the game is to checkmate the enemy King.

NOTE: *It is illegal to expose one's own King to capture.*

STALEMATE: This occurs when a player's King is *not* in check, and he has no legal move on his turn to play. (See Diagram 8.)

DRAW: This occurs under following conditions: (1) stalemate; (2) remaining forces are insufficient for either side to force checkmate; (3) perpetual check, that is, an endless series of checks to which a player may subject an enemy King in order, usually, to avoid imminent checkmate of his own King; (4) recurrence of an identical position three times, with the same player on the move each time—having the right to claim a draw; (5) a player has made 50 *successive* moves during which neither side moved a Pawn or made a capture. (There is a rarely invoked exception to this rule: a conclusive demonstration that a given position requires more than 50 moves, involving neither a Pawn move nor a capture by either side, to force a win.)

Diagram 1

Black

White

Shown in Diagram 1 is the position at the starting point of a game of Chess. Note that a *White* square must always be in the lower right-hand corner of the board with relation to each of the players.

Diagram 2

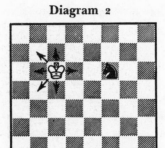

The King, at left, may move to the 6 indicated squares, but may not move to the two unmarked ones diagonally contiguous to him. Those two squares are held by the Black Knight. The King must not expose himself to capture.

In the lower portion of the board, the Knight is *pinned*. He must not move, for the White King would be exposed to capture.

Diagram 3

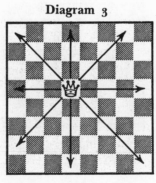

The Queen may move one or more squares in 8 directions, as shown in Diagram 3. The Queen in the center of the board has maximum mobility, a choice of 27 moves over unoccupied lines.

Diagram 4

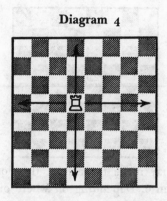

The Rook may move one or more squares in 4 directions, as shown in Diagram 4. The Rook anywhere on the board has a maximum mobility of 14 moves over unoccupied lines.

Diagram 5

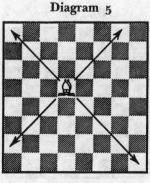

The Bishop may move one or more squares in 4 directions, as shown in Diagram 5. The Bishop in the center of the board has maximum mobility, a choice of 13 moves over unoccupied lines.

Diagram 6

The Knight may move to each of the dotted squares, as shown in Diagram 6. Depending on where on the board the Knight is situated, he has a minimum mobility of 2 moves (when stationed in the corner) and a maximum of 8, as shown. If any or all of the squares surrounding the Knight in Diagram 6—i.e., QB4, QB5, QB6, Q6, K6, K5, K4, Q4—were occupied by White *or* Black pieces, his mobility would remain undisturbed. This is what is meant by the Knight's ability to move over *intervening* pieces. (See also *Knight's Tour*, Chapter 14.)

Diagram 7

The KP in Diagram 7 has the option of moving one or two squares forward (vertically only). This option applies only to the initial move from the home square. The NP may move one square only.

The QP may capture the Black Knight or move one square. If the Black Pawn were to move two squares forward, White's QP would have the privilege of capturing it (on White's QB6 square), exactly as if the Pawn had moved one square only. This is called an *en passant* capture, and if not made immediately following the move by the enemy Pawn, the right to capture the latter is forfeited.

Diagram 8

Diagram 8 illustrates a stalemate position: *if* Black is on the move. The Black King is not in check and no moves are available to the Black side. As it happens, the stalemate shown is an academic consideration, for K and N vs. lone K cannot force a mate.

Chess Notation

There are two principal systems of notation for recording Chess moves *and* Chessboard positions. There are two additional systems (among others less popular) for recording positions only, of which one (Forsyth notation) offers a particular facility for designating occupied and unoccupied squares on the Chessboard. (Note, by the way, that the illustration in Diagrams 1, 5 and 6 is that of the symmetrical 8-Queens arrangement. See Chapter 14.)

1. DESCRIPTIVE OR ANGLO-AMERICAN NOTATION (FOR MOVES AND POSITIONS)

The descriptive notation (Diagram 1, top of following page) is used in the United States and (most commonly) in Britain and in other English-speaking countries. It is the only

Diagram 1

Black

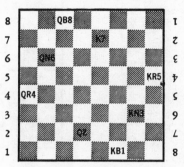

notation widely in use that differentiates the designation of the squares on the Chessboard for White and Black. In other words, a given square has one designation for White, another for Black. (An amusing aside is that the descriptive notation is a horror to Chessplayers of countries where it is not in use. But Americans tend to be confused by the much less complicated algebraic system, described next.)

In the descriptive system, the *ranks* (that is, the *horizontal* rows) are numbered from 1 to 8, for White *and* Black, beginning with the rank *nearest* the player. The *files* (that is, the *vertical* columns) are named for the pieces on the first rank at the start of a game of Chess. Thus, as shown in Diagram 1, the files on the White side of the board, left to right, are QR, QN, QB, Q, K, KB, KN, KR; and they are the same on the Black side of the board but, necessarily, right to left. (By convention, the lower part of the Chessboard is the White side, unless otherwise *specifically* indicated.) The written and pictorial symbols, abbreviations, etc., are as follows:

Chess Notation

Diagram 2

Black

White

Diagram 3

Black

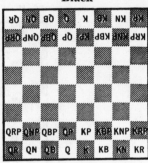

White

Pictorial Symbols for
Position at Starting
Point of Game

Written Symbols for
Position at Starting
Point of Game

King —K
Queen —Q
Rook —R   KR, R on K-side; QR, R on Q-side
Bishop—B   KB, B on K-side; QB, B on Q-side
Knight—N *   KN, N on K-side; QN, N on Q-side
Pawn —P   QRP, QNP, QBP, QP, KP, KBP, KNP, KRP
                    (each, obviously, indentified by the file in
                    which it is originally situated)

* Kt for Knight persists in claiming priority over the more modern N, despite the economy (one letter instead of two) and elimination of possibility of confusing it with K (for King). So strong is the force of tradition that many publications, including the stately *New York Times*, refuse to recognize N. N is used in *Chess Review* and throughout this work. (In notation of Chess problems, S for Knight—*Springer* in German—is common, but, as a rule, only when the algebraic notation is employed.)

Squares on 1st Rank: optionally designated by rank number or by piece on the first rank. Thus, KB1 may be read "King Bishop or King's Bishop one square; or King Bishop square." Similarly, for K1, "King one square" or the preferred "King square."

Precise Identification of Piece *and* Square of Location: using R as an example: R(R2) or R/R2 means "the Rook situated on the R2 square." R/4 means "the Rook on the 4th rank."

Move: The moving piece and the destination square are separated by a dash. P-K4 means that the Pawn has moved to the K4 square; QN-Q2 that the Queen Knight has moved to Q2.

Capture: The *capturing* piece (which is given *first*) is separated by "x" from the *captured* piece (which is noted second). Thus, BxN, the Bishop has captured the Knight; NxQP, the Knight has captured the Queen Pawn; QxN(B3), the Queen has captured the Knight stationed on the Bishop three square. Note that in identifying the square on which an enemy piece is captured, the designation of the square must be that of the side of the capturing piece. If in the last given example the capturing Queen is White, the capture has taken place on *White's* B3 square.

Promotion:

P-B8(Q) or P-B8/Q, the Pawn has promoted to Queen at B8. The symbol for the piece to which the Pawn promotes is either enclosed in parentheses or separated by slant mark (/).

Castling:

O-O, for K-side; O-O-O, for Q-side.

Check:

ch. or ch or + (plus sign)—optional.

Double Check:

dbl. ch. or dbl ch or ‡—optional.

Discovered Check:

dis. ch. or dis ch or §—optional.

Mate:

mate, written out; or ++ (two plus signs); or the number symbol, #, which is usually used in the algebraic notation.

Poor Move:

denoted by question mark (?). E.g., B-N6?, or by two or more question marks, in case of a blunder: NxN???

Good or Excellent Move:

denoted by one or more exclamation points, depending on the degree of excellence: B-N6! or NxN!!

Even Position:

denoted by = (equals sign).

White's Position Superior:

denoted by ± (plus over minus sign).

Black's Position Superior:

denoted by ∓ (minus over plus sign).

The designations of the squares in the descriptive notation (as well as the algebraic) are, in effect, a system of coordinates, for each square is an intersection of file and rank. The relationship between designations for White and designations for Black is much less of a mystery than appears at first blush. Let us return to Diagram 1 where the indicated squares are:

For White (left to right): QR4, QN6, QB8, Q2, K7, KB1, KN3, KR5.

For Black (right to left): QR5, QN3, QB1, Q7, K2, KB8, KN6, KR4.

Do you notice a uniform feature? The relationship is based on the "rule of 9." Deduct from 9 the designated number in the notation for White (or Black) and you have the notation for Black (or White), while the file, necessarily, remains the same. Thus, White's K4 is Black's K5; Black's QB6 is White's QB3, etc.

When a destination is unambiguous, it is customary not to identify it fully as either K-side or Q-side. Thus, Q-N4 is standard notation for "Queen has moved to Knight 4 square," *provided* the Queen can reach one N4 only, not both. It follows that a basic (and troublesome!) consideration in the descriptive notation is avoidance of ambiguity. In Diagram 1 we have an extreme and amusing example. Assume that 8 White Queens are stationed on the indicated squares. What would the move Q-N4 mean? Confusion! Each of 7 Queens can reach *a* N4 square. We must, therefore, specify accurately what Queen is moving to what N4. Q(K7)-N4 is perfectly clear, for identified is the Q (on K7) who has access to one N4 square (QN4) and one only.

There is a logical rule in the descriptive notation for avoidance of ambiguities. Where more than one piece of the same rank can reach a *common* destination, the moving piece must be identified (as in the Q(K7)-N4 example, above). Where a piece can reach a specified square on the K-side (KB3, say) and a piece of the same rank can reach a corresponding square on the Q-side (i.e., QB3), the destination square must be clearly identified. Thus, in the opening moves of the Ruy López: 1 P-K4, P-K4 2 N-KB3. (Note that 2 N-B3 will not do, for 2 N-QB3 is also possible.) Finally, when a piece has access to a square on the same rank in a K-side file (KB-file, say) and a corresponding file on the Q-side (QB-file), the destination square must be clearly identified. Let us consider a Queen on KR5 in Diagram 1. Q(KR5)-B5 is ambiguous; Q(KR5)-KB5 is definite.

Diagram 4

Finally, it is well to remember that excessive identification in the descriptive notation will never cause ambiguity. At worst, it will be considered bad form.

Diagram 4 is Hassberg's 2-mover (see Chapter 9). The descriptive notation for it is as follows:

White: K on * KR8; Q on QB8; R's on KN7 & KN1.

Black: K on KR5; R's on KR7 & KN7.

---

* Sometimes a dash (—) is used instead of "on." Thus, K-R8 etc. Less frequently, the square on which the piece is located follows in parentheses. Thus, K(KR8), etc. For clarity, however, the "on" is standard and preferred.

2 . ALGEBRAIC NOTATION
(FOR MOVES AND POSITIONS)

Diagram 5

Black

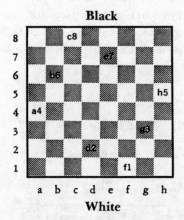

White

As indicated on Diagram 5, the ranks are numbered 1 to 8 from the White side of the board only; the files, left to right—for the White side of the board—are a, b, c, d, e, f, g, h. Thus, the K-file is the e-file, the QB-file is the c-file, etc. As in the arrangement of corresponding symbols in the descriptive notation, the designation for the squares is letter (for file) first, followed by number (for rank). Thus, e5 for (White) K5, d2 for (White) Q2, etc.

A dash between moving piece and destination square is optional; it is frequently omitted. The initial moves in the Ruy López, e.g.: 1 Pe4, Pe5 2 Nf3 * Nc6 3 Bb5 Pa6 4 BxN ** Pd2xB *** etc.

---

* S for N is more frequent (even in English-speaking countries); thus, 2 Sf3.

** Bxc6 is also acceptable, the designation for the square on which the captured piece is situated being substituted for the symbol of the captured piece.

*** d2xB or d2xc6 is also acceptable. See previous note.

The position in Diagram 4 in algebraic notation:

White: Ka8, Qc8, Rg7, Rg1.

Black: Kh4, Rh2, Rg2.

It is to be noted that many of the symbols listed for the descriptive notation (and counterparts for abbreviations in other languages) are used in the algebraic notation.

The pictorial symbols for the pieces are uniform throughout the world.

3. KOCH NOTATION
(FOR POSITIONS ONLY)

Diagram 6

Black

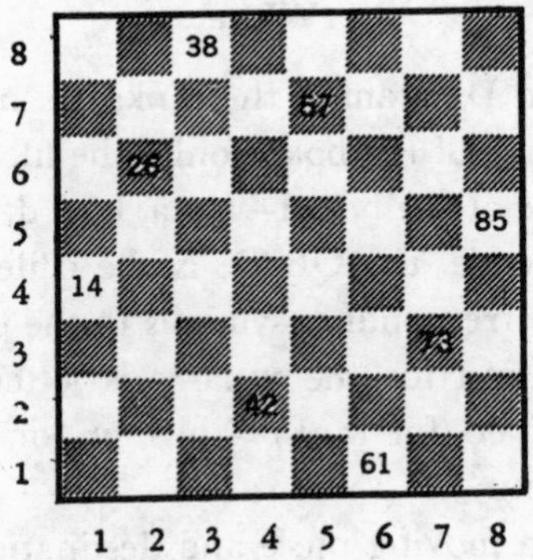

White

This is particularly convenient for designating squares on the Chessboard, and is used mostly in diagrams of Chessboard recreations requiring nonidentification of pieces.

As in the algebraic notation, there is but one designation of the squares: from the White side of the board. The ranks are numbered 1 to 8, from the White side of the board only. The files, left to right, are 1, 2, 3 . . . 8. Each square is designated by a 2-digit number, the first for the file, the second for the rank.

If there is no more than one occupied square in a file, the first digit is left out altogether, and the ranks only are noted, left to right. If there are vacant files, along with those singly occupied, the former are denoted by zero (o). Thus in Diagram 6: 46827135—a most economical notation for squares only. Assume that in Diagram 6 the Queen file and King Knight file are vacant but that the other six squares are in question. The Koch notation for that arrangement: 46807105.

The Koch notation for Diagram 4:

    White: K88, Q38, R71, R77.

    Black: K84, R82, R72.

4. FORSYTH NOTATION
(FOR CHESS POSITIONS ONLY)

In this system, every square on the board is accounted for in the recording of a position. Each square on each rank, beginning with White's 8th rank (and going down to 7th, 6th . . . 1st), is accounted for, left to right, either as vacant or occupied by an identified piece. Standard written symbols are used for the White pieces (K,Q,R,B,N,P); for Black, they appear in lower case (k,q,r,b,n,p). The *total* for the number of vacant squares between one piece and the next on the same rank (or between the piece and the edge of the board) is so designated. Thus, every rank must account for 8 units: the total of the vacant squares and the number of symbols for the pieces on the rank.

Position in Diagram 4 in Forsyth notation:

    2Q4K/6R1/8/8/7k/8/6rr/6R1.

If there are two or more successive ranks on which no pieces appear, the *combined* total of vacant squares is sometimes recorded, in the interest of economy. Thus, for the above: 2Q4K/6R1/16/7k/8/6rr/6R1.

The first example of Forsyth notation is read as follows: Left to right,

8th rank: 2 vacant squares; White Queen; 4 vacant squares; White King;

7th rank: 6 vacant squares; White Rook; 1 vacant square;

6th rank: 8 vacant squares;

5th rank: 8 vacant squares;

4th rank: 7 vacant squares; Black King;

3rd rank: 8 vacant squares;

2nd rank: 6 vacant squares; Black Rook; Black Rook;

1st rank: 6 vacant squares; White Rook; one vacant square.